KU-464-925

ALL TEACHERS GREAT AND SMALL

ALL TEACHERS GREAT AND SMALL

A memoir of lessons and life in the Yorkshire Dales

ANDY SEED

headline

First published in 2011 in Great Britain by HEADLINE PUBLISHING GROUP

1

Cataloguing in Publication Data is available from the British Library

ISBN 978 0 7553 6212 7

Typeset in Adobe Garamond by Palimpsest Book Production Limited, Falkirk, Stirlingshire

Printed and bound in the UK by Clays Ltd, St Ives plc

Headline's policy is to use papers that are natural, renewable and recyclable products and made from wood grown in sustainable forests. The logging and manufacturing processes are expected to conform to the environmental regulations of the country of origin.

HEADLINE PUBLISHING GROUP
An Hachette UK Company
338 Euston Road
London NW1 3BH

www.headline.co.uk
www.hachette.co.uk

To Barbara, of course.

Anyone who thinks they recognise themselves in this book but can't remember the events described need not worry that they're suffering from amnesia. While the events described in this book really happened, the characters are based on amalgamations of real people rather than particular individuals, with the exception of Andy and Barbara Seed.

Acknowledgements

Special thanks to Roger and Pam Hurn for their encouragement to keep believing in this book. My family have been a great help and support, particularly my wife, Barbara, as have many friends, both near and far. I am also indebted to my excellent agent, Kate Shaw, and to the first-class editorial team at Headline, all of whom have gently and skilfully enhanced my writing.

I am grateful to Charlie Butler for his title idea and to Martin Coates for his invaluable input. Finally, I need to thank my former colleagues in teaching and, most of all, the children of Class 3, wherever you are now.

Contents

Prologue

Sylvia

They sat together but were worlds apart. The first child, a girl of eight, was prim and demure. Her pleated skirt was crisp, her hair meticulously tied back and her shoes shining. She was called Sylvia Hammond.

The boy next to her was a year older and considerably larger. His face, glowing with perspiration, was a conglomeration of freckles, snot and mud. The torn knee of his trousers bumped involuntarily against his desk and he squirmed with unbridled energy, chewing at black fingernails and frowning powerfully. He could no longer hold his silence.

'Mr Seed, it's too 'ot in here and this book's boring.'

'Barney, will you please put your hand up if you have something to say.'

I couldn't deny it, though. The June sun streaming in through the large windows made the classroom stiflingly warm. I was reading a story but only half of the twenty-four children were listening. All of them looked hot and uncomfortable; a few were yawning. It had been a long day. I closed the book and took pity.

'I tell you what, Class Three, since you all look so tired, shall we go outside and have a little game?' There was a cheer accompanied by a sudden alertness.

'Can we play rounders?' a voice called out.

'No, not that sort of game – I meant like a thinking game, sitting in a circle.' There was a groan.

'I know!' Barney's hand shot up. 'What about British Bulldog?'

This time I frowned.

A couple of minutes later the class was assembled in a large circle on the cool grass under the chestnut tree outside the classroom. Instinctively, all of them began picking at the grass and daisies.

'Now, who has a sensible suggestion for a quiet game we can play sitting down?' A hand went up right away. It was Sylvia's.

'Can we play "guess the famous person"? And can I go first? I've thought of one already.'

'An excellent idea.' Sylvia had plenty of those. She was a mature girl, and someone I'd found that I could rely on throughout the year.

'Can I whisper it to you, Mr Seed? Then you can help me if you need to.'

'OK, that's a very sensible thought, Sylvia.' I moved a few paces away from the circle of children and leant in her direction. Sylvia cupped her hands, craned towards my ear and spat in it.

'Ooo, sorry Mr Seed.'

'Never mind, Sylvia, I'm sure it was an accident,' I said, applying a hankie, 'Now who's your famous person?'

'It's Hururr Thate.'

'Who's Hururr Thate?'

'What?'

'You said Hururr Thate.'

'I didn't.'

'Sorry Sylvia, you'll have to whisper a bit louder.'

'It's Henry VIII.'

'Oh, right – great idea. The others'll know him from our Tudors topic.' I returned to the circle with Sylvia, relieved that I didn't have to adjudicate on Hururr Thate.

The waiting children were now stretched out on the ground and busy with ants, whistling grass and daisy chains. Fergus had obtained a worm.

'Right, everybody, put everything down and sit up.' They were reluctant, but did so. 'This is how the game works. Sylvia's thought of a famous person and you all have to guess who it is. You can ask her questions, but she can only answer "yes" or "no". We've played this game before, back in the Autumn Term, if you remember.' I certainly remembered it – an endless succession of pop stars. There were a few hazy nods. Sylvia smiled a lot.

'Is it a man?' blurted out Eve.

'Hands up please, or it'll be chaos.' I turned towards Sylvia, who quickly responded.

'Yes, it's a man.'

Nathan's hand went up.

'Is he British?'

'Yes,' said Sylvia, still smiling.

Carol was next.

'Do you know him?'

Sylvia giggled. 'No.'

Malcolm's hand went up.

'Does he play music?'

This time Sylvia looked towards me for guidance. I nodded, recalling that Henry had been very musical, amongst his many other interests.

'Yes,' she said. Suddenly, about fifteen hands shot in the air. I pointed to Barney.

'George Michael!' He looked at Sylvia expectantly. She had her hand in front of her mouth, but her eyes were clearly laughing.

'Er, no.' I pointed at a succession of other hopefuls.

'Elton John?'

'No.'

'David Bowie?'

'No.'

'Michael Jackson?'

'No – he's American anyway, you div.'

After another five similar names, I intervened. 'I think you need to stop guessing who it is, and ask some questions to find out something about the person.' Barney's hand went up.

'Is he in the charts at the moment?' Well, at least it was a start. More hands were raised.

'Does he play guitar?'

'No.'

'Drums?'

'No.'

'I know – synthesiser!'

'No.'

Barney had another try. 'Is he a hairy heavy metal dude, then?'

Even Sylvia had stopped smiling by this point, and my patience was definitely beginning to ebb.

'Look, you haven't learnt anything about him at all,' I said. 'You don't even know if he's alive.' George lifted his arm.

'Is he alive?'

'No.'

There was an undercurrent of muttering at this point, then Jack proffered an answer.

'John Lennon?'

Sylvia's shake of the head brought more grumbling from the children, who had by now slouched back on to the grass. Eve spoke again.

'Can't we 'ave a clue – we're getting nowhere.' It was a very good suggestion: I looked at Sylvia, who responded right away.

'Forget about the music and find out when he was alive.' Good clue. Anita was the first to act on it.

'Did he die this year?'

'No.'

Terry followed up quickly.

'Did he die last year?'

'No.'

I coughed; Isaac raised a hand very slowly, his face creased with thought.

'Did he 'ave glasses?'

'No.'

I stepped in again.

'Think much further back in time, and try to find out what his job was.'

There was a pause and then Hugh signalled to speak.

'Was he a Victorian?' Ah, this was better, and Sylvia tried to make her 'no' sound encouraging. Barney, clearly frustrated, had another go.

'Was he a footballer?'

'No.'

'Was he a politician?' said Rose.

'Errr, not quite.' Sylvia was beginning to get enthusiastic again. I looked at the ragged ring of children. Most of them had given up long ago, but my eyes landed on Hugh. I could see that his mind was working hard on this, and he looked like he was clearly on the scent. Biting his lip, he raised a hand once more.

'Was . . . was he a member of the royal family?'

'Yes! Yes!' Sylvia began to jiggle with excitement. Hugh kept his hand in the air and continued.

'Was he a king?'

'Yes, yes, he was!'

Suddenly, from nowhere, Barney exploded forward from the ground, lifting his whole body with a leap of revelation, and thrust a finger towards Sylvia.

'I've got, I've got it – Elvis!'

Sylvia's patience ran out soon after this and she told them the answer, which produced groans of disappointment. Several children turned around, expecting me to tell them what to do next. They had to wait: I was hiding behind my hankie, wiping my eyes and picturing Bluff King Hal wooing Anne Boleyn at Hampton Court with 'You Ain't Nothing but a Hound Dog'.

This was what I faced every day as a new teacher with my own class: a society of extraordinary individuals who were by turns crazy, inspired, alarming, inert, dynamic, unaware and wonderful. Their capacity for misunderstanding was only exceeded by their enthusiasm and ability to leave me incredulous. No college training, manual, advice or indeed anything could have prepared me for moments like this. I loved it.

Chapter One

Jack

Mrs Fawcett's brown Mini bobbed between the skewed limestone walls along another bend in the little road, and disappeared from view.

'She's not hanging about,' I said to Barbara, my wife, who wasn't listening.

'Oh Andy, just look at the views. It's so beautiful.'

'I can't really – I'll lose her. She might turn off.' Despite my words I couldn't help stealing glances at the flickering green panoramas that appeared in each gateway in the roadside wall. Like a travelling slideshow, every gap presented a tantalising vista of the glorious wide green valley, Swinnerdale, which was to be our new home.

It was late August in the mid-1980s, and we were on our way to the holiday cottage that was to provide temporary lodging, and were following the owner, Mrs Fawcett, up the dale to see it for the first time. As we sped past stone farms, steep fields of brilliant buttercups and dark rising fells, I bubbled with excitement: not only had I just been given my first job as a primary school teacher, but it was in the Yorkshire Dales – a place so overwhelmingly magnificent that the contrast between this setting and our previous home in a town-centre terrace seemed almost too much to take in. To Barbara and me, both twenty-two years old and recently married, it was a real adventure.

We caught a glimpse of a gaunt, square castle on the hillside to our right before a clump of trees secreted it swiftly. Then the Mini's brake lights blinked and Mrs Fawcett shimmied up a narrow road rising in that direction. I could hear Barbara giggling with anticipation as our noisy Alfasud veered after it and climbed the valley side, opening up yet more sweeping views. The cowpat-spattered road steadily increased in gradient, causing me to change gear several times, before bringing the great stone fortress back into view. Next to the castle was a row of dark cottages that seemed absurdly small. Just as we expected to top the road's crest and enter the little village, the Mini disappeared again, this time to the left. Mrs Fawcett swung it round like a rally driver and vanished as if she had gone down a hole. A fat millstone marked the spot where she had turned off; it bore a sign saying *Castle Heywood.* I slowed virtually to a stop and peered at a steep track that plunged back down the hillside between thick trees and high banks before curving away out of sight. There was no sign of the Mini or Mrs Fawcett, but it was the only way she could have gone.

'Be careful,' said Barbara. Braking, however, was never one of the Alfasud's foremost capabilities, and I squeezed extra hard on the middle pedal as the car juddered over the track's rocky surface and pointed down the one in four drop, causing us to slide forward in our seats, and think, 'Where on earth are we going?'

* * *

Brenda Fawcett was married to Arthur Fawcett, who was a governor at Cragthwaite School where I was to start work in a week's time. I remember meeting him after the interview in June, a short leathery-faced man with a genuine smile and a crushing handshake.

''Ow do, I'm Arthur Fawcett – I understand you've got t'job. Aye, well done lad, well done: we're pleased to 'ave you.' I took to him right away, and he sensed that I needed to relax after the tension of the interview. He told me a little about himself: he was a builder in Cragthwaite, down from the school; born and bred in the dale, and now living in the next village along the road at Castle Heywood with Brenda and teenage son, Jimmy.

'You'll be looking for a place to live, lad. Do you 'ave a family?'

'No kids, but I got married last year.'

'Aye, I thought you looked a bit on t'young side to be sproggin' yet. Do you know it in't easy to buy a 'ouse round 'ere so if you need some accommodation, I've a holiday cottage I'm puttin' up, which you can 'ave for a good rent. Here's my number.' He tore the corner off a magazine on the staffroom table and licked on a pencil produced from the breast pocket of his weatherbeaten jacket before scribbling down a number.

'Thanks, Mr Fawcett, that's really kind.' I was amazed.

'No bother at all, lad – you'll be wanting it for the end of August, I reckon, ready to get stuck in t'classroom in September. Aye, it's a nice spot, aye.'

I recalled those words as the car edged down the tumbling lane, guarded by skeletal elms and stout ashes on mossy banks painted with pink dabs of herb robert. And suddenly we were there. The Mini was parked up ahead, and it was indeed a nice spot.

We stepped out of the car and into a new life. Sheltered on a tree-backed ledge on the hillside there was a stout, slate-topped stone house, which looked like it had once been a Victorian railway cottage, accompanied by a jumble of sheds. In the impossibly green field next to it, a little circle of rabbits scuttled in panic at our arrival and fled into the knot of hazels on the bank beside the house. Barbara let out a squeal of delight. To our left, a great picture of Swinnerdale opened up from our elevated position, with the huge bulk of Spout Fell dominating everything.

'There you are, dears.' Mrs Fawcett strode over and woke us up out of our awestruck reverie. She was pointing at a building site about fifty yards from the house, next to the lane. There were piles of stones, wheelbarrows, long pieces of timber and heaps of sand. In amongst the rubble, a small bungalow was emerging. 'Did Arthur tell you that the cottage wasn't quite finished?'

I looked at Barbara.

'Er, no, I don't think he did,' I said.

'How "not finished" is it?' asked Barbara, gingerly stepping between the debris near the door.

'Oh, don't worry, dear – it's fine inside. Arthur's been busy as I don't know what, but he'll have it sorted for you soon.'

It was a relief to discover that the inside of the little bungalow was indeed more or less ready for us to move in. It was spartan – the walls and floors were bare but everything was new and the place smelled clean. Our furniture was following on the next day, although it would be a miracle if the van could negotiate the fearful slopes and narrow track. In the meantime we organised the things we had brought with us in the car, and spent several hours making plans for this temporary home before finding something to eat.

Barbara stood up and stretched. 'I'd better call my mother and tell her we're here – you know how she worries.'

'Oh, I forgot to tell you that there's no phone.'

'No phone. Are you serious?'

'Arthur did mention it to me, sorry. He said they don't put them in holiday cottages and it'd be very expensive to have a new line installed. There's a call box in the village, though.'

'But that's right up the hill. And what if my parents want to call us?'

'I hadn't really thought of that.'

We finished the washing-up in silence.

Barbara scribbled a couple of things on a list then looked up. 'How far are we from the shops in Ingleburn?'

'I'm not sure – hang on, I'll get the road atlas from the car.' The time since our arrival at Castle Heywood had evaporated quickly with the welter of carrying and sorting, and night had fallen without either of us really noticing. When I opened the front door I received a severe shock. It wasn't just dark, it was black. It hadn't occurred to me that there would be no lighting outside, and the vast nothingness beyond the entrance made me realise that I had never really experienced proper darkness before. It was like being locked in a cupboard. Well, I thought, the car was out there somewhere; I remembered parking it just a few yards from the house. I stepped out and in a split second my chest nearly burst with fright as I felt myself falling. Had we rented a bungalow on the edge of a cliff? Then I hit the gravel of the drive with a jolt, which caused me to remember that the outside of the house was not as finished as the inside, and this included Mr Fawcett not yet having managed to put in a set of steps up to the raised front door.

I slid my foot forward carefully in case there were any obstacles, and waggled my hands out in front. I couldn't see my fingers. We really were in the middle of nowhere. Eventually I found the car and the road atlas. A faint grey light from behind the curtains of the bungalow helped me to grope my way back a little quicker. It had taken ten minutes to travel twelve yards. Well, I mused, the Fawcetts had warned us that we would find the pace of life slower in the Dales.

Back inside, the bare rooms hemmed in by the thick darkness suddenly looked less cheerful. I watched Barbara for a moment. She was unpacking the bundles of craft materials she used for making Christmas decorations – something we hoped would bring in valuable extra income until she found a job. I checked how far we were from the shops in Ingleburn. Eight miles. It looked like there was nothing in the tiny village up the hill, and Barbara couldn't yet drive. Was there a bus service? Would there be anyone to make friends with in this lonely spot? I didn't even want to think about the job situation. All the excitement of the early part of the day seemed to drain out of me. Had we made a rash choice?

My mind drifted back to the excitement of first finding the post advertised at college. There were so few teaching vacancies around, especially in North Yorkshire, that I'd simply had to apply, especially as the details made it clear that the school wanted a man. We'd only been married a year too, and were desperate to escape student poverty. To secure any teaching job was an achievement, surely? And there just wasn't anywhere else to live locally, certainly not at the bargain rent that Mr Fawcett was offering. I convinced myself that we'd had no option than to move here.

Three days before the start of term I was back at Cragthwaite School for the first time since my interview. The head, Howard Raven, had suggested that we should meet in order to sort out my classroom for the beginning of the new school year. I felt both apprehensive and energised by the responsibility and size of the task ahead: this was, after all, my first proper job and came on top of the weight of having to move to a new area and find a home.

Cragthwaite was one of the dale's larger villages, possessing a fine wide church, two pubs, a grocery store and, of course, a school. Cragthwaite CE Primary had been built fifteen years earlier to replace both a cramped Victorian building and three other tiny schools in surrounding villages, one of which had just five pupils when it closed. There had been considerable resentment that children from other communities had to be bussed into Cragthwaite, I later learned, although parents soon came to appreciate the advantages of a modern airy building with both a hall and kitchen; facilities that had been unknown in Swinnerdale up to that point.

The school was tucked away at the back of the village so that an adjacent meadow could be used for a sports field. The top of the field rose up the valley's side and commanded a splendid view over the stone rooftops of the village towards the fells. The school had four classes that catered for children of ages four to eleven; mine was to be Class 3, for eight- to nine-year-olds.

Howard Raven emerged from his office when I arrived. He was in his mid-fifties, I guessed, slight and with a stern grey moustache.

'Settled in to the bungalow? I hear that the removal van had trouble bringing your furniture.' His mouth suggested a smile, which didn't appear in his eyes.

'Er, yes – how did you know about that?'

'You'll soon appreciate how small the dale is, Andrew. Now, we've a lot to organise for your new class, so we'd better not waste time.' He held up a neat bundle of papers between thumb and forefinger then flicked through them efficiently. 'Class list, register, contact details, policies, dates for the year, record book and rules.' I was a little taken aback – I thought school rules only existed in Bash Street.

'Is there a planning book? And I need to know which topics I'm timetabled to do this term.' He looked rather bemused.

'Topics?'

'Yes, do you have a set list of themes for the year, like "The Romans" or "Transport", or do we choose our own?'

He surveyed me for a moment. 'I realise that you're straight out of college, Andrew, and that you'll have new ideas, but you need to understand very quickly that we run a traditional school here. We teach the basics very well and other things come second, or not at all.'

He began to march down the corridor that led away from the entrance hall. I followed, feeling more like a pupil than a member of staff. I thought about the exciting child-centred, progressive approaches we'd learnt about on teacher training. Mr Raven seemed to sum up everything that primary education had been moving away from for decades. He produced an enormous bundle of keys from his suit pocket and unlocked a plain wooden door. He opened it a little and, keeping one foot outside, leant in so that his body blocked my view.

'This is the stockroom.' He handed me a small green notebook then locked the door. 'Write down what you need each week – pencils, paper and so on – and give it to Eileen the secretary, on Wednesdays.' He then walked over to the school office and pointed to a small photocopier. 'Please give any copying to Eileen, preferably a day in advance. Staff are not to use the copier or telephone without permission.' The anticipation I'd felt whilst driving into the car park just a few minutes earlier had rapidly dissipated. 'Now, there are a lot more things I need to tell you but I expect you'll be wanting to get into your classroom, so the rest can wait a while. Valerie the deputy head will be along shortly; I'm sure she'll drop in to say hello.' His manner was very terse and I wondered if my face had betrayed too much disappointment when he'd outlined the school's approach to learning. It was a relief to escape the tour and explore my room.

The classroom was outside the main building – a 'mobile' of an early vintage, and showing its age. It was a square grey box, propped up on concrete blocks and sagging in the middle. Inside, it was light and more spacious than I'd expected, however – tatty but reasonably clean, and smelling of floor polish. A little excitement returned as I scanned the bare shelves and thought about the possibilities of what I could do with this, my very own room. I spied a pile of exercise books and picked one up. It was full of English exercises, neatly scribed with a fountain pen. The other books were much the same. Next to them was a small painted bookshelf containing archaic reading books. They were hardback editions, crusty and greyed. Inside, the text was in the jolly lilt of a bygone era; a line drawing of a Brylcreemed boy in shorts confirmed my fears.

'Yes, nineteen-bloody-fifties.'

I jumped, before spinning round to see a stocky female figure by the door. It was Val Croker, the deputy, and teacher of the oldest children. 'Sorry about that, Andy, didn't mean to give you the willies – you do like to be called Andy, don't you?' She flicked a cigarette butt out of the doorway and came into the room. 'This wreck should have been replaced years ago,' she said, peering at the leaning floor and pillars holding up the yellowed ceiling. I regarded her for a moment. She was broad and fierce-looking with tightly curled red hair and cool green eyes. 'Has the Beak given you the tour then?'

'You mean Howard?'

She chuckled. 'No one calls him Howard. We call him Mr Raven and the kids call him "the Beak" . . . or worse. Anyway, don't worry about him – you've got to get ready for your class. Is there anything you need?'

'Lots. I can't seem to find any backing paper for the display boards, and there's no sign of art materials.'

'Don't worry, I've got some stuff hidden away in my room you can have, and I'll lend you a few of my own easier reading books.' She shook her head at the painted bookshelf.

'Did you see inside the infamous main stock cupboard then?'

'Not really – what's he got in there?'

'What *hasn't* he got in there, more like . . .? Mind you, I've not been inside it for ten years or so.'

'Ten years?' I nearly screamed. 'How long have you been at this school, Val?'

'Eighteen. Started out at the old place down the village – now that was a dive. Raven's been here twenty-six years and I daren't tell you about Hilda.'

It occurred to me that I wasn't even born when Raven had started.

'Are all the other staff in today preparing as well?' I asked.

'They'll be in soon but I don't think they'll get a right lot done – they've got all their yacking about summer to do first. Anyway, I'll catch you later.'

After two hours of going through every cupboard and shelf in the classroom I was ready to stretch my legs a little, so I decided to have a nose around the rest of the school. I wandered into the hall first and was immediately struck by its newly polished floor glinting in the August sun. It was quite a large space for a school with only four full-time teachers, and served as a canteen at lunchtimes; dining tables and chairs were wedged into a storage area at one end next to a few baskets of tired-looking PE equipment.

On my way to say hello to the two infant teachers I passed a door I hadn't noticed before. It was half-open, allowing a broad Swinnerdale accent to echo into the corridor.

'You useless damn stupid mop.' A bang and metallic rattle followed. I tentatively pushed the door inwards. A plump backside of checked green nylon greeted me. Its owner was wrestling with a bucket by the look of things. I said hello in a quiet voice so as not to give her a fright. It didn't work.

'Eurrrrghh!' She shot upwards and around with surprising speed, grasping a broom handle ready for defence. 'You gave me a right flamin' shock there!' She put a hand over her imposing bosom.

'I'm sorry, I just wanted to introduce myself.'

'Funny way of doin' it. Any road, you must be the new junior teacher. You're very young.' I was to hear that a lot over the following months.

'Yes, my name's Andy. You must be the, er, caretaker?'

'Caretaker, cleaner, dogsbody . . . the only thing I refuse to do is get footballs down off the roof, not with my ankles, but I reckon you're perfect f'job. I'm Pat Rudds, by the way.'

Pat told me that she wasn't fussy about the state of the classrooms as long as the sinks were empty and the chairs were up on desks at the end of the day. 'If you want yer floor swept it's up to you.' She poked her head round the doorway. 'I think Eileen's just arrived if you want to go and frighten her too.'

I recalled that Eileen Marsett was the school secretary. Looking down the corridor I could see a woman, hands full, attempting to push open the office door with her back. I hurried down to help.

'Oh thank you, Andy. What a gentleman.' Eileen was old-school: a slim, demure person with dowdy clothes and delicate hands. She smiled and placed a small posy of garden flowers into a vase on her desk. 'There, I'm ready to work now. How are you settling in? Is your wife well?'

'Yes, we're both finding Arthur Fawcett's cottage quite an adventure.'

'Oh, he's a dear man though, Arthur. He'll sort you out if you have any problems. Now, do you need anything, home-wise? If you want to know about shops and things just ask me. Ingleburn's a funny old town, especially if you're new to it. And have they shown you where everything is at school? Oh sorry, I'm wittering at you. Listen, it's lunchtime – you go and sit down in the staffroom with the others and I'll come and put the kettle on.'

Feeling peckish, I didn't argue but headed back to my room to find the sandwiches I hoped I'd remembered to bring. I passed Val's classroom on the way back, the home of the top juniors, and stuck my head through the door. It was empty, as were the two large rooms full of miniature furniture that were the domain of Hilda and Emma, the infant teachers. Everyone was in the staffroom.

'Ah, the new boy has ventured to join us!' It was the diminutive Hilda Percival, the Class 2 teacher who, as I was soon to learn, loved nothing more than to give a running commentary on life. 'Come and sit down – any chair will do.' I took the nearest one. 'Except that one, Eileen always sits there.' I leant forward to get up. 'Ha ha, only kidding!' Hilda slapped her knee and chuckled. 'Byy, you're going to be an easy target, lad.'

Val shook her head. 'You can't stop her, Andy – you'll just have to put up with it.'

'We all suffer the same.' It was the Class 1 teacher, Emma Torrington, between bites of a slice of melon.

'Fear not, I'll be retiring soon,' countered Hilda. The contrast between the two infant teachers was striking. Tweed-skirted Hilda was petite, wrinkled and effervescent while Emma was tall, gentle and young, with long straggly hair and clothes that were astonishingly hippyish for a place like Cragthwaite.

'You can't retire,' said a dark-haired woman I hadn't met before, standing at the sink. 'You keep us sane.' She came over to me and offered a hand with a warm smile. 'I'm Sue Bramley, teaching assistant. I help Emma in Class One.'

'And do about five thousand other useful things,' said Val before I had a chance to reply.

Hilda looked at me. 'So, we don't know anything about you, young man, except that you're from York. Where did you go to college?'

'Actually, I've only lived in York a few years; I'm originally from the other side of the Pennines, in Cheshire.'

'Blinkin' Nora, a foreigner,' mumbled Val.

Hilda feigned shock. 'Well, it's regrettable but forgivable – just.'

'Did you train at St John's? I was there six years ago,' said Emma.

I nodded while crunching into an apple but Hilda didn't give me a chance to speak. 'York's a lovely spot but I bet they put you in a town school when you were training. You'll find it very different out here . . .'

Val brushed some crumbs off her front. 'The only thing he needs to know about this school is the playground duty rota and that we each have to give Eileen fifty pence coffee money a term.' I surreptitiously checked my pockets.

'Oh aye, if we forget she imposes biscuit withdrawal – that's serious,' said Hilda.

Emma laughed. 'It is for me – I never have time for breakfast.'

Sue Bramley was reassuring everyone that she'd put up a reminder notice when the door opened and Howard Raven walked in. He took an empty cup to the sink, pouting at the pile of melon seeds that Emma had left on the draining board.

'I've just been informed there may be a new girl starting in Class Two. Eileen hasn't received the details yet but hopefully she'll pass them on to you, Hilda.'

'Oh joy, more empty heads to fill,' she sighed.

Sue looked at the clock and Val shuffled a pile of papers then stood up. 'Right, lots to do, better press on.'

'Me too,' said Emma. I followed as everyone headed for the door.

I spent the next two days travelling between Castle Heywood, helping Barbara to make the bungalow habitable, and Cragthwaite, where I did the same with my classroom, assisted by Val. The cottage started to feel like a home, once we had put up a few Athena posters and found a place for all of our spider plants.

From the start, Barbara wanted to know all about the school. 'So, what's the head like, then?'

'He reminds me of one of those butlers from an old black-and-white film. In fact, I think the whole place is stuck in a time warp.'

'You don't sound too thrilled.'

'Well, the building is modern so I just didn't expect it somehow.'

'What about the other teachers?'

'Well, I've only really got to know the deputy, Val. She's friendly but you definitely wouldn't want to mess with her. Hilda looks about eighty and she gabbles continuously. She's a bit of a joker, too. Then there's Emma who's maybe in her late twenties and takes the little ones. She's a real mystery – just doesn't seem to fit the place at all – she's all bangles and hair. And Eileen the secretary and Sue the NTA are nice . . .'

Barbara stopped what she was doing and looked at me. 'You sound a bit apprehensive about it all – that's not like you.'

I tried not to grimace but I couldn't disguise my disappointment. 'I think it's going to be a lot harder than I expected, that's all.' Barbara gave me a hug and I changed the subject. 'But anyway, what about you? Have you sussed the village yet?'

'Not really, I've been too busy trying to get my tools and things together for making the Christmas decorations. I'll need to get started if I can't find a job otherwise I'll be twiddling my thumbs all day.'

'Did you ask Mrs Fawcett next door about finding work, then?'

'She said we need to get the weekly local paper, the Bilthorpe and something *Gazette* – it's all advertised in there.'

'I'd better drive to Ingleburn, then.'

'No need, they're dropped off in the village. There's no shop but we need to speak to Mrs Partridge up there – apparently she knows everything. She can sort us out with milk too. You see it's all under control.'

I looked at her deep brown eyes. 'But aren't you going to get bored when I'm out all day? We should have got you driving lessons in York.'

'Oh stop fretting, I'll be fine. We couldn't afford lessons and you need the car for work anyway. Mrs Fawcett says there's a bus into town once a day and the decorations'll keep me busy.' She smiled and poked me playfully on the nose. 'Let's have a hot chocolate.'

The final day of the holiday passed quickly and a sense of anticipation bubbled in me as the start of term became imminent, tempered with a good measure of anxiety about being let loose as a teacher. I was looking forward to meeting my very first class, and I had another glance through the class list to try to conjure up characters to match the names: Wilf Bainbridge, Heather Thistlethwaite, Fergus Mudd, Sylvia Hammond. I couldn't wait.

Twenty-four fresh, ruddy faces weighed me up. I was nervous and they knew it. They laughed at the way I pronounced Carol Dinsdale during the register, but not mockingly.

'Tha wants more of a "Dinsdull", Mr Seed,' piped a cheery face from the back. They were very patient as I explained all the things they already knew, like when PE was and where to hang coats. I was desperate to learn who was who, and a few seemed to sense this, beginning questions and answers with their names:

'Malcolm here, Mr Seed; 'ave I to give out the hymnbooks for assembly?'

'Eve. My dad says that you've just come out of college – is that right?'

'Mr Seed – I'm Jack by't way – willus be 'aving 'omework?'

Within a couple of days I knew their names and after a week I knew who they were: who was boss, who were friends, who lived on a farm, who was an offcomer, who liked maths and who didn't, who did the talking and who did the working. It was great fun going home each evening to fill Barbara in with all the details of the rich personalities under my charge.

'You look exhausted, poor thing,' she said to me on the first Friday evening.

'Never mind that,' I said, snuggling up to her on the settee, 'I want to know how *you're* getting on – what's happening in the village?'

'Well, considering there's only a castle, a church and about ten houses, not a lot.'

'No scandal then?'

'Ha! Well, only the arrival of a couple of strange incomers down here.'

'Have you met Mrs Pheasant yet?'

'Mrs Partridge, you noodle. Oh yes, you can't miss her – she spends all her time gardening at the front of her house. I think it's so she can spy on what's going on. Actually, she's really friendly.'

'I thought there was nothing going on.'

'Well, you know, she likes to keep an eye on everyone's doings. She already knew that we'd come from York and that this was your first job.'

'How'd she manage that?'

'That's what I asked. It's because everyone seems to know each other in the whole dale. In fact, from what Mrs P says, they're all related. You probably won't believe it but all the families except three in Castle Heywood are Partridges.'

'Val told me it was like that – jungle drums.' I stifled a yawn. 'The same farming families have lived here for generations, apparently. Anyway, did you manage to sort out the milk and papers?'

'The milk we collect from two old sisters called the Miss Kirks – it's from their nephew's farm in the village. The papers are left in Spence's stick 'ut – that's Mrs P's brother-in-law at the end of the road.'

'What's a stick 'ut?'

'Fancy not knowing that . . . I'll take you up there tomorrow. But anyway, I've been through the *Gazette* and the only jobs are in Bilthorpe, which is hours by bus. Oh, and someone down the dale wants a pig man.'

'Don't we all . . .' We giggled for a moment and Barbara flashed her lovely smile. 'But what *are* you going to do with yourself all day?'

'Oh something'll turn up job-wise and I've already started cutting some new decorations. Perhaps we can go to Hauxton on Sunday and see if there are any craft markets there.'

Barbara was very upbeat but I knew she was missing her friends from York. What would happen when the newness of everything wore off?

'Actually, I've already made a new friend,' she said, as if reading my mind. 'Ada Gill. She lives up in the village – Mrs Partridge introduced us. She's really sweet, I can't wait for you to meet her.'

'Er, Ada doesn't sound like a spring chicken.'

Barbara smiled. 'No, she's what my mother would call a spinster. But she does keep chickens and she's going to supply us with fresh eggs. And just wait until you taste her baking . . . it's very old-fashioned but heavenly, reminds me of your granny's.'

'But will you be happy spending your time talking to elderly ladies?' Part of me wondered whether she was trying to make herself believe it.

'She's fascinating, honestly. Her house is like going back to the Victorian era with stone-flagged floors. She still has a mangle! And, she has three cats and you know I can't resist cats.'

I wasn't completely convinced but by this point my eyelids were descending of their own accord.

As the early weeks passed, one problem that I had to overcome was the language. Yorkshire people have some fine expressions of their own, and as time went on I gradually became used to the vagaries of the local dialect and the turn of phrase used by the people of the Dales and their children in my care, although a few expressions still befuddled me. One instance of this was their use of the word *off*. I asked Val about it one morning before school.

She was typically blunt. 'Everyone says, "I must be off", don't they? It just means going. What's up with you?'

'Yes, they do but the way they use it here doesn't make sense to me: people say "I'm off out", which is OK, but yesterday I heard "I'm off shopping".'

'What's wrong with that?'

'Doesn't that mean they've had enough of shopping?'

'Don't be daft. They would say "I'm right off shopping" if they mean that.'

'What about "he's off courtin'"?'

'Oh shut up and mark some books.'

Despite Val's lack of help, my understanding of this linguistic matter reached a new level of insight one peculiar September morning early in my first term.

Eight-year-old Jack Raw was a solid citizen. Until I met him, I had no idea that human beings could be wider than they were tall. His arms and legs were like giant babies' limbs, and his chest was a formidable expanse topped by a neck which could have supported at least three heads. Jack's face was soft and amiable, however, testifying to his tender personality. He was always equipped with hearty greetings, and was almost old-fashioned in his morning enquiries when entering the classroom:

'Grand day, Mr Seed. Are y' keeping well then?'

'How's Mrs Seed, then – all proper?'

'I don't know about that tie, Mr Seed; old 'un, is it?'

I enjoyed these little exchanges with the portly Jack and so did everyone else in the class. But although Jack was indeed a character, and undoubtedly robust of body, the same could not be said for his thought. Jack was as slow and steady as the Whitby tide. When questioned in class, he seemed to have the ability to draw his eyes back into their sockets, leaving deep gloomy recesses. It was almost as if his brain were saying, 'Aye up, tricky one here – come on inside, eyes – I need all the help I can get with this . . .'

Jack and schoolwork just didn't get along. Pencils snapped in his brawny fingers, pages curled up in front of him and all his books fell apart. It seemed like numbers and letters were his foes, to be fended off and regarded with deepest suspicion at all times. But as much as he loathed academic work, Jack loved anything practical: the hands which could never grasp a pen properly were nimble masters of a hacksaw; hammers, drills and rasps were like old friends, controlled with energetic purpose and accuracy. He leapt at any opportunity to help a classmate fix a model or to demonstrate how to extract a bent nail. Jack similarly excelled in the school garden, so enjoying outdoor tasks that he would frequently get carried away. It was a dangerous move to turn your back if you had asked Jack to make a hole for a bedding plant; when you looked round he would be down in a chasm fit for a coffin, manically flinging dirt all over the paths and grassed areas with a simple grin.

Jack was legendary for his strength, and Jack's mother was legendary for her absence notes. Jack was frequently away 'badly' and would always appear after a day or two clutching the corner of a cereal packet or a grey, rolled-up fragment from an old envelope, bearing a blotchy message. These 'letters' were small masterpieces of vivid fiction, detailing whole series of incredible circumstances that conspired to keep Jack away from school. I often wondered how she never made it as a scriptwriter. One of her best detailed a particularly bizarre natural phenomenon:

> *Deer Mr Seed,*
> *I am sorry that are Jack was not at school yesterday. He put on such a groth spurt in the night that nun of his clowthes fiited im next morning so I had to take him to shops.*
>
> — *Mrs R.*

It was after one of these brief sojourns that Jack turned up to school looking very strange. He waddled into the classroom, smiling as ever, but with both ears wedged full of pink toilet paper. He was keen to tell me something.

'HEY, MR SEED.' (Louder than usual.) 'I'M OFF DEAF.'

'You're what, Jack?'

'I'M OFF DEAF.'

'What do you mean?'

'DOCTOR SEZ AF TAF OPERATION.'

'An operation – what for?'

'HIS GUNTA PUT GROMICKS IN ME EARS, SO I'M OFF DEAF.'

At this point, our baffling bellowed conversation suddenly made sense – it was the good old Yorkshire use of the word *off* again: he meant 'I'm going to be deaf'. The strange thing was, he seemed very pleased about it all. I couldn't wait to read the absence note for this one (it reminded me of the time when another child had pus leaking out of a lobe, and was overheard telling his friend that he had dire ear). Jack was very keen to explain the intricacies of the operation as he saw them and so the conversation continued for some time, with Jack proudly pointing out his comical ear plugs to every child who entered the room for registration. He eventually finished our exchange with a typically fine dialogue:

'AYE, I'M OFF DEAF I AM.'

'So, you won't be able to hear anything?'

'NO, THAT'S RIGHT.'

I looked once more at the tissues. 'Can you hear me now?'

'NO.'

Chapter Two

Carol

Mid-September brought four days of rich amber sunshine that drew Barbara and me out of our cottage in the early evenings and up the hill to the village. We made the walk every day to collect milk and the local newspaper, but the glorious scenery and invigorating Dales air made the journey much more of a pleasure than a chore and our doubts about living in such an isolated spot were temporarily evaporated by the landscape's splendour.

The steep road was edged with banks of blackthorn bearing their enticing blue-black sloes and jostling with wild roses and elders, whose clusters of fruit weighed down every branch. Tall wisps of rosebay willowherb nodded in the breeze and further up the field, walls were hidden by rows of blackened sweet cicely, its upright seed pods like miniature overripe bananas. The air carried the gentle fragrance of aniseed. I unexpectedly found myself with a strong urge to know the names of all of the flowers I passed on this delightful amble.

Barbara stopped and stared ahead. Heywood Castle had suddenly loomed into view: a magnificent stone fortress with sheer sides of rusted stone peppered with yellow lichen and scaled by clusters of brave wallflowers. With massive towers and dark windows, impossibly dramatic, it must have terrified visitors in the distant past who approached the village along this tranquil lane. We reached the castle, with the tiny village sheltering in the shadow of its towering bulk, and stopped to rest. Its back was shattered open by centuries of relentless storms and further ransacked by locals who made welcome use of the good building stone while the structure was uninhabited.

A little church was curiously positioned behind the castle, its modest square form completely dwarfed by the soaring walls only twenty yards away. It was nonetheless dignified, standing upright with its miniature box-like tower, bare and uncomplicated. The view over the dale from here was worth our breathless trek alone, and we stopped again to survey the sun's tracing of Spout Fell's immense form. To our left, the village stood on its lofted hillside shelf, a broad empty strip of grass with a few quiet cottages, each weighed down against the constant wind by great thick slabs of stone on the roof. As always in a Pennine village, Land Rovers, tractors and pickups were strewn about. The only movement apart from the swaying ashes on the green came from swallows skimming the grass for insects and yakking on the overhead wires in groups of six or seven.

'Now then youngsters, what are you up ter?' Mrs Partridge raised herself from her knees as we passed her pristine little front garden, a bunch of purple daisies in one hand. 'Fetchin' yer paper 'n' milk I expect.'

'And enjoying this beautiful day,' said Barbara.

'Aye, September doesn't come any grander'un this – mek most of it!' She was a tall woman of indeterminate age with a windswept visage. 'Have you a job yet, then?' she looked at Barbara.

'No, I'm just going to check the *Gazette* again.'

'Well, yer wasting time there if you ask me. There's no work in the dale unless you're a farmer or a builder and they don't make cheese round 'ere any more, more's the pity. What did you do before, lass?'

'Well university until summer last year—'

'University, eh?' Mrs Partridge interrupted. 'I only know one person who's been to college and that's Felicity ovver yonder but she's a bit, well, superior, if you get my drift.' Her shoulders rustled as she said it. 'Anyroad, sorry pet, carry on.'

'Er, and then while Andy did his teacher training last year I worked part time as a barmaid and did waitressing at a hotel while I was looking for a full-time job.'

'Oh, interesting . . .' she said, raising her eyebrows, 'Well, the trouble is that everyone round here does about five part-time jobs so there aren't any going. My William – that's my eldest son – he's the postman in't' morning, cooks at the pub in Crackby in the evening and helps out at me brother's farm rest o' the time, y'see.'

Barbara made a determined effort to resist the doom-mongering. 'Well, I do crafts as well so I'll just have to keep busy with those.'

'She makes beautiful wooden Christmas decorations,' I added, noting the level of intrigue in Mrs P's eyes.

'What, for shops you mean?'

'No, we sell them ourselves at craft fairs – do they have craft fairs round here?' said Barbara.

'Well, they do in Kettleby – lots of tourists there in summer – but you'll be wanting something in November or December I would've thought. Bilthorpe maybe? How did you get into that, anyhow?'

'We went to Austria last year and saw some in a shop. I thought I'd have a go at making some similar ones. We sold lots in York.'

'Oh, right, well, it's different . . .' Mrs P looked extremely doubtful.

I grabbed Barbara's hand and pulled her away saying that we had to get going while thinking to myself that the whole village would be aware within minutes that I was keeping my wife at home doing joinery.

We headed for the farm at the end of the village, to 'Spence's stick 'ut' as Mrs Fawcett had memorably named it. The 'ut was a small doorless stone outbuilding attached to a barn, and inside was a pile of newspapers. I picked one up and we headed for the Miss Kirks' dairy. On the way, Barbara waved to Ada Gill, who was bringing her washing in. She wore a headscarf and waddled towards us on lumpy legs.

'Now, Barbara, I've got that Be-Ro book for you, and a curd tart,' she called. 'You can't go wrong wi' a Be-Ro book.'

'You go and chat, I'll get the milk,' I said.

I knocked on the Miss Kirks' ancient door. It opened slowly, revealing their bulky nephew Edward assaulting the remains of magnificent Yorkshire high tea: a round table arrayed with sandwiches, pies, cakes, buns and tarts all on china dishes. One of the frail ladies led me round the side to a crate of green-topped farm milk in her cool dairy. I took a couple of pints and sighed at the wonderful simplicity of life here.

* * *

School, meanwhile, was far from simple. There was so much to learn and so many ways to do things wrong. At least I wasn't alone: the first few weeks had enabled me to get to know the other teachers quickly, and it was a relief to discover that they were more than willing to accept a new apprentice to the trade.

The Class 1 teacher, Emma Torrington, continued to intrigue me. She was only six years older than me, but seemed impossibly experienced and energetic, fuelled by a tremendous love for children. She was as sweet as she was disorganised, which was reflected by her chaotic appearance: wild hair of an indeterminate hue and abundant cottony clothes in vibrant colours, weighed down by pounds of jewellery.

I'd plucked up the courage to ask Val why Emma was here when she clearly didn't fit the school's traditional outlook.

'Good question and you probably won't believe the answer,' she said.

'Go on.'

'Well, for a start she gets away with things because the Beak's scared of little ones.'

'You're kidding! He doesn't look like he's frightened of anything.'

'Oh, yes he is – it's because they're still untamed and have to be allowed to play. He can't cope with kids who aren't tied to desks in silence.'

'But surely he could have found someone more, er, conservative than Emma when she got the job.'

'Oh yes, there was someone in the running but Emma pulled out an ace at the interview.'

'What d'you mean?'

'She wore a "really lovely dress". His words.'

She had to be having me on. 'Val, that just can't be true.'

'I told you you wouldn't believe me.'

It was perhaps no surprise that Hilda Percival, the Class 2 teacher, despaired of Emma's frenzied approach to teaching; they were such polar opposites. Hilda herself was a legend in Cragthwaite. She seemed to know everyone in Swinnerdale and had probably taught half of them during her forty years in the classroom. Small, crumpled and sharp as glass, Hilda had a wit that carried the force of a potent disposition, and sorry was any child who crossed her. Her lectures about good behaviour were, I soon learned, as rich a feature of the school as any fitting or fixture: her preferred subject was the boys' toilet and, more specifically, the quality of the 'aiming' that led to its foul odour. She despaired about this to the six- and seven-year-old boys she taught, then despaired some more in the staffroom at break-times, in between despairing about Emma in the classroom next door. Somehow though, however much she complained and rebuked, there always seemed to be an eddy of laughter around Hilda Percival.

It was Hilda who gave me a shock one morning by announcing that Howard Raven was looking for me.

'Don't worry – it's just something about your new subject leader role.'

'My what?'

'It was all in the advert when you applied for the job, wasn't it? We all have to be an expert in some aspect of education these days, you know.'

I cast my mind back and recalled the wording of the newspaper advertisement for the post: *The successful candidate will be responsible for the development of Design and Technology throughout the school.* It hadn't occurred to me that now that I had the job, I was actually expected to do something about this; nervously, I turned towards the headteacher's office.

Howard Raven passed me a thick green document. There was no hello.

'I haven't time to go into it now but you'd better read this,' he said, and disappeared, clutching a heavy armful of similar official-looking booklets. It was titled *The New Curriculum: Design and Technology in the Primary School*, and was crammed with bold-typed lists of expectations, aims, objectives, targets and the like: looking at it made me feel almost queasy.

The government of the day had decided to shake up the education system: they wanted to streamline everything, hoping to ensure that each teacher in the country knew exactly what he or she was supposed to be teaching and how. With this in mind, every subject taught in the primary school was awarded one of these curriculum documents, and every school was told that a teacher must be selected to co-ordinate each subject. Up to this moment I had felt quite pleased with myself that I had been given such a responsibility, particularly as a new teacher. I hadn't realised that I was, in fact, landed with 'D&T' because no one else wanted it. It soon became clear that ours was such a small school that every teacher was required to lead several subjects anyway.

Now that I read what was expected of me, the awful realisation dawned that this was indeed a bum job: Design and Technology was new to most primary schools, and teachers who were up to their eyeballs with countless new demands in English and Maths didn't want to know. When my colleagues found out what they were expected to teach in this Cinderella subject they were surely going to go spare, and I would bear the brunt of their disgruntlement.

The document was written in a strange semi-technical language that had no home in the average primary school: it was full of references to systems, product design, mechanisms, structures and other nonsensical jargon. It seemed like the average seven-year-old would have to go from sticking yoghurt pots on top of egg boxes to aerospace engineering within a term. I decided that it was probably just difficult to read because it was new and I was new to it – everything would all be perfectly clear the second time I read it. It was worse the second time. The third time I looked at the words but my mind had given up and was thinking about what was for lunch. This was bad news.

A couple of weeks later, having talked to a few teachers from other schools and seen a couple of explanations of the new curriculum in proper English, I began to piece together a vague idea of what primary teachers were supposed to be doing with their children in Design and Technology lessons. It was still very frightening, but at least it was now somehow tangible. The gist of the matter was that children had to design and make lots of really good things then test them and improve them so they would be *really, really* good. But it was no use children making models of Tudor houses or puppets from lolly sticks – the 'outcomes' that the children were to make had to meet proper needs, like in the real world, according to the new document. Every teacher who read the curriculum agreed on one thing: whoever wrote it was clearly unhinged. Children didn't make (or indeed do) anything at school to meet a need – they did it because the teacher told them to. But teachers, it seemed, weren't to be asked about these matters, and so I spent most of a dreary late September weekend wondering how I was going to address my new responsibility.

By late Sunday night I hadn't done too well. In fact, I'd done nothing. I knew what Jack Raw felt like when he said, 'I'm stook.' Well, actually, one decisive thought had been adopted: the only way that I was going to get D&T going in Cragthwaite School was by setting a good example myself. I needed to do a really spectacular project that would inspire the other teachers and children – something to get the whole thing off to a great start. The trouble was that I couldn't think of any needs that could be met by wizard new technologies created by eight- and nine-year-olds.

Barbara came in with a cup of tea. She looked at me and then at the document on my desk. I heard a sigh.

'This is for young kids to do? I can see why you've been so miserable all weekend. Who wrote this twaddle?'

'I don't know and I don't care. All that matters is that I'm supposed to know how to do all this.'

She put her arms over my shoulders. 'I thought that someone from another school had explained it to you.'

'They have, but I don't know how to start teaching it with my class. We're supposed to identify a real-life problem to solve and then fix it – in my case with gummed paper and string, since that's all there is. Have you got any brainwaves?'

'Maybe you should break something in the classroom so that

the children can make a new one. At least there'll be a genuine need.' Barbara looked very pleased with her suggestion, which was more than I did.

In the end I didn't have to wait long for the answer.

Tuesday's staff meeting began with the Beak announcing that a lady from the Royal National Institute for the Blind would be visiting the following week, and that she would be showing a video to the whole school about the work of the organisation. I wasn't listening very hard, but I scribbled the date and time in my diary like everyone else, then went back to worrying about the D&T document. The rest of the meeting passed me by until the end; the last item on the agenda was a killer.

'I'd like all subject co-ordinators to present a summary of their new curriculum documents at next week's meeting, along with a list of suggestions for implementing them.' For some reason he looked at me sternly when he said this part. Had I said something to upset him?

Mrs Spoonwick from the RNIB was not a very thrilling speaker, and I spent the first part of her talk machine-gunning brutal stares towards my class who were fidgeting in extremis.

'Now I have told you a little about the work of the Institute, children, I am going to show you all a film about what it is like to be a blind person, and about some of the things which help blind people to have a better life.' There was a small cheer as the hall curtains were drawn and most of the lights turned off. The video fizzed into life, and the children's attention was recaptured instantly.

The film was excellent. It centred on a teenage boy who had been born blind, and a sweet old lady who had gradually lost her sight. Both characters spoke openly about their everyday problems, and the children were fascinated to see and hear about what seemed like another world. The teenage boy demonstrated a number of useful gadgets which had been provided for him by the RNIB, including a folding white stick, rattling football, and a clever device for indicating when a cup was full of water. It took me a good few minutes to realise that what was being demonstrated was real technology, and a further few seconds to see that it had been purposely made to meet a specific need. I rushed out for a pad to make some notes – this was exciting.

When I returned, the real star of the video was being featured – the delightful old lady. She was ancient, tiny, blind, but fantastically independent and uncomplaining. She gave a guided tour of her home to show how it had been carefully adapted to meet her needs.

'There's only one thing I have real trouble with,' she said. 'Cupboard doors. I can't tell if they're open or closed and I sometimes walk right into them – not nice that isn't.' I made a note and mentally planned a whole series of D&T lessons in that moment. The children asked a multitude of questions when the video was over, even the fidgeters in my class, and I was delighted that they were as interested in the subject as I was. I loved that old lady.

When Thursday afternoon's D&T session arrived I was ablaze with enthusiasm for our new project: Technology for the Blind. I couldn't wait to get started, and I was convinced that the class would be just as eager. A group had been chosen to make designs for folding white sticks, and another to try to come up with new ideas for inventions suggested by the film. The rest of the class were going to tackle the cupboard door problem. Several children had suggested that it might be possible to make cupboard doors that closed automatically, and this seemed like an excellent problem to solve. I had raided Beasley's supermarket in Ingleburn and managed to find enough large strong cardboard boxes to act as cupboards; the box lids made perfect doors with which to experiment.

After half an hour, the classroom was buzzing with furious activity: the sounds of cutting, sawing, hammering, gluing, stapling, taping and drilling were punctuated with bursts of animated conversation about joints, hinges and handles. I could already see some ingenious solutions to the cupboard problem beginning to take shape. Wilf and Cameron had rigged up an admirable system with a piece of string tied to a door via a cotton reel pulley; when the door was opened it raised a ball of plasticine, the weight of which closed the door when it was left open. I was going to take a closer look at another idea involving a Lego motor when a large margarine box was shoved into my side. It was Carol Dinsdale; she giggled apologetically.

Carol was a cheerful, quiet girl with long limp hair and a sallow complexion. She was the type of child who it was somehow hard to get to know – she rarely offered information about herself or her family and was easily overlooked in a classroom of characters. I made an inward resolution to pay her more attention in future, but it wasn't the first time I had done this.

'Mr Seed, me an' Tracey 'ave 'ad an idea for the cupboard door. Can we 'ave some laggy bands – I mean elastic bands, please?'

'Of course, Carol – there's a pile on my desk.' I remembered that Eileen the school secretary had left me some yesterday; she was a wonderful ally in my recently established campaign to find resources for the children. Howard Raven clearly had no intention of spending money on subjects like Design & Technology, despite all the demands of the curriculum. But right now I was too absorbed in the classroom's atmosphere of creative excitement to dwell on the matter. I wondered whether to follow Carol to try and observe her making skills, but was accosted by two more pairs of boys asking for advice before I could move. In fact I didn't escape from that corner of the room for at least twenty minutes; many of the class's first ideas had by now been tested and exultant children were beginning to head towards me to demonstrate their creations, along with a few rather more downcast individuals seeking inspiration.

I was about to stop the class and allow a few children to show the others what they had already achieved when Carol bounded towards me again, with Tracey in tow.

'Mr Seed – look at ours, it really works!' I had never seen her so animated; I was delighted, and immediately asked for a full demonstration. The box had a number of roughly hewn holes, both in the top and 'doors'. There was a tangled coil of wire in two of the holes at the top, attached to the thickest elastic band I had ever seen. I recognised it as one of the ones that the postman used to secure the huge bundles of mail that arrived at the school every morning. The other end of this piece of industrial rubber was fixed to one flap of the box, again with large amounts of wire.

There was no slack in it. The girls had obviously practised the scenario: Tracey went round the back of the box and grabbed its sides with strong hands. Carol positioned herself at one side, with her left hand on top of the box and her legs well spaced apart. She looked up at me.

'Are you ready?'

I wasn't sure.

'Er, ready.'

Carol tensed her body and began to heave the door of the cardboard cupboard open. I stood back. Several other children were watching and the classroom went strangely quiet. Carol's knuckles turned a bloodless ivory as she fought against the enormous tension of the giant rubber band, the poor box twisting and warping with the strain. I wondered whether to intervene, but Carol gave a final pull so that the door was clearly open. She looked up again, and blinked as a bead of sweat rolled into her eye.

'Now watch it close automatically, Mr Seed'.

It certainly closed all right: Carol snatched her hand away, as if she had suddenly found herself too close to a crocodile. WHAM! The lid ripped back, and the whole box leapt a couple of inches into the air. Carol beamed. Tracey beamed. I thought about the little old blind lady. To my amazement, Malcolm Willoughby and several other watching children murmured their approval at the efficiency of the design.

'Er, that's fantastic, girls,' I said. 'Can you try to find a way to slow it down just a little when it closes now?' It was tempting to simply tell them to abandon the design but I needed to hold on to the spirit of the new curriculum: test and improve. Also, I didn't have the heart to appear in any way critical of their idea when they, and the watching children, were so delighted with it. I barely had time to check out the progress of some of the other groups when the two girls were back.

'We've improved it, Mr Seed,' said Carol.

'We've added weights to slow it down,' said Tracey, placing the cardboard box in front of me once more in a very satisfied manner. The box looked much as it did before, with the great inner tube of a rubber band wired to the top, except that there were now two large metal one-kilogram weights dangling from the front. They were the black hexagonal type with metal rings, and they were attached to the door of the model cupboard with two more outsized elastic bands; they dangled at the front, and knocked together on their bungees with a clank of latent danger. I was too mesmerised to react.

'Can we demonstrate it to the class, Mr Seed – please? Pleeease!' I had never seen Carol Dinsdale like this before.

'Of course you can, girls.' I gulped and told everyone to sit down. Maybe this was a good opportunity to do some of the evaluation activities that the new technology document kept referring to.

By the time the class had reluctantly settled back into their seats, the two girls had set up their box on a table at the front where everyone could see. Carol gave an eloquent introduction, explaining the problem they were trying to solve, and how they had already tried it with just the rubber band. The class listened intently.

'We 'ave added two weights to slow the door down and now we are going to demonstrate 'ow this works.' Once again Tracey took up her wide supporting position, and Carol grasped the cardboard door firmly, ready to heave it open. The two black weights swayed and clanked. The watching children were very impressed. With a couple of strains, bracing her whole body, Carol levered the door open. I stood a little further back. When she let go I was amazed to see the door slam shut just as quickly and violently as before. It was immediately followed by the two huge black weights swinging round in a terrifying horizontal arc like a medieval bolas. They smashed brutally into the front of the box, which was still being admirably held by Tracey Pratt. Both girls were smiling – they obviously considered the demonstration a major success. This seemed like a great opportunity for some class discussion.

'Well, thank you, girls – very impressive.' The class murmured their agreement. 'Now, can anyone suggest how this design might be improved?' I expected a rush of hands. There were none.

'Do you think that the door closes as well as it should?' No response. My voice began to rise a little. 'Remember – this is a kitchen cupboard door for a blind person. Could it be better in any way at all?' One or two children shuffled, but still no one answered. The metal weights were still swinging; I was almost cross now. 'Right. Listen. There is a little old blind lady in her home and she has asked the vicar round for tea; she decides to use her best china, which is kept in this cupboard. She's a tough old bird and she somehow manages to get the door open. She reaches up for her antique teapot, and then lets go of the door, safe in the knowledge that it will close automatically. As she lets go, two enormous pieces of iron come flying towards her. Is this going to work?' There was a moment of silence. Most of the faces still stared blankly forward. I was becoming really impatient.

'What's the answer then?'

Malcolm Willoughby's hand began to ascend. Joy – at last!

'Yes Malcolm?'

'She could wear a crash helmet.'

I was relieved to reach the staffroom after the final bell. Hilda pushed a steaming cup of coffee across the table towards me as I relayed the tale.

'Well, rather you than me doing this technology business, that's all I can say.' She headed towards the door, chuckling. I felt sure that she carried on talking as she walked away down the corridor: it sounded distinctly like, 'The blind leading the blind . . .'

Chapter Three

Malcolm

'Ever been to Northumberland, Andy?'

Val's question took me by surprise. I was sitting in the staffroom half asleep with weariness at the end of another exhausting day with my class. I had no idea that teaching could be so physically strenuous, in addition to being mentally and emotionally draining.

'The boy needs iron tonic,' piped Hilda, before I could answer. 'When I was at college doing my teaching practice, the head wouldn't let me into the classroom before I'd had two teaspoons of iron tonic.'

Val smiled; it looked like she'd heard this before.

'Er no, I've never been. Why do you ask?' I said.

'Tasted rank, that stuff,' interrupted Hilda again.

'Your class's residential trip goes to Northumberland,' continued Val. 'It's in June next year – I expect we'll both be asked to go.'

'That tonic used to make *me* go,' said Hilda with big eyes. 'Byy, I was out to that lav across the yard like no one's business.' I tried to concentrate on Val, who didn't even seem to notice Hilda's ramblings.

'Won't that be difficult with both junior teachers away, Val?'

'There needs to be a male and a female member of staff and he likes me to be there as deputy head. You obviously need to go because it's your class; I reckon Mr Raven'll be glad of a break too – he's been on the last four trips himself. He's going to have a word with you about it tomorrow.'

'I wonder if you can still get that stuff?' Hilda was still oblivious, but the thought of a few days away with the children perked me up, and I questioned Val about the details for the next twenty minutes. The trip took place every two years, and involved five days away on a tiny island just off the Northumbrian coast called Oswalfarne. It sounded quite an adventure for juniors.

The following day, Howard Raven filled in more details about the visit and confirmed, in his usual semi-formal manner, that he'd like me to go. He also explained that arrangements needed to be made several months in advance so that parents had plenty of time to save the £65 that the trip would cost for each child.

'Right. I'll send out a letter to parents tomorrow, giving details about the trip and the date for a meeting where they can ask questions; you'll need to be there too, of course.' After a silent scan of the wall displays, he left my room, leaving me feeling very excited and already planning to go up to Oswalfarne with Barbara, perhaps at a weekend, to explore.

There was even more excitement at the end of school a day later when I announced the visit to the class. A tremendous babble of anticipation immediately swept through the room and animated faces turned to their neighbours with plans and suggestions for who might share a room in the hotel. Amongst the fervour, there was one face, however, which didn't light up; in fact, if anything, Martha Micklegate looked upset by the news of the trip. She sat quite still and looked down with her large eyes. I was both surprised and intrigued by Martha's reaction, but decided not to question her about it in front of her friends; I'd wait for a quiet moment the next day.

In the event, I didn't have to wait, and it certainly wasn't a quiet moment when I discovered the reason for Martha's gloom. At quarter past eight before school the following morning, my classroom door opened with a boom like a mortar, and into the room marched a fearsome-looking woman pulling a reluctant girl in tow. She strode right up to me and waved a piece of paper in my face. I recognised it as the letter about the residential visit and I recognised the girl as Martha.

'What's all this about sixty-five pound for a blinkin' trip?'

'Hello, Mrs Micklegate, is it?'

'Yes, it is and before you say anything else let me get one thing straight: Martha's not going on this pointless trip cos I aren't paying sixty-five blinkin' quid, or even one penny.' I felt the blast of her breath across my eyes.

'Would you like to sit down to talk about this, Mrs Micklegate?' I tried to remain calm but my heart was racing. Poor Martha stood well back, cringing with embarrassment. Her mother, meanwhile, ignored my question and continued her aggressive bluster.

'Why should we 'ave to pay for school stuff? School's supposed to be free, isn't it? I pay enough in stupid rates and taxes.' Her chin was jutting forward and strands of thin hair fell across her cheeks as she spoke.

'The trip isn't until June next year, Mrs Micklegate, and we've sent out the letter in September to give parents plenty of time to save up the money.' I realised very quickly that this was the wrong approach. A finger jutted towards my chest in rhythm with the snarl of her reply.

'There's not going to be any money and I don't care if you give me ten years' warning – where school's concerned, I aren't paying for owt. I can't see the point of this trip anyway.' I stepped back behind my desk and pretended to look for some papers. There was no point in arguing with this woman. Her eyes, huge and burning, dared me to challenge her but I was ready for a full retreat.

'I, er, think you'd better see the headteacher about this, Mickeys Misslegate. He's in charge of the trip.' Two children's faces appeared through the door, wondering what all the noise was about.

'I intend to go and see 'im, and he's going to get the same mouthful as you. She's not going and that's that.' With a snatched turn and stomp she was gone. My heart was thumping in the sudden silence of the room. It was my first 'concerned' parent.

That night I poured out the whole story to Barbara, who was as upset for poor Martha as I was. She nestled up to me, saying she was sure that something could be done about the situation and suggested that perhaps Val could help.

'And have you asked the Beak?' she added.

'I daren't ask him for anything. I really don't think he likes me.'

'It can't be a personality clash because he hasn't got one.' She let out a snicker.

'But I don't know what I've done wrong, that's the trouble.'

'You'll just have to win him over by doing amazing work with the kids. It's still the first term – he just doesn't know you, that's all.'

'Maybe it isn't just me. Eileen the secretary always looks brow-beaten and miserable when he speaks to her.'

'Poor thing,' said Barbara. 'She's really sweet when I talk to her on the phone.'

'Anyway, what about you? How was your day?' I asked, aware that I was allowing school to hog our conversations again.

She twisted round so we were facing each other, and said, 'I rang my mother this morning.'

'How is she?'

'Well, she wasn't in a great mood – she's really frustrated that she can't call us when she wants to.'

'Yeah, but she always speaks German to me on the phone even though I don't understand a word.'

'Well, that's because she *is* German. She just kind of slips into it.'

'But she can speak English really well.'

'Anyway, the reason she wanted to call was that she's arranged a trip to Hildesheim at short notice. My granny's having a minor operation in a fortnight and it gives my mum an excuse to see some of her relatives and friends over there.' Her voice betrayed an edge of shiftiness.

I began to suspect I knew where this was going. 'And . . .'

'And she wants to know if I'd like to go along.'

'Would you?'

'Well, yes and no. Of course I don't want to leave you here but I would like to see my oma.'

'Well, that's OK. Why don't you go – it'll be a nice break for you for a couple of days.'

Barbara twiddled the hair at the back of her neck. 'It's a bit more than a couple of days.'

'How "more"?'

'Two weeks.'

My shoulders slumped. 'How many relatives has she got?'

'Well, there's quite a lot of travelling involved and she doesn't want to miss anyone out. She likes to have me there too, of course.'

'But two weeks . . .'

'You can cook, sort of, and you'll be fine. You can go for lots of walks and I won't be there to slow you down.'

'But I'll miss you.'

Barbara ignored the pathetic little boy expression. 'There are other advantages too – my mum always buys me clothes and things while we're over there: all sorts of things we can't afford.'

'Yeah, but they're always so . . . German.'

'Well, I'm not going to bring back anything for *you*.'

'Not even ze leather pants?'

'Stop it!' She playfully pushed me: I lost my footing and cracked an elbow against the door. 'Ooh, sorry.' She picked me up as I feigned serious injury. 'I'll miss you as well, you fruitcake.'

The next morning, children began to arrive at my desk with reply slips from their parents giving them permission to go on the Northumbrian trip. I watched out for Martha, but she didn't turn up for school.

At morning break I looked for Val before remembering she was outside on playground duty. It was starting to drizzle as I walked outside and a slender Class 2 boy rushed past me with the bell before ringing it feebly. A few children took notice and began to drift towards the door but most of them carried on playing. Then the ground shook.

'STOP!'

One hundred children froze in an instant. The thunderous boom of Val Croker's voice seemed to echo off the fells across the valley. I stopped too. She surveyed the statues with a slow sweep to ensure that there was no movement in any quarter of the yard then gave the next order.

'Class One, line up now.' Within seconds they'd formed a tidy queue. She continued through the classes with sergeant major efficiency until the whole school walked silently into the building.

'How do you do it?' I said.

'How do I do it? I tell 'em.'

'But when I tell them to stop or to line up there's always someone chasing a ball or messing around.'

'You've got to sound like you mean it. You can't be nice in this job – growl like you've got sharp teeth. Kids like proper authority provided it's fair because they know where they stand.'

I asked her about Martha as we walked inside. Val twisted her face.

'I know her mother. Tight as a whale's arse, that woman. She won't change her mind and there's not a right lot we can do about it.'

A pall of frustration seemed to reside over the rest of my week in the classroom. Martha returned to school a couple of days later looking pale and despondent, and her friends shared her misery when they heard the news. It seemed that everyone in Class 3 was going to Oswalfarne except her.

Only one thing lifted the fog that week: the Technology for the Blind project, which continued to gather momentum in the classroom, despite the numerous setbacks and inability of the class to make anything remotely approaching a sensible evaluation of the work.

From the very start, several children had greatly admired the natty folding white stick that the blind teenage boy on the RNIB video had demonstrated; in particular, they loved the ingenious way it folded. The boy had been shown boarding a bus, and as he took his seat he seemed to simply flick his wrist, causing the stick to magically collapse into three jointed pieces, which he swiftly pressed together and popped into a bag. There were whispers of 'cool' and 'I want one'.

When the class started to devise their own designs for innovations for the blind, several children had set off to plan and make folding white sticks. There were two boys who were particularly enthusiastic about this project: Barney and Wilf. They came bounding up to me early in the first session.

'Take a look at this, Mr Seed – we done a design f'the stick.' They thrust a slightly crumpled piece of A4 into my hand, and gave me a guided tour of the drawing on it.

'We've 'ad a mint idea—' Barney stopped and looked around to check that no one was listening. He cupped his hand round his mouth, and beckoned me nearer, while Wilf simpered. 'We're gunna use magnets!' I jerked upwards – it was the loudest whisper I had ever heard. The design did look good and the boys must have noticed my reaction, as they pressed home their claim to go ahead.

'Can we start making it now, Mr Seed? We know where there's a really good stick.'

'And it's white,' added Wilf.

Now I should have been gravely suspicious at this point, because I knew that there were virtually no resources in the school for this sort of activity, despite my ongoing intention to beg for offcuts of wood at the secondary school, but the two lads were so eager and excited that I said, 'all right', and watched them gallop away. After this, I scanned the room and was delighted to see every child busily occupied with the work; the atmosphere in the room was fairly buzzing with constructive discussion and purposeful activity.

Then the head came in.

As the weeks of my first term at Cragthwaite Primary had passed by, I gained the growing impression that Howard Raven didn't like me. He certainly didn't seem to approve of anything that went on in my classroom: whenever he entered the room he would always sidle about, eying what the children were doing and saying nothing, save for the occasional loud 'tut'. Sometimes his face would take on a mask of mounting disgust as he watched what was happening, which made me nervous and dispirited.

Somehow we'd started off on the wrong foot and the fear arose that this might affect my chances of passing my probationary year as a new teacher. How it had happened remained a mystery but one thing was certain: Howard Raven would have the final say in the matter. I'd just have to work hard to stay on the right side of him.

'Well,' I thought, looking round at the class beavering away at their technology, 'surely he's not going to be tutting today – even *he* must be really impressed with the work that's going on now.' As usual, he didn't say anything, but drifted silently over to watch Barney and Wilf working on their white stick for about thirty seconds. He didn't tut, but came over darkly to where I was standing and said, 'Mr Seed, could you please explain to me why those two boys are sawing a rounders post in half?'

I couldn't. I mumbled something about it probably being an old one, whereupon he fired a look of sour disapproval in my direction and then headed towards the door without saying anything more. My feelings of elation and excitement dissolved in an instant. I wandered over to where Barney and Wilf were still sawing, just to have a check. It definitely was a rounders post.

I really felt like cutting the lesson short at this point and reading a story to the class instead, but someone revived me, and indeed the whole project, with a piece of sublime inspiration.

Malcolm Willoughby was a joker. He had the look of a boy who was always up to something and most of the time he was. When he wasn't up to something he was giggling: the sight of his cunning smirk was frequently an omen of illicit whisperings and goings on at the back of the class. Despite his appetite for digression, Malcolm played a central role in our technology project, and went on to create something truly memorable.

I didn't expect Malcolm to be greatly affected by the video of the blind old lady, but he clearly was. For once, he sat still and passed no comments, and after the film asked a number of intelligent questions, which revealed a side to his character that raised him considerably in my estimation.

From these questions, it emerged that Malcolm's chief concern for unsighted people was dental hygiene. For some reason, he was convinced that the little old lady would never be able to find her toothbrush in the darkness of her life. Despite the woman from the RNIB assuring him that this wasn't a problem, Malcolm returned to the classroom gravely concerned. When the opportunity to make something to help blind people arose, Malcolm saw his chance. Like many of the children in the class, he emerged from the discussion at the end of the first Design and Technology lesson with a clear idea of what he wanted to do.

'Can I make something so that the old lady won't lose her toothbrush, Mr Seed?' There was an unmistakable seriousness and sincerity in his speech which I had never heard before. I meant to say, 'Well, Malcolm, finding a toothbrush isn't really a problem for blind people – we were told that, weren't we?', but what I actually said was, 'Yes Malcolm, lovely idea.'

A couple of days after this, the children had brought bagloads of resources from home, and the practical sessions were under way. Individuals, pairs and small groups talked and worked with hectic energy on white sticks, self-closing cupboard doors and other wondrous inventions. A continuous stream of children came over to me throughout the lesson with drawings, questions, designs, prototypes, models, problems and ideas. It soon became apparent that this project was going to need several more sessions, and I began doing some mental adjustments to the timetable: I was anxious to make the most of the children's tremendous motivation for this work. After about half an hour had passed I decided to make an announcement to everyone; I was just about to tell the class not to rush because I would give them at least two extra sessions when Malcolm appeared in front of me.

'Ave finished,' he said. He hadn't giggled all afternoon. I looked down, expecting to see a design on paper or a hastily assembled model but his hands were empty. I was mystified. Malcolm noticed my reaction and armed his mouth with the first stages of his trademark smirk. 'It's here,' he said, and took a step backwards, lifting his jumper a few inches as he did so.

He was wearing a brown plastic belt, and just beside the buckle was a hefty block of wood tied on with a remarkable length of string. Malcolm raised his jumper a little more to give me a better view and extended his grin. A large tube of Colgate toothpaste was nailed to the wood. I shouldn't have been surprised – this was, of course, the classic Dales way of fixing things, confirmed to me by the woodwork teacher at Swinnerdale Secondary School who related that whenever he taught joint-making, a big rough hand would inevitably be raised with the accompanying question, 'But suh – wa don't tha jus bray a larl' nail through it?'

Malcolm could see that I was now thoroughly impressed and decided to hit me with the full range of features of his mobile dental unit. He reached into his pocket and drew out a fluff-tousled toothbrush, which was also tied to the block of wood with a piece of string. I was just about to congratulate him on his craftsmanship when he held up a hand.

'There's one more feature,' he said gleefully, and reached behind his back. After a few seconds of squirming and fiddling he finally produced an empty yoghurt pot, which had, evidently, also been attached to his belt by some mysterious means. 'This is to spit in,' he said. He had clearly thought of everything; a blind person need never again be without oral cleansing equipment. The smirk was triumphant. I was speechless.

Malcolm wanted to show his 'Brushman' to the class, but I thought it deserved better, and decided that a proper showcase was needed for this and the many other wonderful inventions that were being produced. I therefore arranged for the class to make a special presentation of Technology for the Blind in assembly on the following Friday.

I managed to find a couple of extra hours in the week for the children to finish off the various models, but this left no time to rehearse for the assembly; I would just have to risk it. The work was so good that I was sure we didn't need to practise anyway.

Early on Friday morning, the models were taken into the hall and carefully laid out on tables before the other classes arrived – all, that is, except Malcolm's: he was so inordinately proud of his invention that I let him wear it beforehand, even if he did look decidedly strange with a great lump under his jumper and a yoghurt pot on his bottom.

Class 3 were chattering eagerly as they lined up to go into assembly to show their work. The rest of the school and the staff were sitting quietly while a strangled version of the *New World Symphony* crackled out of the tiny cassette player in the corner of the hall. Howard Raven stood solemnly at the front, daring any child to twitch. The models looked wonderful.

The children gave a series of superb talks about what they had done, relating it all back to the RNIB video of the previous week. I was proud of them. Carol demonstrated her once deadly automatic cupboard with the fluid assurance of a Tupperware rep, whilst Tracey explained its use of new thin elastic bands with aplomb. These, and every other invention were greeted with admiring applause from the audience. I did cast a nervous glance over to the Beak while the white sticks were being folded and unfolded, but even he looked forgivingly impressed; this was a triumph indeed.

Malcolm wanted to go last, in the fashion of a true showman. When the time came, he stepped up with confidence. All the children in the other classes knew him as a joker and expected something funny, glancing sideways at each other with elbows twitching. But on this occasion, Malcolm was transformed. He unveiled his creation with a sincere disposition and went on to describe every stage of its construction clearly and succinctly, adding details of all of the various features of the design. The assembled audience of four- to eleven-year-olds thought it eminently reasonable that the toothpaste was nailed on to the wood, and greatly admired the provision of the secret yoghurt pot.

'Are there any questions?' declared Malcolm when he had finished. A single hand went up from one of the top junior girls in Class 4.

'Can you give us a demonstration of how it works, please?' Usually, a child in Malcolm's position would turn to the teacher for guidance at a point like this, but such was Malcolm's confidence that he immediately began unscrewing the lid of the toothpaste tube. He drew the green brush from his pocket once more and deftly flicked away the resident coat of fluff from the bristles. A red and blue worm of paste was then exactingly applied. The infants sitting in the front row were hugely impressed, both by Malcolm's awesome device and his complete mastery of its operation. Malcolm held the brush in his left hand and, unhurriedly, twisted the toothpaste lid back on to the tube. His cocky old self was completely in command here – he was going to enjoy making a show of brushing his teeth in front of the whole school.

Everyone's eyes were fixed as Malcolm lifted the toothbrush. Just as he bared his teeth, the brush pinged back down with a sudden jerk, flicking the globule of toothpaste up into the air. The string was too short. Malcolm gave it a heave. It was still too short. Finally, he craned forward in desperation, like someone trying to lick his chest. The tip of the brush just about reached his bottom lip. He gave it a contorted waggle as the audience's concentration began to disintegrate into a squall of guffawing and pointing. Malcolm needed rescuing so I began to clap to ensure a premature end to the demonstration and to save further embarrassment. Everyone began to applaud, even amongst the cheers and laughter, but, amazingly, Malcolm didn't want to give in; like many great inventors, he had total faith in his creation. He wiped the toothbrush on his trousers, carefully returning it to his pocket, took a bow and, before walking back to his place, calmly produced the yoghurt pot to receive an extravagant purple spit.

To this day, the 'Brushman' remains one of my favourite pieces of work by anyone.

Chapter Four

Terry

I walked into the staffroom on Monday lunchtime to find everyone there except for Howard Raven. I was still on a high after my class's memorable assembly. Hilda noticed my arrival.

'Well, I hope you don't think we're all going to be making inventions for the disabled, young man. It's all I can do to teach my kids to hold a pencil.' Emma rolled her eyes while Sue Bramley looked over to me and smiled.

'I thought the models were great.'

'Well you've certainly stirred things up,' said Val. 'Half of my lot were asking why can't they do technology this morning.' There was definitely a grumble in her voice.

'I just wanted to give my class a chance to show their work,' I said, slightly perplexed but also pleased that it had got everyone talking.

'My little ones enjoyed it but they didn't really understand it,' said Emma.

Val continued, 'You've got Pat chuntering about the mess, too. She was in a right mood when she got to my class on Friday after school.'

I recalled my conversation with the cleaner before the start of term. 'But Pat told me she doesn't mind mess.'

'Aye, but she's never had to clear up sawdust, wood glue and bent nails before,' said Val, without looking up from a pile of marking. I half-laughed, as usual never quite sure just how serious Val was.

Hilda reached over for a biscuit. 'Raven's unhappy when a child gets out of its chair. He won't know what to make of you, Andy. He doesn't do change.'

Emma chuckled. 'That's a bit rich coming from you, Hilda Percival – you're still using those lesson plans from 1947.'

'I blame rationing. It's my make-do-and-mend outlook.'

Val finally looked up. 'Go and see the doctor, Hilda – he'll give you something for your nostalgia.'

Everyone laughed, although the mirth wasn't enough to dispel the doubts that inhabited my mind as I left the room. Was I going to fit in at Cragthwaite?

The village was beautiful – arcs of comfortable stone houses surrounding a long tapered green, sheltering under the protection of Spout Fell. It had a lovely name too: Applesett. Could this be the place for us to live?

Barbara and I loved the little bungalow at Castle Heywood, but we knew we couldn't stay there long, and needed to find a house to buy before winter. The trouble was that there simply weren't very many houses for sale in Swinnerdale, particularly places that we could afford. We discussed the matter constantly, and dreamed of owning our own little stone cottage, but nearly two months of fruitless house searching had passed since we had first moved up to the dale. The vast majority of homes for sale were well beyond our limited means, and the cheaper houses that did come on to the market seemed to be snapped up instantly: there was fierce competition between people looking for holiday cottages and local first-time buyers, which meant that many places were sold before details became available. In a close-knit community like Swinnerdale, word soon got round that a house was due to come on to the market, and very often the deal was done privately. This was a frustrating state of affairs for Barbara and me, and we wasted hours trudging around the overpriced leftovers that were all the estate agents seemed to offer. As much as we loved Castle Heywood, the fact that the bungalow was only a temporary home made us anxious to find somewhere before the cold weather took hold.

Our only chance seemed to be persistence, and a routine soon emerged where I would call into each of Ingleburn's three estate agents on the way home from work, in the hope of hearing about a property new on the market. It was a tedious business, and after a while I became such a familiar figure in the three offices that I simply poked my head around the door and raised my eyebrows to await the inevitable shake of the head from whoever was behind the desk.

It was on this recurring mission that I found myself one late afternoon in October. Barbara was in Germany with her mother, and the thought of returning to an empty house didn't raise my spirits after a long and tiring day of squabbles in the classroom. I pulled open the door of Millers Estate Agents with a heavier feeling of resignation than usual. Joanne, the affable secretary, gave her usual shake of the head, leaning it to one side as she did so. I must have looked even more glum than ever because she called, 'Wait, Mr Seed!' as I let the door go. I caught the handle and looked back in.

'There is one in Applesett just come in . . . It's a bit over your price range, but it's a really nice village.' I'd not been to Applesett but the name was familiar from the guidebooks that we studied when first moving up to the dale. Well, there was nothing to lose I supposed.

'When can I go and see it?'

'I'll give Mr Crockett the owner a ring now.'

Half an hour later I was standing on Applesett village green, breathing in clean reviving air and admiring the fine solid Dales houses bordering its rough grass. It was easy to locate the house for sale from Joanne's description. For a start, it didn't face on to the green; it was gable side-on, almost as if it was too embarrassed to present itself fully in the company of the other dignified dwellings. Neither was it symmetrical, like the majority of its neighbours, but rather it carried a lopsided profile towards the road, with a curious double-decker bay window – no doubt a Victorian addition to a much older building. It also appeared to be the only house in the village that was not built entirely from stone: it had been given a kind of dowdy brick extension on the side which had been painted a tired mushroom colour in a frail attempt to blend in with the honeyed greys of the surrounding buildings. The name didn't help either – it was called Craven Bottoms.

The house wasn't actually an eyesore, but it was awkward and incongruous – if it had been a child, its mother would certainly have told it to keep out of sight in polite company and not to touch anything for fear of breaking it. Yet, for all its lack of beauty and dignity, it stood firmly on the green in one of the finest villages in Swinnerdale. I knocked on the door.

'Now then lad, tha' must be Mr Seed – come on in then.' Mr Crockett was a short, broad and neckless guide, quite fierce and obviously not enamoured with taking people around his home. His technique was to rush from room to room jabbing his stubby finger at the door as soon as I had stepped through it, to suggest where we should go next. After about fifteen seconds on the ground floor, during which time he said nothing at all about any of the rooms or features, he darted for the stairs.

'Er, Mr Crockett – do you think we could slow down a bit? I need to make a few notes for my wife. She's away at the moment.' He looked at me as though I was daft.

'Aye, a suppose so, aye.' He shifted from foot to foot. I took out my notepad and pen and went back to the front door to have another look at the entrance hall. The first thing that struck me now that my eyes had time to rest, was that the hall, a long passageway, sloped upwards at a not inconsiderable angle. In fact, it required quite an effort to reach the end of it. At least the downhill journey was a jaunt.

The living room at the front of the house was the first door that opened off the hall and right away I was impressed by its high-ceilinged airiness and the amount of light flooding in through the large bay window at the front. Mr Crockett followed me in, suspicious that I needed another look at this room after the good four seconds I'd been given earlier.

The view from the window was wonderful: the whole village with its wide green, market cross and swaying ash trees sloped away, framed by the dale's distant north side. I was about to make some notes about this delightful panorama for Barbara when I noticed the carpet. A sudden feeling of nausea swept through my head, causing me to grasp the window frame and blink hard. I had seen many grim carpets on our recent house-viewing excursions – the dale seemed to hoard a concentration of particularly disturbing 1960s experimental designs – but this one surpassed anything I had previously encountered. It consisted of giant swirls of brown, purple and green, which gave the impression that someone had been breakdancing in sick. I looked up quickly, headed for the door and climbed the hall to the dining room.

This room was altogether different: a shaggy, chocolate-brown carpet, mercifully unpatterned, faced a much lower-beamed ceiling. The walls sloped outwards as they rose and the window at the far end of the room revealed their extensive thickness. Two old glass-fronted cupboards full of frightful ornaments bordered an unsightly 1950s tiled fireplace. The log fire crackling away in the grate gave the room a tremendously cosy feel, however, and I scribbled a few more notes, accompanied by Mr Crockett's pungent breath on my shoulder.

Our first house in York had been a 'two-up two-down' terrace, and thinking of the possibility of having two good-sized living rooms filled me with excitement. Despite its quirks and lack of perpendiculars, I was really taken with this house, not least because of the village itself. Then I saw the kitchen. The house was obviously quite large, and I was beginning to wonder why it wasn't far more expensive; here was one of the answers. It was a room to test the creativity of even the most eloquent estate agent. For a start it was tiny – I instinctively drew my elbows inwards as I turned to survey its walls, and noticed that Mr Crockett didn't try to follow me inside. Secondly, it looked like it had been constructed by someone with a grudge against the owner. A few withered cupboards sat next to an array of garish sticky-back plastic covered shelves. The only work surface was a scarred piece of Formica. I cast my mind back and tried to recall if Valerie Singleton had ever done a full-sized kitchen on *Blue Peter*. The ceiling's greying fibreboard sagged down in a grisly bulge, and the whole room was terminally damp – I surreptitiously pencilled 'axe job' on the pad and headed back to the hopping Mr Crockett.

Craven Bottoms certainly had character: there was a utility room that used to be a paint shop, a garage where my head scraped the ceiling, and a back yard full of frogs. The bathroom was mysteriously located halfway up the stairs, and the three bedrooms were all on different levels. Strangest of all was a large walk-in cupboard at one end of the landing. It was painted pink inside with a small mirror fixed to the wall, and had a blocked-up doorway at the far side. Mr Crockett reluctantly explained that there was a cottage at the back of the building and at one time the two houses had shared this cupboard as a bathroom. An ancient widow called Mrs Tiplady had lived in the cottage with 'bathroom rights' for over fifty years. I wrote 'bathroom rights' on the pad and enquired with Mr Crockett how much he was asking.

It was £6000 above our limit. I suddenly faced a terrible dilemma: not only would buying this house involve borrowing considerably more than we had planned, but I would have to make a decision without Barbara even seeing the place. If I delayed even for a few days it would be snapped up by someone else – that was certain.

The next day I was back at school thinking about a different kind of quandary I'd faced several weeks earlier.

I recalled the slender, awkward boy sitting with his head buried behind folded arms, his nose touching the desk, his whole body unmoving. I had only asked him where he lived, and he had stared towards me briefly in terror then shrivelled into this foetal position without saying a word. I looked around the classroom at the other children for help, feeling bewildered at so extreme a reaction to so simple a question. It was explained to me by Heather, one of the older girls, that Terry always did this when people he didn't know spoke to him, and that it was nothing unusual. Feeling powerless and almost ashamed, I decided just to leave him alone, and after fifteen minutes or so, he obviously felt that the coast was clear and slowly lifted his head. This had happened in the first week of term, and I didn't speak to him again that day.

Terry Spickels was an inert, ashen-faced boy with special needs. He was kind-natured and lovable but excruciatingly shy, and wouldn't even look me in the eye for the first few weeks in the class. As time went on, however, the emotional barriers that separated us were gently dismantled by my good-humoured encouragement and his gradual understanding that I posed him no threat.

Eventually a relationship of trust developed in which Terry began to emerge from his shell.

I established an underhand campaign of making him smile by doing slightly odd things when I was near to him, such as sticking my tongue out slightly when no one else was looking or, when giving out worksheets, offering one to Terry then not letting go when he took it, and having a mini tug of war with him. One of the most satisfying aspects of my first term at Cragthwaite was to see Terry gradually gain in confidence and begin to respond with nods, then, after a few days, answer simple questions and enquiries about his well-being; it was a great delight to see him growing so quickly. There was, however, one aspect of school life where Terry remained a terrified and bewildered innocent as the term went on: football.

Virtually all of Terry's friends came along to the after-school football club which I ran on Tuesdays, and Terry's mother, despairing that he would never join in anything, had browbeaten him into attending from the start. He arrived immaculately presented at the first session, resplendent in a spanking new, crisply ironed replica Leeds United kit, with glossy black boots, huge shinpads and matching socks pulled up high. He was obviously proud of his appearance and I commented how smart he looked, to give him a boost.

When the training began, I noticed Terry sidle off to a corner and pretend to be preoccupied with something important in his pocket. Then, as the other children dived into the net bags to get the best footballs, he took up a posture of deep thought, one hand philosophically propping up his chin. He looked like he was considering my instruction to 'get a ball' as a question of great gravity to be weighed and inwardly debated for some time, or perhaps to be referred to a higher authority in due course.

Over the weeks, Terry developed a whole range of advanced participation avoidance routines: he would normally warm up with a few bouts of fetching his ball (which had mysteriously rolled away again), then do a couple of minutes of brisk shirt-tucking before moving on to his favourite, a hard session of rigorous shoelace tying. This often took us into the practice match period, the time when he truly came into his own. Whereas the other children rushed after the ball like a pack of magnetic puppies, Terry developed a genius for staying well away from it. He smiled whenever I bawled, 'Get into a space!' He was always in a space. He knew it and I knew it.

But I left him there. He was happy, and being such a gentle, good-natured waif, I didn't have the heart to make him join in.

As the term wore on, Terry kept up his strict routine. Every football training session he turned up – beautifully presented in his bright white kit, kept well away from the ball and the other players, and went home. But as the fair days of September were left behind, and we were assailed by scouring winds and rain in October, I sensed that Terry was getting fed up.

It was a particularly dark and damp afternoon, and I noticed Terry standing alone, shivering. It had been raining on and off for three days and the school football pitch had become a squelching black quagmire, pockmarked with thousands of stud prints, and almost completely devoid of grass. As usual, the players were mobbing the ball, and the standard of play was desperate, so I decided to stop the game and call the players towards me for further coaching on this tactical detail. Terry ambled over from his isolation to join us.

As I talked to the children a remarkable thing happened. I was scanning the pink steaming faces for traces of comprehension when I noticed that Terry was actually listening intently; not only that, but I knew instantly that he actually understood the point I was making – it was as if a spark had penetrated his outer defences and ignited the fires of recognition within. Perhaps his self-enforced observation of the other boys' toiling around the ball had aroused in him the dormant knowledge of a better way. At any rate, it was obvious that this faint awakening had swiftly become a firm resolution to join in the game and do something positive, perhaps spectacular.

As the players dispersed I held on to the ball and watched Terry. It was a defining moment in his life: his jaw was set and there was a fierce determination in his eyes.

I gave the whistle a blast and threw the ball into play, purposely quite near to Terry. For once, he didn't back off towards his far corner. He was facing the action and standing ready, like an Olympic athlete waiting for the starting gun, his whole body tensed with coiled energy. And suddenly bang! – off he went towards the ball, and bang! – down he went into the mud, vertically, like a collapsing chimney. In his eagerness to become a hero, Terry had neglected the very bootlaces he had tied and retied a thousand times. None of the other children even noticed but my heart broke for him.

Slowly, he released the wet clay's vacuum-like grip and rose up, like a B-movie swamp monster. He had Denis Healey eyebrows, a five-inch nose and must have weighed a great deal. He wiped more mud into his eyes with his dripping sleeve and mewed, 'My mum'll kill me,' before trudging towards the school and tripping over his laces a couple more times. It was all over in that moment. I knew he would never come to football training again.

It was watching Terry wander across the field during afternoon break that brought this episode to mind as I stood outside on playground duty the day after looking round Craven Bottoms. After ringing the bell I came inside to find a grim-faced Howard Raven standing over two of the younger boys from my class, Charlie and Nathan. They were both rigidly staring up at him, pale and small, while he lambasted them.

'I have made it perfectly clear on numerous occasions that children are not allowed to stay inside at break-times. You're both aware of this, aren't you?'

The boys nodded meekly.

'The rules are simple: you go outside and you stay outside. You can go to the toilet at the start or end of break but not in the middle. Am I making myself clear?'

They nodded again but I could see that Nathan wanted to speak. The Beak continued, flecks of spittle gathering in the corner of his mouth.

'The cloakroom is for coats and bags, it is not for ill-behaved boys or for anyone else. People who hang around in cloakrooms are the ones suspected of taking things when they go missing.' He stared at the pair. Nathan opened his mouth.

'Mr—'

'If I find either of you in here again at playtime you'll be punished.'

I felt as if I was being made to wait; he must have seen me there but my presence hadn't been acknowledged. I spoke up for Nathan.

'I sent the boys inside, Mr Raven. Charlie was feeling unwell and I sent Nathan in here to sit with him – they're both sensible and quiet.'

He looked at me askance then at the boys. 'Oh, I see. Well why didn't one of you tell me that? Anyway, Mr Seed is new and perhaps he's forgotten that children do not come inside at break. If Charlie is unwell then he should be at home; if he's at school then he can go outside.'

I felt myself flush and was just about to speak when he turned and walked away. The boys looked at me, my reddened cheeks unmissable. They scuttled into the classroom while I tried to compose myself for facing the class. The girls' toilet door opened and Pat Rudds appeared, holding a bin bag. She must have heard the whole episode.

'At least he talks to you. I don't even get the time of day.' I said nothing. She waddled back to her cupboard while I stopped at the door with a thumping heart and racing mind. All of a sudden, everything seemed to be too much: Martha's mother; my technology work unsettling the staff; having to make a decision about buying a house while Barbara was away; and now the Beak belittling me in front of pupils.

A few weeks ago I had felt that I was beginning to get to grips with the routines of the job and understand the children; my enthusiasm was rubbing off on the class and learning was growing. Somehow, the events of the past few days had stolen that excitement away, leaving me with a cold emptiness and the recurring thought that I didn't fit this place.

Chapter Five

Eve

The hill up to Castle Heywood village was a steep trudge at the best of times, but the weight of trepidation seemed to turn it into a small mountain as I headed for the old red telephone box to make two vital calls about buying Craven Bottoms. It was already dark outside as I deposited a pyramid of ten-pence pieces on the small black shelf and debated who to call first: Barbara in Germany or my grandfather in Wales, the only person I knew who had £6000. Common sense told me that I should telephone my grandfather first since there was no point in getting Barbara excited about the possibility of a house if the money wasn't there.

I began to dial the code for Hanover.

After a protracted series of clicks and beeps I heard a faint elderly voice make enquiries in German. I began to hurl ten pences into the slot.

'Ja . . . hallo . . .' *Beep beep beep* . . . 'Wer ist da?'

'Hello . . . er . . . guten . . .' *Beep beep beep*. I fired more coins into the grey box and deeply regretted messing around in French lessons and so not being allowed to take German at school.

'Hallo . . . wer ist da?'

'It's Andy – is Barbara there?'

'Wie?'

'Is Ba—?' *Beep beep beep.* In my rush to feed the machine I knocked the pile of coins on to the floor. I was desperate not to lose the line: I bent down quickly, grabbed some of the money and stood up, cracking my head on the steel shelf before trying to force a lump of sheep poo into the slot.

'Are you still there?' I wailed, trying to rub my head, hold the receiver and clean doo-doo off the queen's head all at the same time.

'Andy? Is that you?' I had never been so glad to hear a muffled crackle before.

'Yes, it's me, Barbara – hope you're OK. Listen, I'm in a phone box and I've got no time to chat but I think I've found a . . .' *Beep beep beep.*

'You've found a what?'

'A house – in Applesett.' There was a tiny distant whoop.

'That's wonderful – is it pretty?'

'Well . . . er . . .'

'Does it have a modern kitchen?'

'Not very modern.'

'Has it got a nice big garden?'

'Just a small one, but it's got a back yard with frogs.'

'Oh. Are carpets and curtains included?'

'Yes, unfortunately.'

'Well . . . as long as it's not damp.' For once I was glad of the beeps. The ten pences were disappearing fast so I mentioned the money and followed it with the big question.

'If we can get the £6000 shall I go ahead and put in an offer?' There was an expensive pause.

'OK.'

The next phone call was, if anything, worse. My maternal grandfather, a retired bank manager, had built up a tidy pile of savings from stocks and shares. He wasn't rich, and lived a very modest lifestyle along with my grandmother in a small bungalow on the North Wales coast, but he had mentioned to me that I shouldn't be afraid to ask for a loan if I was ever in need. After feeding the call box with the last few coins I relayed to him a frantic assessment of our general situation, peppering the explanation with apologies about the hurry I was in.

'Well, you need a house, Andrew, that's for certain,' he said. So far so good. 'And you can get a mortgage but you're still a bit short?'

'That's right.'

'Well, how much do you need then?'

I gulped generously. '£6000.'

There was silence, and once more I thanked the beeps.

It was only years later, during a conversation with my mother, that I discovered the effect that the figure had on my poor grandfather. By all accounts, he was expecting me to ask for something like £50, and nearly had a seizure when I mentioned the amount. I pictured my grandmother reviving him with her smelling salts (having never forgotten the time when, along with my sisters, I asked her if I could try them myself, and nearly hit the ceiling with shock). The really strange thing, however, was that he said yes. Once the last ten pence had silenced the beeps, he croaked that he would arrange the money, as long as I understood that it was loan.

The following day I called into Millers Estate Agents in Ingleburn at lunchtime and put in an offer for Craven Bottoms. Midway through the afternoon I was trying to teach Class 3 about the difference between a continent and a country when Eileen sidled in, clutching a piece of paper. She stood at the door and waited until I'd finished speaking.

'Sorry to interrupt. I've a telephone message for you, Mr Seed. It's from Joanne at Millers. She said could you ring her back about, well, it sounded like cradle bottoms.'

Twenty children sniggered and I saw Carol nudge Tracey. As soon as the bell went I skipped out into the village to the call box, excitement overriding my frustration that staff weren't allowed to use the school phone. Joanne confirmed that Mr Crockett had accepted the offer. It was done.

The sense of responsibility somehow eased at that moment and I felt a quiet elation that we would soon have a home of our own in one of Swinnerdale's finest villages, even if my wife hadn't yet set eyes on it.

October also saw the class embarking on a new History study: The Tudors. I carried out hours of background reading about the period, my own knowledge being thin at best. It was hugely enjoyable familiarising myself with great characters like Henry VIII, Elizabeth I and Walter Raleigh as well as momentous events like the Armada and Great Fire of London. As I accumulated information and pictures, and formulated ideas for classroom activities, I found that my recent anxieties were simply pushed aside by the excitement of the theme.

My enthusiasm couldn't be held back. It was simply part of me and essential to every good teacher, I told myself. Cragthwaite Primary School would just have to cope with it.

Even though officially the school didn't carry out 'projects', I couldn't help myself going beyond lessons with dull textbooks. In fact I arrived at a plan that was sure to cause further contention. I mulled it over long and hard but I simply couldn't let it go. I decided that in order to instil the children's own enthusiasm, a class trip should be organised to start the work off, and I knew the perfect place.

Preston Blaise Hall was a magnificent Elizabethan country house situated about twenty miles east of Swinnerdale in the Vale of York. I had first been introduced to its charms by an eccentric retired neighbour in Castle Heywood called Peter Hedge. Peter was a voluntary guide at the hall, being a keen amateur historian with a passion for great houses. As soon as I had told him that I was going to be teaching about the Tudors at school, he insisted that I should bring the class on a visit to Preston Blaise and that he would give a guided tour tailored to our needs; he wiggled his wild eyebrows and almost bounced with excitement as he described the wonders of the place and how he would have no trouble in arranging a special price for us. There was just one problem: I would have to ask Howard Raven for permission to go on the trip.

The following day I was standing in front of him in his gloomy office. He looked me up and down. 'What precisely is the purpose of it?'

'I think it will bring the whole subject of the Tudors alive for the children. It'll help them find out how they lived, see what they looked like and, well, inspire the class to learn.'

'I've taught history for over thirty years and I never needed a whole day out by motor coach to motivate the pupils. They learned because they were told to.'

I tried not to imagine his thrilling lessons but rather stood my ground. 'I'm planning to do extra English and Maths beforehand to compensate and I'll carry out a preparatory visit to ensure the day is well planned.'

'And what about Martha Micklegate?'

'If you agree, I'd like to ask for a voluntary contribution of a pound each from parents to cover the cost. That should satisfy Martha's mother.'

He waited for a few seconds then drew together his lips. 'Very well, it can go ahead on the condition that sufficient funds are raised in that way.'

I loosened my collar as I walked away, hoping that I hadn't been too forthright. He clearly thought that I wouldn't collect enough money but he didn't know how I planned to wind up the children with enough anticipation to unleash an epidemic of pestering.

About two weeks before the trip, I arranged to meet Peter Hedge at the Hall for a preparatory visit. From the moment I stepped out of the car park and looked down the long, grand drive leading up to the house, I knew that this day was going to be special. Two lines of imposingly sculpted giant bushes led my eyes towards the building – a dramatic symmetrical façade of tall windows and crumbling lobster-coloured brick. It was a wonderful building, even more beautiful than Peter had described, with its great climbing chimneys and elegant bays. If the exterior of the hall was impressive then the interior sent me into a state of complete astonishment: it was a feast for the eyes that left me in awe of the skill of the seventeenth-century craftsmen, and in admiration of the marvellous way it had been preserved unchanged for centuries. The dark oak panelling of the rooms created an eerie, evocative atmosphere, particularly as nearly every wall displayed masterful period paintings of the Blaise family's ancestors staring out of black shadows with fierce eyes and extraordinary clothes.

Peter bounded across the vast Great Hall when he saw that I'd arrived and immediately began pummelling me with information about the carvings, statues, beds, fireplaces, priest holes, and huge angular pieces of furniture. I made pages of notes about every room, trying to imagine the details that would particularly make an impression on the children. It was a surprise to find that there were almost as many interesting things to see outside: an extraordinary donkey wheel for pulling buckets of water from the hall's well, a delightful collection of carts and carriages displayed in the stables and a beautifully maintained walled garden. Surely there was something here to appeal to everyone in the class.

Peter finished the tour by telling me the Hall's own infamous ghost story. This was the tale of the unfortunate Charles, son of one of the house's owners, Percival Blaise, in the eighteenth century. According to the story, Charles was tragically run over by his father's carriage on the drive while hurrying to meet him returning from a long journey to London. It was said that the poor young boy could still be heard running along the drive on quiet evenings, or even seen sitting in his father's carriage, now preserved in the stable block next to the house. This eerie yarn was the icing on the cake for me – I knew full well that all children adore ghost stories, and I left Preston Blaise that day with a tremendous feeling that my first school trip as a leader would be an overwhelming success, if I could just ensure that it materialised.

On Monday morning I sat in assembly thinking about the visit and how I would announce it to the class.

Howard Raven stood at the front of the hall droning out a story about St Francis. I wasn't the only one whose mind was elsewhere: a number of children yawned silently with heads down and several were staring blankly out of the window. The small infants at the front were squirming. I noticed Hilda fighting to stay awake at the piano.

During the dreary hymn I wondered how hard the Beak must work to achieve so little rapport with an audience. My college mantra that teaching was all about changing children's lives seemed laughably inapplicable here. As Class 2 filed out sluggishly at the end, Sue whispered to me.

'We've had that story at least four times since I've been here.'

In stark contrast to the children's reaction to the assembly, there was a spontaneous cheer of excitement among my class when I told them about the possibility of the visit to Preston Blaise Hall. As the tenor of my earlier conversation with Howard Raven had led me to suspect, day trips had been somewhat rare events at Cragthwaite School before my arrival, and it was refreshing to see that the children were even more pleased than I had expected. I was just about to describe the Hall to them when Eve Sunter's hand shot up. Eve was an irrepressible character from West Doddthorpe, down the dale – Val had warned me about her when I first arrived at the school. 'Born busybody, that girl. Never shuts up, and always has her nose in other people's business.' Although I quickly found out that Val was undoubtedly right in her assessment, I couldn't help liking Eve: she was as blunt as porridge.

'Mr Seed, how much can we tek with us?'

'How much what, Eve?'

'How much spendin' money?'

'Eve, we don't even know if the trip can go ahead yet. We need your parents' permission and we need enough money to pay for the bus and entry to the hall.' There were lots of murmurs from the class but Eve seemed to ignore my point completely.

'Do we need a packed lunch and if we do, can we take cans?'

'Erm . . .'

'And can the girls 'ave the back seat on the bus?' A choral moan erupted from the boys.

'I'll decide all of those things later.' Eve's hand was still waggling in the air. 'You can ask more questions after I've told you about the place we're visiting, Eve.' She looked faintly disgusted as she lowered her arm, and whispered something to Tracey. I then began to describe Preston Blaise in detail to whet the children's appetite, both for the visit and for our study of the Tudors in general. It was disappointing to see eyes glaze and chins flop on to hands within just a few minutes – they obviously didn't share my passion just yet. I decided to give them a break.

'Are there any questions about Preston Blaise Hall?' Eve didn't raise her hand at all but spoke first, as usual. 'Do they sell ice-cream?' I was just about to give up on telling them any more when I thought I would have one last try at arousing some interest in the actual purpose of the trip.

'Does anyone here like ghost stories?' I asked. The quiet mutterings of discontent stopped immediately and even Eve broke her slouch. 'Well, there's a two-hundred-year-old ghost at Preston Blaise Hall, and you never know when it might appear next.'

I regretted saying that particular sentence for some time afterwards. I made many mistakes in the early part of my teaching career, but I really had no inkling of the trouble that I'd unleashed that afternoon. When I followed this by saying that I wasn't going to tell them the ghost story there and then and that they would have to wait for the day of the trip there was uproar. As ever, Eve led the way.

'Go on, Mr Seed – tell us now. You can tell us it again on the day, you can. We love ghost stories. Go on, Mr Seed, don't be tight – it's not fair.' But I stood firm; Charles would wait.

Within two days we had enough money for the trip and every child had consent to go, even Martha. I was delighted but I did wonder whether I might just have racked up another black mark from the Beak for proving him wrong. I sought out Val.

'You do seem to get him in a mood. I've noticed it myself.'

'But I haven't really done anything, have I?'

'Maybe he feels threatened by another male presence. There

hasn't been a bloke teaching at this school for yonks.' I didn't like the way she avoided the question.

The door opened and Hilda walked in.

'Ooh sorry, I hope I'm not disturbing anything.'

'Don't tell me,' said Val. 'You'd like to borrow my stapler.'

'How did you guess?'

'You don't have to be Sherlock Holmes – you've borrowed it nearly every day for the past fifteen years!'

'Well, mine's broken.'

I couldn't believe I was hearing this. 'Can't you ask for a new one, Hilda?'

'Hah, that's a good one!'

'You could always buy one yourself, of course,' said Val, almost smiling.

'Behave yourself, Miss Croker. I've given my body, soul and mind to this school over the last forty years; I am not giving my savings as well. Cheek!'

Val shook her head and I laughed.

'Anyhoo,' said Hilda, 'What's this about a Class Three school trip?'

I told her what she already knew. 'But don't you ever organise visits, Hilda? Your infants would love it.'

'Of course. We do a nature ramble every spring.'

Val snorted. 'You mean you take them for a ten-minute walk round the back of Sunters' farm.'

'Well, that's enough for me at my time of life – it's too windy, this village.'

She left and I asked Val again if my class's trip would widen the apparent rift between myself and Howard Raven.

'Hmmm, doing all these new things isn't helping, that's for sure. I'd just keep your head down for a bit if I were you. Right, I've got to go and scare two miscreant boys now.'

She disappeared, leaving me with a furrowed brow but also with a hope that I could win her as an ally.

Over the next fortnight before the visit, two things happened. First, I finalised details of the trip with Peter Hedge, who suggested that on the day we finish the guided tour with the ghost story and that I should tell it to the children rather than he. This surprised me, as I suspected that Peter would probably be able to adorn it with extra layers of mystery and drama, but I did agree, thinking that it was probably best if I was in control in case the class became too excitable, bearing in mind their reaction in the classroom.

The second thing that happened in this period can only be described as ghost mania. Over the next few days it transpired that Eve Sunter was determined to prepare the class in every way possible for meeting the school trip ghoul. She told the perpetually nervous Heather Thistlethwaite, in terms of cold certainty, that there was a ghost in the girls' toilets, and Heather told the rest of the girls that Eve had seen a ghost and that she was only going to use the infants' loo from then on. A few days later, Heather Thistlethwaite's mum came in to talk to me after school to see if I could do something about the girls scaring each other.

'Our 'eather 'ad a sleepover with three of her friends on Friday, Mr Seed, and she won't stay in her room on her own now; she says Eve Sunter kept them up all night telling scary stories, and she told our 'eather that there were scrabbling noises under her wardrobe, and now she's in a right state, Mr Seed – she's hardly slept at all over the weekend. Could you have a word with that Eve please because our 'eather says she's scaring all the other girls 'n'all.'

Soon afterwards the boys started shouting 'Boo!' behind each other, and ghosts were promptly banned in Class 3. I announced that I would not tell them the 'real' ghost story on the trip if they carried on. I looked very grave and they all looked very grave back, except for Eve, whose mouth was sucked inwards and whose eyes flicked from side to side.

Amazingly, there were no more mentions of ghosts until the day of the trip, when excitement overrode everything else. A pleasingly uneventful coach journey ended with the children snaking around the side of the hall to see the donkey wheel. I had arranged with Peter to start here and then meet him inside after the day's first visitors had finished their tour. The children were fascinated both by the cavernous well and by the wheel itself. This was rather like a giant wooden hamster wheel about twelve feet in diameter, suspended vertically and attached to a winding mechanism that hauled huge buckets of water from the well. As soon as they saw the wheel, the children begged for a go inside it, and Clive Lambert led the way. He was the largest child in the class and generally the one in the largest amount of trouble at any given time, but he had been very well behaved up to this point, and furthermore, was probably the only child in the class who possessed enough bulk to overcome the wheel's considerable inertia. There were whoops and cheers as Clive awkwardly climbed into the structure; I was reassured by the memory of Peter telling me that it was quite safe.

I asked everyone to step well back, and told Clive to start walking forward very slowly, adding that I would hold the big wooden spokes to help control the speed. Clive gave his hips a quick waggle of bravado, aimed a pale grin at his friends, and pressed forward against the rising inner curve of the wheel with his hefty boot. The wheel creaked and moved about an inch. There were derisive hoots and a sarcastic cry of, 'Oh wow!' from Eve, who was orchestrating the watching mob, as usual. I tried to calm everyone down but didn't help particularly when I said, 'Come on, be quiet, and give him a chance – just remember this was actually designed for a donkey.'

Clive grasped a spoke with either hand and leaned much further forward. The wheel creaked again and reluctantly began to rotate. Clive took another step and had to release his hands as the spokes he was holding moved behind him; the wheel edged further round – it was moving properly at last and the class now clapped their approval. Clive looked unsteady and seemed unsure when to step forward, but the wheel didn't wait for him and he was forced to keep his feet moving: it was obviously more difficult than it looked, and I attempted to slow the wheel down by pulling against the massive spokes as they went past. My efforts were embarrassingly ineffective, however, and each time that Clive was forced to step forward by the rotation of the wheel he added greater momentum by inadvertently pressing down hard on the rim in front of him. It was obvious that the wheel was picking up speed. The class started cheering more loudly, and exhorted Clive with cries of, 'Burn it, Clivo!' and 'Go donkeyman!' egged on by the boisterous Eve. I tried to get Clive to slow down but he had started to panic and paid no attention, but rather made increasingly desperate attempts to steady himself with his hands against the flailing spokes. We could all hear the heavy wooden bucket thundering up the well as the great wheel trundled bumpily round with its captive boy wobbling, dancing and sweating within.

I had no idea how to stop it and was about to send another child for help, when Clive decided to take radical action himself. He had long given up any notion of slowing down the wheel with his feet and decided that if he held on to it without running then it would at least stop accelerating. He made a sudden lunge to the side and grabbed one of the passing spokes with both hands. The wheel barely registered this bold move, and began lifting him bodily around and upwards. Everyone watched in horror: would the wheel take him right over? His cheeks, seconds before the colour of tomatoes, were now starkly bleached, and his eyes looked as large as golf balls as we watched him sail past and rise. Up he went, his feet now dangling, and further up. The wheel creaked and slowed down. The class were silent. Clive reached the top of the wheel, clinging on with his stout fingers and making strange raspberry noises. The wheel gave a couple of heavy jerks as the boy dangled from its apex, holding him in the balance, as if debating whether to let go or carry on with its sport and turn again. I looked up and prayed that it would stop; Clive looked down and made another raspberry sound, then let go. He clanked on to the great central axle, flopped back down to the bottom of the wheel and dived through the spokes towards me in one heroic movement before the wheel could spin him again. He stood up and asked to go to the toilet. I was speechless.

* * *

It was only half past ten; the visit had made a rather more eventful start than I had expected. At least things would be calmer inside the stately old house. Once we'd entered the Great Hall, Peter greeted the class with towering enthusiasm and launched straight into the early history of the house before I could even introduce him. I looked round to see if everyone was listening and noticed Eve shuffling to the back of the group pulling faces which suggested that she was already dying of boredom. She located Anita Thwaite for a chat and extracted a glob of chewing gum, surreptitiously planting it under the polished black top of the 1672 oak banqueting table before I could reach her. Peter was already heading for the next room and waving his arms flamboyantly at the huge gilt-framed canvases of kings, lords and dukes along the way. At least most of the class seemed impressed by the place, and I was pleased to see a few children making notes and others pointing at features that they had been told to watch out for. Peter stopped outside the elaborately decorated dining room and began to ask the class questions about the different objects on display: the dark wall tapestries, the spectacular ornamental silver service and a richly featured Dutch clock.

'The furniture is, of course, by Chippendale . . .' he intoned. Not one of the children's faces registered, except Jack's. He leaned over to me with a smile and whispered, 'Mah mum likes watching them on telly.'

The children greatly enjoyed the different bedrooms with their wobbly four-poster beds, and the tales of priests in priest holes, which Peter told with great relish. Even Eve was drawn in to listen by this point, and I was both delighted with the class's interest and relieved that we had reached the last room without breaking anything irreplaceable.

'Well, children, that's the end of the tour of Preston Blaise Hall, said Peter. 'Mr Seed is going to take you to the stables now, I believe, and show you some of the wonderful old carriages we have there.' He gave his two shrub-like eyebrows a last theatrical wiggle.

'Right children – wasn't that wonderful?' I didn't wait for an answer. 'What do we say to Mr Hedge?'

'Thhhaaannnnkkkkyoooouuuu.' The response was long and loud enough to satisfy Peter, and I marched the class into the cool brightness outside, and towards the walled garden for lunch. Along with Mrs Alderson and Mrs Hugill, the parent helpers for the trip, I greatly enjoyed sitting and watching the children run round, excitedly exploring the garden after their sandwiches. They were hemmed in safely by the walls and were able to expend pent-up energy on the wonderful oversized games which had been so creatively incorporated into the garden's design: giant chess, draughts, hoopla; and a lovingly crafted miniature maze. There were seats in the shape of animals and little gazebos everywhere – and quite soon the whole class had disappeared in search of yet new treasures. It was time to try and round everyone up for the stables, so I set off calling out for them to return to the gate as I went. I found most of the children in the maze, and they had great fun pretending they couldn't find their way out. Near the centre I heard a couple of voices on the other side of the hedge: it was Eve and Anita.

'Come on Eve – Seedy's just called – we've got to get back.'

'Oh, what's the rush. He hasn't even told us the ghost story yet. Do you believe in ghosts, Anita?'

'I believe in 'em but I aren't scared of 'em.'

'Well, I definitely aren't scared of 'em. Come on, let's go then.' I crept away quickly with that guilty feeling you always have when you've overheard someone talking about you. After this, I let the children look at the carriages in the stables with their stiff dummy passengers in period costumes, then, to groans, made them fill in a worksheet from the information boards before finishing with some sketching. Eve then asked me for the third time about the ghost story, and I agreed that it was time. The sheets, pencils, drawings and boards were gathered up and I took the children through to the visit's last port of call: the dingy high-ceilinged tack room where Percival Blaise's lustrous black carriage loomed. There were quiet gasps of awe from the children, and I asked them to gather close in a hushed voice. The atmosphere was perfect for a ghost story: the children were tired after a long day and wanted to listen; the room was damp and gloomy; there was a musky quietness all around, and best of all, there was the old sinister carriage itself, right before us, complete with a mean-faced dummy of Sir Percival sitting in its murky interior, wearing a towering top hat.

I drew out the story as much as I could, emphasising the desperation of the poor son Charles, longing to see his absent father, describing the achingly long, cold journey from London, the beating noises of the horses' hooves and the ceaseless jerking of the carriage caused by the terrible roads. The class were rapt – every eye was held by mine and every word was able to leave its mark. Eve was at the front for once, and was transfixed by the tale, particularly when I increased the pace as the boy heard the onrushing carriage hurtle through the gates and down the drive.

'Charles yelped and began to run down the long drive towards the magnificent carriage, towards his father, and he could now see it approaching through the last faint light of dusk. He waved his hands and shouted, expecting his father to look out of the window and see him, but still the carriage raced on between the great bushes, as if the driver was unaware of how close they were to the house. Charles ran on and cried louder; still the carriage came . . .' Several of the class gulped quietly and more than a few eyes turned glassy as I continued and relived the boy's tragic end. I then went on to relate to the class how the gardener had heard the sound of a child running along the drive on more than one occasion a year after the event.

'And worse than that . . . the family stopped using the carriage after the poor driver went insane, claiming that whenever he looked at the carriage it would start to shake of its own accord, and that he had seen the pale figure of a child sitting inside and crying . . .' At this point, a very strange thing happened: Eve's eyes, which were almost as wide as Clive's had been in the donkey wheel, actually began to get wider and she suddenly looked as pale as death.

'The carriage is moving – it's shaking, Mr Seed!' I was just about to tell her not to be daft when I detected a faint movement in the carriage to my right. A thin top-hatted head moved into the carriage window from within. Eve Sunter took off vertically, like a Saturn moon rocket, and let out a scream with enough power to wake China. I had never seen a child move so quickly, nor attain such a height without being thrown, and I never have since – it was truly remarkable. Peter Hedge opened the door of the carriage and said hello while Eve and several other children cowered back, holding their chests. He lifted his hat, winked an enormous eyebrow at me, and walked back towards the house, muttering that another group was waiting for him.

The bus was pleasantly quiet on the way back to Swinnerdale. Clive sat on one of the front seats, and Eve sat on the other, and not a mention of a ghost story was heard.

Chapter Six

Fergus

The air was filled with drifting midges, picked out by a mellow sun. From the hillside, a steady haze defined distances, shrouding the far fells in ever more cloudy whites and blues. I looked down on the village where I hoped we would soon be living: a huddle of tight stone cottages with piecrust roofs and square windows set in bouldered walls.

It was a glorious Saturday in mid-October and I couldn't resist another walk in the fields around Applesett. I loved the moss-clad walls here with their mottles of gold, white and crackled yellow lichen. Further up, the sycamores on the lower ridges of Spout Fell were turning grey, and bunches of handsome orange rosehips hung, embellished by the light. Rabbits bolted into the gorse ahead of me as I explored the path. I scanned this exquisite place, trying to imprint every little scene in my mind, to describe to Barbara.

Ahead, a clutch of farmers with busy dogs were patching up a collapsed old sheep fold, speaking in blunt, deep tones. The gently buffeting breeze carried the dale's sounds everywhere: the appeals of birds, the warble of a lamb or the long murmur of a shed-bound cow, each accompanied by the gentle rush of the beck dropping down from Buttergill, the hidden valley behind the village. It was time to go but I took one last look towards Applesett with its long, low farms. The scene could have been centuries old but for a Land Rover and stack of oily silage bags. To me, it was perfect.

Barbara's return to England was both a wonderful and daunting moment. I drove to meet her at Bilthorpe Station where she appeared, loaded with bags, looking lovely in a cotton dress. I rushed up to her for a classic railway platform hug.

'I've missed you so much,' I said in squelchy slur, trying to kiss her at the same time.

'I've missed you too. But it's so lovely to be back.' Her eyes twinkled with excitement. 'Can we go and see the house right away? I can't wait.'

I nodded but my mind was like a stuck record: 'What if she doesn't like it? What if she hates the village? What if it's too far from town?' I babbled the whole way on our journey to the village, extolling the virtues of the place and dismissing the significance of every one of the house's negative features. I hardly let her get a word in about Germany or explain why she'd had her hair permed, something I wasn't entirely sure about. On our arrival, the first part of the test was won easily: as we crossed the village green, an autumn gust pierced the clouds and a shaft of vivid sunlight elucidated the open beauty of the location.

'Is the house really here? It's so lovely,' said Barbara. The sight of Craven Bottoms at the far end then put me back on edge.

We stepped out of the car. Two women standing in front of a house across the green turned to watch us. I smiled and gave a nod. Mr Crockett had allowed us to tour the house alone, which raised my spirits. They were further lifted when I looked at Barbara's face as she stood in the living room. 'But Andy, you didn't tell me it was this big. We'll have room for all our stuff – this is fantastic.' As we went round, she didn't seem to notice all the details that made me grimace on my initial visit. Barbara was much more of a visionary: she saw potential, space for development and room to spread out. And there was another reason she was extremely keen.

'Andy, I think you've done exactly the right thing. It's not just this house, even though I do like it. It's the timing that's right, too.'

'What, because we need to move out of the bungalow?' I was a little confused by her semi-cryptic tone. She moved close and gave me a hug. There was a look in her eyes I'd never seen before and her voice was strangely mangled.

'Andy, we're going to have a baby.'

The Preston Blaise trip had been memorable for several reasons. Of these, I tried to blot out the most unnerving, and resolved to concentrate on the history of the Tudor house itself, and how it represented the glories of the period. The class was set to work on research and writing, on paintings and collages, and producing lists of monarchs and famous people of the time. They greatly enjoyed all this activity, and were particularly hungry for stories about the heroes of the Tudor age: Drake, Raleigh, Shakespeare and of course, Queen Elizabeth herself, and were even more keen to hear about the excesses of Henry VIII and his battles with Rome. All of this went very well, and I was especially delighted with the magnificent displays of work that the children created right round the classroom walls, but there was one previously planned activity that hadn't yet materialised: drama.

When I first visited Preston Blaise with Peter Hedge the previous month, and learned some of the rich tales associated with the place, it occurred to me that perhaps we could weave some of these into a short play back at school after the visit. Foolishly, I had described this idea to the class as a possibility too. A fortnight after the trip, however, no one had mentioned the suggestion: the children had been so enmeshed in other work on the Tudors that I began to think that it had been forgotten. This was no small relief, as I quailed at the thought of the children trying to re-enact the donkey wheel disaster for their parents. Then Josie Birkett came up to me in the classroom during English.

'Shouldn't we be starting the play by now, Mr Seed? Time's getting on.'

'Er, what play's that, Josie?' What a stupid thing to say. She was an intelligent person, and now looked at me as if I were three.

'The history play – the one you said we would do after the trip.' Anita Thwaite overheard this, unfortunately: 'Oh yerr – we're gunna do a play, aren't we!' She was just too loud, and soon there were cries from all over the classroom.

'When can we start?'

'Can we do some today?'

'Can I have a big part?'

'Will it be all about Preston Blaise, then?'

And then came the killer: 'Can we do the ghost story?'

The noise suddenly rose to a crescendo, with shouts of, 'Oh yessss!' and, 'Go on, pleeasse!' and 'Can I be the ghost?' I had to shout myself, to calm them down. I said I would think about it, but it was clear what was going to happen, and I felt myself buckling under the weight of the class's collective will, just looking at the excitement on their faces.

Over the next week, I was bombarded with further requests, suggestions, demands and jokey threats, so I began to plan a short play centred, inevitably, around the ghost of Preston Blaise Hall. A small group of able, enthusiastic writers was chosen to put together ideas for a script and the thing began to take shape; I even became quite excited about it myself. After a few days, I was presented with a pile of scraggy-looking papers by Josie, along with Penny, Nathan and Hugh, the other writers. They were almost popping with excitement.

'It's finished. Read it now, Mr Seed, can you?' Penny was silently clapping her palms together and all four of them sported enormous grins of self-satisfaction.

'Well done, all of you,' I said. 'It's lunchtime now, so I'll take it with me and read it in the staffroom.' They seemed happy enough with this and ran off towards the cloakroom, elbowing each other with wild giggles.

The script, set in 1755, was not for the faint-hearted. Percival Blaise was the main character, a decidedly charmless dastard who treated everyone he met with frightening contempt, and regularly kicked his dog to extinguish any sympathy the audience might muster for him, which was rather unfair considering that we all knew that he was going to inadvertently run over his own son.

Percival's coach driver, who was given the curious name of Marmaduke Snort, also featured quite heavily. This man must have been a dextrous individual, as according to the script he only had one arm, and frequently lit his pipe while on the road. The tragic son, Charles, was painted as a sensitive and innocent victim of corrupt adults. He liked football, and at one point considered running away to become an engine driver. All of the characters spoke lines from recent films and adverts that the children admired. The most striking feature of the play, however, was the frighteningly violent treatment of poor Charles's death under the wheels of the coach. Every anatomical detail was covered as the unfortunate child's body received an amazing array of injuries. It was not a quick death, either – it went on for four pages.

When I reached the end of the script my coffee had gone cold and break was nearly over. Emma was leaning over my shoulder and reading the last page.

'Heck, that's gory – you're going to need lots of ketchup to perform this. Who's going to see it?'

'Well, the kids want to do it for an audience, but having read the script I think this is going to be a radio play just for voices.' I didn't want a repeat of my 'show-off' assembly.

Eileen looked up. 'Ooh, no one in school's ever done one of those before – how exciting.'

I was just about to tell her not to get too excited when Hilda burst in, mid-sentence, followed by Val.

'I kept asking him, "Are you all right?" but I could see that he wasn't,' said Hilda. 'The poor little lad was the colour of a parsnip.' Val put the kettle on while Hilda continued. 'Well, he started to gag so I just picked him up and hurled him in the toilet. Well, not right in, anyway, but it was just in time.'

Val barely reacted. 'Has he gone home?'

'He has now, but only after Raven came into the toilet to see the evidence.'

'Lovely, just when I'm eating my lunch!' said Emma.

Sue Bramley, the teaching assistant, grimaced. 'It's all sorted now but the smell in those boys' lavatories is unbearable.'

This set Hilda's wrinkled finger wagging. 'It's because they don't—'

'—Aim straight. We know, Hilda – you've told us five thousand times,' said Val.

'Well, I don't know why we can't have ping pong balls like Hauxton Primary.'

Now I was really confused. 'Ping pong balls in the toilets?'

Hilda nodded. 'Aye, you put one in each bowl and it gives them something to aim at.'

'Pat Rudds is convinced they'll get flushed away and the Beak thinks someone'll fish them out and play with them,' said Val, heaping coffee into a stained mug.

'Well how come they work at Hauxton, then?' Hilda cried, just as Howard Raven came in.

'Ping pong balls again?' he said, grinning humourlessly. Val rolled her eyes as Hilda considered making another appeal before thinking better of it. The atmosphere in the room changed in an instant, as it always did with the head in there. We talked about the weather for five minutes then everyone headed back to the classrooms.

Over the next few days I made some drastic but necessary changes to the play script, added a few minor characters to provide more parts, and typed it up. The children were a little disappointed with the idea of performing the piece as a radio play, but some did agree that staging the coach accident scene could present one or two technical challenges that might overstretch our resources. This didn't prevent several individuals making suggestions for how it might be done; Barney assured us that his dad could get an old cart and that he wouldn't mind being run over by it. Rose offered to bring in her pony, which immediately led to a spate of others asking for a ride at playtime.

'It'll only crap on t'yard,' grumbled Jack.

I cleared my throat. 'Anyway, all this can stop because we're doing this as a radio play and we need to make a start. Who would like one of the main parts?' Nearly all of the hands went up.

'Why aren't there many parts for girls?' called out Eve. This was going to be really hard. All the boys wanted to be Charles Blaise, and there was also the question of reading and acting skills. Several of the less able children were really keen to take part in the play but would struggle with the lines. It was also clear that there just weren't enough parts to go around anyway. At this point, with a number of children turning purple with the sheer physical exertion of extending their arms to improbable heights in an effort to secure a leading role, I had a brainwave.

'I'll give you all the chance to audition for a part, and anyone who doesn't get one can perform sound effects.' After all, there was no shortage of action in the drama to convey acoustically.

In the end, the dashing Cameron Dent was chosen to be Percival Blaise, George Walden was given the part of Snort the driver, and Sylvia Hammond surpassed all others as the pathetic hero, Charles.

Several other small parts were added to accommodate more actors and most of the class seemed happy with the arrangements. The less able readers were delighted to be in charge of the sound effects and they were each issued with a noise and a suitable implement with which to produce it. Amongst this group was one of the great characters of Class 3, Fergus Mudd.

Fergus wore bottle-bottom glasses and never closed his mouth. He was the palest and most freckled child I had ever met, but he was also the most enthusiastic. Whatever activity I proposed to the class, Fergus would respond with a loud, 'Yessss!', even when others groused. I often used to imagine testing out the limits of Fergus's fervour for school activities:

Me: *Right, children, we're all going swimming now.*

Fergus: *Yessss!*

Me: *Maths next, everyone.*

Fergus: *Yessss!*

Me: *Remember, you all have fifteen spellings to learn for tomorrow.*

Fergus: *Yessss!*

Me: *There are paper towels all over the boys' toilets again – you'll have to clean them up during playtime.*

Fergus: *Yessss!*

Me: *The school nurse is going to give everyone six injections today.*

Fergus: *Yessss!*

Me: *Right, two volunteers to jump off a cliff, please.*

Fergus: *Yessss!*

Fergus was a delight to teach because of his enthusiasm, but he was not the most brilliant star in Cragthwaite's galaxy, so I gave him the simple but important task of making a banging sound for the dramatic moment when the coach hit poor old Charles. I had started handing out parts at half past nine and by the time I had organised Fergus's group with their sound effects it was quarter past eleven: I was horrified at the amount of time it had taken, and told the class that the first rehearsal of the play would have to wait until later in the day because of the need to catch up on other work; this produced a welter of groans and a small 'yesss' from Fergus.

There was art in the afternoon and a lot of mess to clear away. As three o'clock approached, Eve appeared at my feet.

'Mr Seed, you promised us that we could rehearse the play and look at the time now.' I had completely forgotten, which made me annoyed – I really didn't like rushing things. Despite the lack of time, the remaining tidying was quickly completed, so scripts were handed round and equipment for sound effects was given out. There were only twenty minutes of the day left, no real time to organise the reading properly: the children would just have to show some initiative.

There was a ticklish excitement in the room as the actors started speaking their lines, and the rehearsal began well. Cameron, Sylvia and George put real gusto into their parts and the expectation grew as each short scene passed and the story's desperate climax neared. It had been decided that the coach accident itself would mainly be represented by sounds: there was to be the sound of approaching horses' hooves, building up in volume (Jack with the ubiquitous coconut shells); the sound of a boy's feet running (Carol, using her shoes on the floor), followed by George's coachman's cry of, 'Look out!' A dramatic pause was then to be followed by a bang, provided by Fergus, who assured me that his hand thumping on the table would be more than sufficient.

The moment of the play's disaster approached with surprising tension. Jack's coconuts went to work. We all looked towards Carol, who blushed as she clattered her feet on the floor. George cried, 'Look out!' in a dread scream, and all eyes were fixed on Fergus as we braced ourselves for the tumultuous crash of the great black carriage ploughing into the unfortunate youth. Fergus lifted his hand and let it flop on to the table top with all the force of a Cabbage White landing on a daisy. There was no sound at all. A huge groan went up around the room; the moment was lost. Fergus smiled. I tried not to look too cross, but the wall clock clearly showed that there were only five minutes of the school day left, and the people in the last scene were anxious not to be left out.

'Oh Mr Seed, we 'af ter do that scene again – it's got to be done right.' It was Eve, as usual, and everyone agreed. I scurried over to the bookshelves and picked up a large encyclopaedia volume, handing it to Fergus.

'Use that to make the bang, Fergus, and please do it louder. Right, quickly, let's run through the accident scene again – everyone quiet.' The actors rattled off the lines leading off to the crash once more. Jack's hooves clattered in, followed by Carol's urgent feet. George's 'Look out!' heralded Fergus's sure redemption. The book was there, but instead of lifting it up and slamming it on the table, he hit it with his hand, just as before. The thick imitation leather let out barely a sound, and again the class was in uproar. Outside the classroom window, two homeward-bound infants passed by clutching coats and lunch boxes, but I could not let this end there; I was as frustrated as everyone else. I picked up the book and lifted it with both hands.

'Oh Fergus – use your head! We need a big bang.' To demonstrate I thumped down the volume on to the table with a force that made several pencils jump. Fergus seemed to like the noise and took the book in both hands, placing his tongue between his teeth for extra concentration.

'OK, same scene once more,' I said, trying not to reveal my enormous angst. One or two of the children who needed to catch a bus were looking fretful about the time. As the moment approached, I glanced over to Fergus. His eyes, grotesquely huge behind stout lenses, were fixed on the script and he was holding the book well up with both hands; surely this time . . . The next moment had a somewhat surreal quality, and I still sometimes wonder whether it really happened. As Jack galloped the coconut shells together, Fergus began to raise the heavy book even higher – it looked like he was really going for it this time; Carol's tired feet went to work again and signalled the now familiar cry from George. The scene was set, and Fergus didn't disappoint. He raised the encyclopaedia another notch, and with a spectacular burst of energy, brought it crashing down on his head.

Fergus survived this self-inflicted assault – his skull was clearly well built, and a greater concern was probably the chaos that ensued amongst the other children afterwards. Several of them simply burst out of the room to tell others what had happened. I had to tell someone too and, after the bell, went looking for Val. She was with a parent, however, and Hilda, Sue and Eileen had gone home. Emma was in her room, rebuilding the Wendy house; I recounted the episode in detail.

'It actually doesn't surprise me,' she said. 'Remember, I used to teach him when he was five. He used to get up to all sorts then. His speciality was, erm, fiddling.'

'Fiddling?'

She looked down to make it obvious.

'Oh, *fiddling* . . . at five?'

'Oh, yes,' she said. 'Fiddling fives are ten a penny, girls too. It's completely innocent – they don't know they're doing it.'

I clearly had lots to learn. Emma noticed my surprise and smiled. 'You'll get to know everything in time. The kids really like you, you know, and not just Class Three. I think you're good for the school.' She looked around and lowered her voice. 'Try not to let Raven get to you – we've all had our troubles. It's like the dark ages this school sometimes.'

I thanked her and slipped out, feeling a sense of reassurance that I wasn't alone.

The play was eventually performed – successfully too – but when it was finished I was relieved to say goodbye to Preston Blaise and its ghost for a long time. And I never asked Fergus to use his head again.

The following day I was in the middle of a mercifully calm English lesson when the door creaked quietly open and Howard Raven slunk in. It was another of his 'surprise' visits but I consoled myself with the knowledge that the children were at least all sitting at their desks writing.

He floated round the room like a spectre, intermittently craning to assess individuals' work, his face as stony as ever, his bottom lip hinting at disapproval. I noticed that the children didn't chat to him or offer to show their work like they did with other visitors to the classroom, but rather kept their heads down in almost guilty silence.

'Mr Seed, why are these pupils writing on paper?' He spoke from across the room, taking me aback.

'They're writing poems, Mr Raven.'

'I can see that.'

'Well, it's so I can put some of them on display on the walls.'

'English work, as far as I am concerned, should be in English exercise books. I also think this class needs more time on comprehension, grammar and spelling, rather than poetry.'

The children had all stopped writing, and a number who needed help with their work were waiting in a small queue next to me. 'Can't we talk about this another time, Mr Raven?'

'There's no need to talk about it again. I've made things clear.' He glared around and then departed. Once more I was left beetroot-faced in front of the children.

As soon as the lunch bell rang I sought out Val. I simply had to know what the Beak's problem was with me. She proffered me to sit down.

'Several teachers at this school have had something similar at one time or another.'

'But he doesn't treat you like that, does he?'

'No, he doesn't.' I couldn't imagine Val standing for such a public affront, or even a private one.

'So why is he picking on me?'

'Well, have you asked him yourself? It sounds like you've every right to confront him.' This notion had begun to grow in my mind but I sensed that Val knew more.

'Not yet, but just tell me what *you* think the reason is.'

'Right, well, I would have thought it was obvious but let me spell it out, even though I do not want to be dragged into this.' She was clearly itching for a smoke. 'He's been in teaching a long time but there's been more changes in the last five years than the other thirty, I reckon.

'He just wants to see out his retirement quietly in a nice village school and he can't face all the government initiatives like the new curriculum, or movements like child-centred learning.'

'OK, but what's all that got to do with me?'

'Can't you see? You represent all this progressive teaching and change in his eyes. It isn't personal – you're just an easy target: young and green. He probably thought you'd just do as you were told.'

'So he's taking out his frustrations on me?'

'Well, that and he feels threatened because he knows damn well that he couldn't do half the things you do with the kids.' I was just wondering whether this was a compliment when there was a knock at the door and Eileen appeared.

'Sorry to disturb you but there's a call for you, Val.' The deputy head looked grouchy as she left the room but I walked out feeling a whole lot better.

* * *

Back at home my mind was full of babies and the changes that a child of our own would bring. Barbara was incredibly thrilled by the prospect but I felt a strange mixture of joy and trepidation. Coming on top of settling into a new job and buying a house, the news left me reeling, and life seemed to be in total turmoil as October neared its end. I tried to imagine what it would be like to be a father, but kept seeing a rather disconcerting picture of myself coming home to a miniature Jack or Eve after a long day in the classroom. Barbara, meanwhile, went straight into plan-making mode.

'We're going to need a cot and somewhere to change the baby and a pram and pushchair, of course. Isn't this exciting?'

I put my arms around her. 'It is exciting – it's wonderful.' I was so glad to see her so happy after all of our recent worries. 'I only wish all these things didn't cost so much. We already owe my grandpa thousands for the house.'

'Oh, you don't worry about money at a time like this. There are ways and means.'

I eyed her suspiciously. 'How come you know so much about this parenting business all of a sudden?'

'I suppose it's one of those feminine things, the mothering urge or whatever you want to call it.'

'Hmm . . . It amazes me how you can be so calm about it all – I'm still getting used to being a husband. I think I'm a one urge at a time man.'

'You'll change when we have a squidgy little baby all of our own to cuddle, I'll bet.'

'It's the brown squidgy stuff I'm worried about.'

'Oh, don't be ridiculous – you can manage a bit of poo. And *do not* for a minute think that you aren't going to change your fair share of nappies or clear up the piles of sick.'

'You make parenthood sound delightful . . .' We both grimaced then laughed, although privately I couldn't quite shake off my fears about what it would really be like.

Chapter Seven

Hugh

The last week at school before the half-term break brought news of even more changes. It came during one of Howard Raven's staff meetings. Usually on these occasions I would be fighting to stay awake, but this time an announcement from the head woke me up with a jolt.

'This may come as rather a surprise to you all, but after a lot of thought I've decided to take early retirement. I'll be leaving the school at Christmas and a new head will be appointed. County are putting out advertisements this week.' There was a short period of silence, broken only by a cough from Val who, for once, seemed quite taken aback; it was as unexpected for her as for the rest of us. Howard Raven smiled, enjoying the slight shock effect that his words had on the circle of teachers. 'Does anyone have any questions?'

Eventually we came to our senses and a short discussion about practical matters followed. I didn't ask anything, not least as my mind was full of conflicting emotions: part relief, part disbelief and a peculiar sense of guilt that he might be leaving because of me. I couldn't wait to escape the room and talk to Val as the Beak explained that he had intended to see the year out but had been advised that the regulations on retirement were soon to change and that it might be financially beneficial to leave sooner rather than later.

The meeting finished late with everyone keen to get off straight away, so I raced home to tell Barbara the news.

Her eyes were agog. 'What! Really? That's unbelievable – what's brought this on?'

'He was planning to go soon anyway but it's something to do with a new county policy on retirement, I think.'

'Well, blimey, how good is this?' She stared at me for a moment. 'The end of an era . . . how do you feel?'

'Relieved; I won't need to go and confront him now.'

'Good, I was worried about that. You've been so upset you might have clouted him.'

'I wasn't that bad, was I?'

'Well, let's just say the strain did show now and again. Anyway, it doesn't matter now – let's walk up to the stick 'ut to celebrate.'

The following day Howard Raven was out at a Heads' meeting and Val announced that we were all going to the Top Pub for lunch.

'Mrs Hyde can sort out the kids – that's what she's paid to do.' I thought of the beleaguered dinner lady, facing 100 rowdy children, although Eileen said that she'd better stay behind to man the phone.

'Is this a celebration, then?' said Emma, as her purple and gold cotton top drew curious glances from the lunchtime regulars at the Crag Hotel.

'Of course not,' said Val, with a wicked glint. 'We always come down here at the end of half term, don't we?'

'I wish we did,' said Hilda.

Val dug in her bag. 'I'm getting these, by the way – what's everyone having?'

Ten minutes later the five of us were tucking into fat beef sandwiches with only one topic of conversation. Sue, in particular, was animated.

'Val, I refuse to believe that you didn't know he was planning to leave. You know everything.'

'He told one of the governors – Arthur Fawcett – and that's all, honestly.'

'The man's a law unto himself,' said Emma. 'Anyway, I think the school can only gain – it's about time we had a change.'

'I wonder who we'll get,' said Sue.

I looked around. 'You're uncharacteristically quiet, Hilda.'

She chuckled to herself, her mouth half crammed with crusty bread. 'I was just thinking: some people cause joy wherever they go, and some whenever they go . . .'

Our raucous laughter caused everyone in the bar to turn round.

'Come on,' said Val. 'Sup up, we've already got the village tongues wagging – don't want to make it worse. Plus it's ten to one already.' She gulped the rest of her pint and I followed suit, while Hilda wailed that she still had a quarter of a sandwich left.

'Stick it in your handbag,' said Sue. 'It can be your mid-afternoon snack.'

I enjoyed that afternoon as much as any in my first term at Cragthwaite, although Class 3 thought it very odd that for once I was the one going to the toilet.

When the week-long half-term break arrived, Barbara and I found ourselves in Applesett, moving our belongings into a small stone house opposite Craven Bottoms. The house, called The Shippon, was another holiday cottage, belonging to a couple from Sussex. After a lot of thought and planning, we decided that it would be really helpful to be near to Craven Bottoms so that work could be started on the house as soon as the sale went through.

I opened the back of the van that Arthur Fawcett, our builder neighbour, had kindly leant us and looked at the pile of boxes, all neatly labelled by Barbara.

'Ay up, you must be the new schoolteacher at Cragthwaite. He's very young, don't yer think, Alec?'

I turned round to see a fresh-faced woman of about fifty wearing a quilted jacket next to a weatherbeaten tower of a man with tousled hair and deep-set eyes.

'I'm Mrs Dent from the village store just a few doors down, by't' way, and Alec Lund here farms at top.'

'Ow do,' said Alec in an accent so thick it was almost comical.

Barbara came out of the house, having opened all the doors. 'Oh, hello,' she said. I introduced her to our new neighbours. Alec nodded and said, 'Expectin' too, ma missus sez.'

'Well, you seem to know all about us,' said Barbara. I suspected Mr Crockett had spread the word.

'My sister-in-law is Hilda Percival's cousin,' said Mrs Dent, 'So, y'know . . .'

I was just about to say that we'd better crack on unloading the van when Alec stepped forward and grasped a box in each of his two mammoth hands. 'Your lass shunt be liftin' – I'll get thee fettled.'

The van was emptied in no time thanks to Big Alec, as we discovered he liked to be known, and Barbara and I sat down inside after Mrs Dent thoughtfully brought us some milk for tea. The warm welcome felt like a confirmation we were doing the right thing after the difficult decision to leave Castle Heywood.

'This is perfect,' said Barbara. 'I can just nip across the green and get on with decorating at the house.'

'Remember that Arthur said it's going to need a lot of renovation first.'

'Craven Bottoms. It's a stupid name – shall we change it?'

'Not on your nelly. It's got character.'

Barbara looked out of the mullioned window. 'Applesett is lovely. And what a luxury, having a shop. No stick 'ut, though.'

'But there's the pub, the school and the chapel.' It was strange, but we still needed to convince ourselves about the move.

'True,' said Barbara. 'There'll be a lot more people around and I won't have to heave a pram up the side of an alp every day.'

'We'll really get to know the village living here.'

'And the phone's nearer too.'

We stood up and agreed it was time to start opening boxes in the various rooms. The Shippon was a snug little converted stone barn, once belonging to the old farm next door. It was sparse and simple inside, but also clean and very homely, and the owners had agreed to let us have it through the off-season at a bargain rent. Barbara opened the windows upstairs and we heard the sound of children playing on the green outside. She sighed.

'You know, it might sound daft, but I'm going to miss living in the middle of nowhere.'

'But not with a baby.'

'No, you're right, not with a baby.'

'Hey – that is super!' The two boys were looking at a pencil drawing of a fox, and Hugh Richmond was speaking. It had to be Hugh; no one else in the class, or indeed the whole of Cragthwaite, used the word 'super' – it just wasn't Dales vocabulary. Then again, Hugh was no ordinary Dales boy. He had only arrived at the school this September, having been privately educated beforehand, and it was evident that his once wealthy parents had fallen on hard times. The Richmonds inhabited Shawby Hall across the dale, a stately pile set among several acres of parkland and graceful beeches, and they created quite a stir when they arrived at Cragthwaite Primary. The unmistakable aristocratic air of the parents made me wonder whether Hugh would be able to settle in the class, but from the moment he shook my hand and revealed a cheeky grin, I sensed that here was someone with more than enough character to meet the challenge.

At first, there were suppressed titters in the room whenever Hugh spoke: his fruity accent was delivered with such vibrant clarity that every word could be heard a mile off, and yet it quickly became clear to everyone that he was kind, modest and delighted to have the chance to make lots of new friends. Soon enough, Hugh was accepted – the class realised that he was a normal boy despite his posh voice and, as the term went on, he established himself as a popular character.

Just occasionally, glimpses of Hugh's privileged background emerged to produce delectable moments of humour in the classroom. One of these occurred after Hugh formed an unlikely alliance with Isaac Outhwaite, a quiet, lean farmer's lad who lived in a tiny cottage near Millscar. The two boys, although radically different in many ways, shared a love of nature, and animals in particular. They were always out together looking for badgers or birds' nests and spent hours sketching pictures from books. Hugh couldn't help enthusing loudly about Isaac's drawings, but soon realised that saying 'super' was not the done thing. He made a tremendous effort to adapt to the local boys' linguistic vagaries and I recall smiling to myself when I heard him trying to use the latest popular expression in the playground one day: Isaac had suggested that Hugh might like to come round to play with his ferrets. The response was a deliciously superior, 'Get on!'

On another occasion the class was creating a database about houses. Every child was asked to fill in an information sheet with details about his or her home: type of house, roof material, location, and so on. Hugh created quite a stir when he arrived at school with his piece of paper and an argument soon broke out, with several children involved.

'What's the matter over there?' I questioned.

Hugh looked indignant. 'It's Clive, Mr Seed – he doesn't believe my house has seventeen bedrooms.'

* * *

I was not surprised to discover that our next-door neighbour in Applesett knew the Richmond family. Piers Asquith was a retired major and another upper-crust personality. Unlike Hugh's parents, he was rather brusque, however, and I felt that whenever we met, or just exchanged pleasantries, he somehow disapproved of me. He had stern eyes that were always in shadow under a flat cap, and he spoke in a series of challenging growls. Major Asquith also had some strange habits: one of them was taking his black Labrador out for walks in the dark – baffling given that the village and surrounding roads and footpaths were unlit. Perhaps his army officer's training gave him advanced night vision. It was on a thick, late-November night that I passed him on the village green.

'Evening,' he barked.

'Oh, evening, Major Asquith.'

'Where are you off to then?'

'I'm going to the pub – there's a, erm, darts match.'

'Oh.'

'Bye.' But he was gone. More disapproval; I tramped across the green to the pub.

The Crown Inn nestled amongst the long bent row of weathered cottages at the edge of the green, facing the rising flanks of Spout Fell. It was one of the last of those rural havens that were once to be found all over Britain: a real village pub. At the social heart of Applesett, it was a proper community centre that still belonged to locals rather than visitors, and was undoubtedly another of the place's treasures. The building's thick walls, low ceilings and rich dark wood interior, warmed by a huge perpetual log fire, created a splendid atmosphere in which to relax and talk.

The Crown's landlord was called Dennis Helliwell and he had made Barbara and me feel wonderfully welcome from the first night we visited the pub the previous month, soon after our bid for Craven Bottoms was accepted. He was a short, oval, relentlessly cheery man who made an admirable licensee, and who undoubtedly added greatly to the pub's popularity. Dennis was also a keen darts fan and had run a team in the Upper Swinnerdale League for years. It was his great ambition to win the league but one thing always seemed to hold the team back, and everyone knew what it was: Dennis himself. Although he loved the game and played and practised every week, Dennis was not actually very good at darts, and an otherwise strong team always seemed to miss out on the prizes because of this. Reluctantly, he decided to look for another player.

It was into this situation that Barbara and I stepped when we shut the pub door against a harsh October's wind on that first visit. After a long chat with Dennis, where he filled us in on many of the pleasures of living in Applesett, I noticed the dartboard in the corner next to the door marked *Toilets*. I had played and enjoyed the game while at college, and had briefly joined a spectacularly dreadful pub team in York before moving up to the Dales.

'Is the dartboard used much, Dennis?' I asked.

'Certainly is – we have a fair team chucks on a Tuesday – do you play yourself?'

'Well, I can play, but I'm not that good.'

Dennis suddenly looked very interested. 'Come on then, I'll give you a game.'

I was very surprised that he just left the bar and strode over to the board to find some darts for me. I asked Barbara if she minded, and she seemed quite happy for me to play. The darts that Dennis produced were good ones, and after a few minutes I was well ahead in the game. Luck seemed to be with me, as I also hit the double to finish with my first dart. Dennis looked impressed.

'How would you like to join our arrers team?' he asked. I was amazed and certainly taken aback by the question – we had been in the pub for just an hour, and I had only played one game. 'I wouldn't mind . . . er . . . that would be great.' Barbara agreed that it seemed like a good way to get to know a few people in the village, and Dennis's enthusiasm made it almost impossible to say no anyway. It was only later, of course, that I learned that he was actually giving up his own place in the team for me.

Over the next month I became acquainted with the team and played a few matches, doing reasonably well against admittedly weak opposition. Two things about the other seven members of The Crown darts team struck me right away: first, they were all enormous; and second, they were all local farmers or builders. I felt very conspicuous as both the only incomer and as a teacher; at least I could take consolation in being tall. They were certainly a friendly bunch, however, and I soon came to greatly enjoy the droll banter and gentle teasing that was their trademark. The team captain was John Weatherall – a wiry builder and one of three brothers whose family had lived in Applesett for several generations. John was a great encourager and constantly toured the room on match nights telling you how the other team couldn't even hold their darts straight, 'never mind throw 'em'. He also had a very winsome habit of massaging your neck and shoulders for a few seconds as he passed behind you giving last-minute advice – most

Dales men wouldn't dream of carrying out or receiving such an action, but with John it was somehow natural and completely acceptable.

Big Alec I'd met on our first day in the village when he helped us unload the van: a hulking great brute of a man with hands that entirely enclosed his pint glass, and a mouth and stomach that could empty it in a single surging pour. Although he was as friendly as the rest of the team, I was always slightly wary of Big Alec; I felt that a wrong remark might just cause him to swat me like a fly with one of his outsized arms. Later on he did like to drop a few disparaging remarks about teaching not being proper work, but I never had the courage to tell him that I thought riding round all day in Land Rovers, tractors and quad bikes looked far easier than imparting all knowledge to twenty-four extremely demanding kids.

'Cheesy' was the none-too-flattering nickname of another member of the team, Andy Cheeseworth. He was also a builder and a young athletic character who excelled at all sports. Cheesy was one of those laid-back people with a natural warmth, who seemed to be popular with everyone, despite having the most outrageously scraggy long blond hair and unfashionable beard. He never bothered with practice on darts nights, and didn't seem to get at all nervous like many of us, preferring instead to loiter at the bar swapping earthy jokes with the other locals.

Vince was a great friend of Cheesy's and the star player of the team. He was a broad, swarthy, handsome man, quietly spoken and completely modest. Everyone else in the team was quick to tell me two things about Vince: one that he was once good enough at arrows (they never said 'darts') to turn professional, and second that he had dartitis. I'd heard of dartitis before and always assumed that it was a joke condition, being the inability of a thrower to let go of the dart when aiming at the board, but everyone who told me looked quite solemn during the disclosure. I also found out from Vince himself that he gave up the idea of making money from the game after breaking his arm badly three times: it seemed that he was also unsurpassed at falling through ceilings as a joiner, with not a few of the dale's older cottages refusing to tolerate his sixteen-stone frame.

Paul farmed just outside the village on the road to Skirbridge. Most farmers talked about beasts and prices when in the pub, but Paul only ever discussed girls, cars and football – he was a Manchester United fanatic, and more than once I saw his ruddy features glowing scarlet as he reacted passionately to criticism of his beloved team. Paul always arrived at matches with our single 'outsider', Bri. He was only from Shawby, about five miles across the dale, but I later heard that the move from his own local pub and team the previous season had caused quite a stir. This was yet another example of a phenomenon that never ceased to amaze me about Swinnerdale: not only did everyone know everyone else – many being related, of course – but everyone seemed to know what was going on there, down to the last dot and comma, despite the dale's considerable length and moorland terrain.

The final two members of the team were known as DD and DW: Dave Duggleby and Dave Whiterow, two more local builders. DD was a six foot six tree trunk of a man who threw darts so hard that the pub walls shuddered when he was playing. He was also the possessor of a scandalous wit and frequently drew booms of laughter from the team as we travelled to away matches. His side-kick, DW, was almost as large, but altogether saner. He was a wholly likeable person, thoughtful and mature, although only in his early twenties – what the locals called 'steady'. He was also saving to get married and so went easier on the beer than most. I was ridiculously pleased to be amongst this group of burly working men, and it helped me to feel accepted into the dale far more quickly than would have happened otherwise; something that led me to be grateful to Dennis for many years.

Although we made a winning start to the season, The Crown was not top of the league. That position had been held, and held for many years, by our team's fiercest rivals – The Black Bull from 'oop'dale', as they always said, in Kettleby. We were due to play them in late November.

'Aye, it's about time we knocked that lot off thes perches,' said John. 'We just might stand a chance now Dennis 'as given over.'

'Well, this is the best team we've 'ad at App'sett since I can remember,' added Paul. Big Alec slammed down his pint on the bar. 'Aye, let's give the buggers a reet scare.'

This was the darts match that I walked across the village green to join, when I passed Major Asquith and Jet.

The Crown was busier and noisier than usual that night, and there was a definite edge of excitement and tension about the place. You could see it on the faces of the players as they queued up at the board to practise: there were fewer of the usual larking jibes and a far greater level of concentration helped each man to guide the thin tungsten missiles towards the treble twenty region of the board. I joined the line and watched Paul taking a throw. A girl came and stood next to the board, waiting to cross the line of fire to reach the toilet door. There was no way to avoid darts games when going to the toilet in The Crown – the door was in the corner and the board was right next to it. This unfortunate layout often led to some very near misses, particularly when visitors were around in summer, and the players were well used to having to stop in mid-throw, often allowing people to pass with a quip of, 'Don't worry – I'll get you on the way back . . .' or similar. But there were no wisecracks from Paul this time, and he carried on with his throw, making the girl wait nervously: it was clear that the Applesett lads really wanted to win this match. I took my first practice throw and scored twenty-six. Nobody said anything.

At half past eight the pub door crashed open and eight monsters walked in, heading straight for the bar. It was unmistakably the opposition, and to my disbelief, they were even bigger than our team. There was a brief bout of nods and 'now thens', and a number of Applesett glasses were drained quickly so that they could be charged while the Kettleby players had a practice. I watched them fitting the tiny plastic flights into the ends of their darts with crusty sausage-like fingers. Each man stepped up in silence and flicked his darts towards the board with startling accuracy: there was a treble in every throw, and no one missed the twenty. I picked up my glass and moved to the bar like the others.

There was quite a queue to be served, and while waiting I was drawn into a conversation with one of the village's most ancient and fascinating characters, sitting on his favourite stool in the corner. Sam Burnsall was ninety years old and had lived in Applesett all his life. He was born at Low Bottom Farm near the beck and now occupied a grand old house at the top of the village. Sam was a wonderful person to listen to and never missed a night at The Crown, where he could share stories with other farmers, old and new, and anyone else who was blessed enough to catch some of his tales of Edwardian days in the dale. Sadly, Sam was now so frail that he had taken to driving down to the pub, at a steady four miles an hour, even though he lived only 300 yards away. A few whiskies were the only things to bring his shaky hands relief, he claimed, and more often than not they also caused him to forget to put his car lights on for the slow drag home.

Despite the formidable strength of the upper dale team, we matched them game for game, with DD, Paul and Cheesy throwing brilliantly to make the score 3–3 after six rounds. There were great barrel-chested roars of 'arrers!' when anyone hit a ton or more, which happened frequently, and the tumultuous clattering of heavy hands and beer glasses against table tops when an Applesett dart landed in the finishing double. Inevitably, or so it seemed to me, I had been drawn to play last, against Old Albert, whoever he was. I was consoled by the fact that our best player, Vince, was still to play, however, so we were unlikely to lose even if I had a stinker. Despite being armed with this knowledge, my nerves were steadily building up and I was pleased when John came over to me with a quick massage and quiet word.

'How yer doin' then?'

'Bit nervous,' I said, knowing that he would pass on some

encouragement and bold captain's psychology. He patted me on the head.

'Go and score Vince's game will yer, lad.'

Scoring in any darts match was bad enough, but the whole of the crowded pub was watching this game, anxious to see our star player stuff the opposition. I sloped over to the chalkboard and wrote 501 twice then drew a wobbly line in between. Before joining this team, I thought that I was quite capable when it came to mental calculation – after all, I did teach it – but the builders and farmers of Applesett in this rural corner of Yorkshire put me to shame. Not only were they lightning quick at adding totals and subtracting the scores as soon as the darts hit the board, but they also knew exactly which treble and double combinations were required to achieve any finish. And now I had to score this game in front of them all; I edgily drained my pint glass for fortitude.

Vince won the toss and stepped up to the board, looking calm and strong. I cleared my throat and croaked, 'Quiet please – game on!' Amazingly, the babbling stopped and a respectful quietness embraced the smoky room. I was even more nervous now. Vince leant forward and scythed three beautifully straight darts into the twenty sector of the black and red board.

'Sixty,' I whispered. At least this calculation wasn't tricky. Vince's opponent, a mammoth snorting bull of a man with a nose and neck the colour of blood, was already throwing. His darts slammed into treble twenty, treble five and eighteen. There were cries of 'guurrddd arrers!' from the Kettleby team. My brain started pinging numbers inside a beery head. The bull man snatched his darts out of the board and snorted, 'Ninety-three.' I chalked 407, then rubbed it out and put 406.

'Four o eight,' said Vince, who was waiting to throw. I changed the number and stared hard at the board. The game continued in a similar vein, with Vince scoring more and more heavily while helping me with the chalking, and the bull man just staying in touch. The room nearly erupted when Vince pinned a magnificent 140 to leave himself needing double top to win the game. The bull man responded with sixty, but still required well over 100 to finish. Then disaster struck. Vince pushed his boot against the wooden oche and leaned forward: we all believed that his next dart would put The Crown 4–3 up and therefore assure that defeat by the auld enemy was impossible. He drew back his wrist, touching the Union Jack flight against his chin like a deadly sniper squeezing the trigger. There was complete silence. Beneath a taut mouth, his forearm, poised like a praying mantis, twitched then extended in a smooth line. I expected to see the dart slip easily into the double twenty, but it never left his hand. He drew it back again: obviously an extra aim was needed for this vital throw, but the same thing happened. Vince's arm reached forward but drew back the slim metal barrel just at the moment of release. Murmurings and shufflings pierced the calm, and John edged nearer to the board, looking fretful. Vince just stared forward and continued to swing his dart back and forward as if in a trance, his chest rising and falling, his mouth in a lipless grimace. I heard more than one whisper of, 'It's t'bloody dartitis again.' I was the only person in Vince's line of vision but I felt completely helpless: I looked over towards John for direction just as something whizzed past my ear. Vince had let go. The dart clipped the wire just above the double twenty. Suddenly the tension erupted with screams of, 'Goooo on, Vince lad!', 'Fill yer boots!' and, 'Put it to bed!' The power of the strange condition over Vince's body seemed to be broken by this burst of support, and he let go of the next dart first time: its point was buried in the centre of double top and the place went mad.

It was now 4–3 to us and I had the chance to seal victory for The Crown. My first three darts scored five, one and five. Old Albert, using ancient brass arrows which looked like cartoon bombs, hit 100. He fired them from the hip in a sideways action. My next shaking dart bounced off the wire, finishing up in a half-full ashtray, and that set the standard for the remainder of the game. I also managed to land one dart in the back of another, to jeers of, 'Aye up, it's Robin Hood!' Meanwhile, Old Albert bagged another three hundreds: he smelt of sheep and had noisy teeth, but effortlessly finished the game off on the next throw but one, leaving me on 296. I went to buy him a half pint, in the loser's tradition. No one spoke to me at the bar – there was nothing to say; we had lost our best-ever chance of a famous victory. A minor consolation arrived after I handed a grinning Old Albert his drink: Dennis brought out a steaming tray of home-cooked pie and pea suppers for the players. He handed the first one to me and whispered, 'Don't worry, lad, he once left me on 400.'

The delicious pie and peas did little to revive me, and I left the pub feeling that I had let everyone down. Not even the comical sight of Sam Burnsall motoring up the village at four miles per hour with no lights on could raise my spirits. I crossed the green and began fumbling for my house key when I heard a strange commotion from a few yards up the road. I couldn't see anything in the darkness and so wandered over towards the noise. The shape of a stationary car emerged out of the gloom, and I could hear a muffled voice shouting.

'Back off will you, man!' I was baffled. Nearing the scene I could make out the stooped figure of Sam Burnsall. He was searching about beside his car trying to locate the mystery voice.

'I'm under here, you old fool, back off!' Sam couldn't see the frantic figure of Major Asquith pinned under the front wheels, still holding his dog lead.

'Back off, you bugger!' I raced over and told Sam to let off the handbrake, desperately trying not to laugh. The car rolled a few feet back down the sloping road and the supine Major came into sight, with Jet, his black Labrador, standing bemused alongside the incident. Neither of them seemed to be injured. Sam apologised, but the Major refused help to get up; his Barbour was dusted off and the ritual walk was resumed, with the sound of intense muttering trailing off into the night. I never did find out just how Sam had managed to run him over travelling at such a dawdle, but I somehow felt a lot better about the darts match after the incident. 'Get on!' as Hugh would have said.

Chapter Eight

Tracey

Two Christmas cards and an official-looking letter dropped on to the stone-flagged floor of The Shippon's hallway. I looked at the postmarks: it was unbelievable that December had come around so quickly.

'Any good news?' called Barbara from the kitchen. She sounded more tired than usual – a recent bout of morning sickness was clearly taking its toll.

'Well, it's not brilliant. The mortgage company have got their survey results for the house and they're unhappy about the condition of some of the window frames.' We were both thinking the same thing: where would the money come from? We talked about it for a while but found ourselves weighed down by gloom.

Barbara suggested a bit of fresh air might cheer us up so we headed down to the village shop. Mrs Dent was outside swabbing the windows with gusto.

'Now then, you two. How are you liking The Shippon, then?'

'It's lovely,' said Barbara, trying to sound upbeat, 'and it'll give us a chance to meet a few more people in the village – Andy's got the darts team but I don't really know anyone yet.'

'Oh, you will, soon enough. And everyone knows who you are, don't worry about that. Now would you like some bread because I've just got some fresh in?'

I left Barbara chatting in the shop and went to say hello to John Weatherall who was unloading ladders from his pickup outside the smithy on the green just a few yards away. The small, ramshackle building acted as a store for his building equipment. I noticed that he didn't lock the ladders inside but just pushed them through a large hole in the wall above the door.

''Ow do, lad,' he said with a wink. 'And don't worry – I won't mention arrers.' I returned a weak smile.

'Do you just leave all your tools and stuff here? Doesn't it ever get nicked?'

'Never 'as done yet. If you ever need to borrow ladders you know where they are – just come and help yerself.'

I thanked him and waved to Barbara as she came out of the shop.

John nodded across. 'It's a wonder your lass got out before dark the way that woman in there talks.'

'You obviously know Mrs Dent, then?'

'Should do, since we're cousins.' This came as no surprise; in the short time we'd been in the area it rapidly became apparent that there was an intricate web of family ties right along the dale.

'So who else is related in Applesett?'

'Well, that's a question. I could be all day on that 'un.' He scanned the village and pointed to a tractor flinging muck across a field behind the chapel. 'Well, for starters Big Alec there's my brother-in-law – you know 'im – and that kid taking dog furra walk yonder is his niece. Then, see Old Sam Burnsall at the top, he's Cameron Dent's great-grandfather – the lad you teach.'

'Is Mrs Dent related to Cameron, then?'

'In a distant way, aye. It's like that round here, Andrew – you can't get away with a fart. Reet, got to go and stick me head in some drains.' Barbara arrived as he trundled off in his pickup, flashing her one of his cheeriest winks. I was glad to see a little more colour in her cheeks.

'Mrs Dent's suggested that I go with her daughter to the Mums and Tots group in Skirbridge on Thursday,' she said. 'It'll be a good chance to suss it out early and get to know a few people round and about. She'll give me a lift too.'

'Hey, perfect timing!' We headed back to The Shippon in lighter spirits.

At Cragthwaite Primary, the business of school life reached a new and hectic level as preparations were made for all the traditional end of term events. Everywhere in the school, children were acting, singing, rehearsing music and turning out cards, calendars and Christmas decorations with the efficiency of a wartime production line. Ordinary lessons were further disrupted by a succession of smartly dressed visitors being given guided tours through the classrooms by Eileen the secretary. These were the interviewees for the headship of the school. As with all such candidates, each was desperate to impress, and in particular to show how interested he or she was in children and what they were doing. It was the middle of the week when a tall, elegantly coiffured woman smiled her way across my room and approached Jack, who was busy colouring in a Christmas card.

'That's a lovely robin,' she said, still smiling.

'Who are you?'

'I'm a teacher.'

'Well, where's your class? Shouldn't you be teaching them?'

'Not today, I'm having a look around your school.'

'Can't be bad.'

At this point Tracey Pratt, sitting next to Jack, decided to join in the conversation. Tracey Pratt was, as her father had once memorably told me, one of a long line of Pratts that had inhabited the village of Cragthwaite since time immemorial. She was a fascinating child, someone without inhibitions, prone to constant fluctuations of mood and emotional turmoil: when things went well for Tracey she screeched with delight, but if she so much as lost her rubber she was pitched into spasms of black despair in the blink of an eye. She was always interested in visitors, too.

'I like your perfume,' said Tracey to the tall woman. 'Do you not think you've overdone it, though?' The woman flushed, and let her smile slip beyond recovery. Tracey continued. 'You must be one of them that's trying for Mr Raven's job. My dad says that they're having interviews today. Your jacket's nice too, if you like grey. What d'you think of our school then?'

'I think it's a lovely school.'

'They've all said that. Suppose you 'ave to really. D'you think you'll get the job then?' At this point I intervened to rescue the poor woman, who was looking decidedly trapped, even though I was enjoying Tracey's forthright interrogation. The poor girl was always putting her foot in it, even when she meant well. I also needed to gather the class's attention: there was, I'd discovered, oodles to prepare this month. In addition to making cards and calendars, we had to learn carols for the carol service, decorate the hall for the Christmas dinner, plan games and organise prizes for the class party, and, most importantly, rehearse and build a set for the term's great finale: the Christmas panto. The show was all my idea. In a moment of madness back in October I had volunteered to write and produce a pantomime after I had asked Val if the school put on any kind of play for the end of term.

'The infants always do a nativity,' she said with more than a hint of disinterest, 'but the juniors have never done anything like that while I've been here. The Beak's not into plays.'

After this conversation, I went to see Howard Raven, who said that he was 'happy' for me to put on a performance with the juniors as long as I took all responsibility for it. His very lack of enthusiasm caused me to start planning immediately, and the idea of a panto sprang to mind. Somehow I felt that it would be immensely liberating for the children to do something with fun at the centre – the whole place seemed to have been starved of it. This all happened, of course, before the ill-fated Class 3 play about the ghost of Preston Blaise Hall. Since then, my confidence in the success of the idea had plummeted drastically, but *Jack and the Beanstalk* was going ahead and it was now down to me.

With so many activities based around Christmas going on, I decided that a good place to start would be to go over the wonderful story of the birth of Jesus. I felt sure that the children would know the story only too well, so I began by asking them to write out the events of the nativity in their own words. The results were shocking.

According to Class 3, Jesus was born in an amazing number of places, including Jerusalem, Nazareth, Bethlehem and Egypt. The stories featured an interesting array of characters too, ranging from Moses to someone called John the Basher. At least Mary and Joseph managed to feature in most of them, along with the stable – although the menagerie of creatures in there at the birth was quite phenomenal, with oxen, asses, horses, sheep, pigs, dogs and cats all getting in on the act. Several other notable contributions caught my eye:

Mary and Joseph lived with a donkey in Nazareth.
The angle said, 'You are going to have a daddy.'
Mary and Joseph were going to pay their taxis.
Mary rode on a bonkey.
In the stable was a ship and an oxo.
Jesus was born in a pig trof.
The three kings gave Jesus gold, myrrh and a woolly jumper.

It was fairly clear that they needed to hear the story once more.

As I pulled into Applesett I was looking forward to telling Barbara about John the Basher but seeing the village shop reminded me that she'd been to the Mums and Tots group in Skirbridge that morning and so would no doubt be excited to give me all the details.

I knew something was wrong right away. As I opened the door there was no radio or sound of Christmas decorations being made or busyness. Barbara was sitting in the living room, stony-faced.

'Whatever's the matter?' I'd never seen her like this before.

'They're revolting, that's what's the matter.'

'What, the Skirbridge mothers?'

'No, their offspring.'

'You mean the cute little toddlers?'

She turned and virtually spat at me. 'They are *not* cute! They are noisy and rude and ill-behaved. Cute is the last thing they are.'

'Er, well, perhaps it was just a bad morning?'

'I think not: someone actually said they were better behaved than usual.' I offered to make a cup of tea; she ignored me. 'What I can't understand is, there were three or four of the snotty-nosed little oiks throwing tantrums, and the mothers were just sitting there letting them get away with it. They didn't do anything. If it had been me there would have been some action, I can tell you.'

'I get the picture, but little kids are like that, Barb.'

'I never used to run around, screaming and not doing as I was told at that age. My mother would have skinned me.'

'Yes, but you were a nice little well-behaved girl, and an only child.'

She stared at me for a moment. 'But, but . . . what if *our* baby turns into one like that. I'll run away.'

'You won't, it's normal. It's that phase thing they go through. I'm sure I was occasionally like that at three, and so were my sisters, but a sharp word from Mum or Dad soon sorted us out.' It was a relief to see some of the tension drop from her face. 'Kids do behave better with proper discipline.'

'I suppose you're right.'

'I'm sure I'm right.'

'Well, there's a first time for everything.' She almost began to smile at her own remark. 'I must just have a frighteningly idealised view of what young children are like.'

'It certainly scared me.'

'Stop it.' She gave me a gentle push.

'Anyway, mothers give birth to babies, not toddlers.'

She nodded and wiped an eye. 'Do you think I'll cope then?'

'Course I do. You'll be a fantastic mother.'

'You're not just saying that to shut me up?'

'I'll ignore that and I'll make that cup of tea now.'

'It's a good job I like you.'

With interviews and long deliberations amongst the school governors now over, we found out who our new headteacher was to be. Her name was Joyce Berry. Joyce was not the tall woman with the big hair, but she was the staff's favourite among the candidates. Unlike many of the others, her warmth and smile seemed genuine, and we were all delighted that she had been given the post – even Val seemed pleased. The next fortnight gave us barely a moment to think about the following term's changes, however, and Val's mood soon returned to its usual gruff equilibrium as we went into Christmas activity overdrive.

The carol service took place at the village church in sub-zero temperatures: the children forgot most of the words of the carols and were told off by the vicar for playing with the kneelers. My class's Bible readings were scarcely audible, and the world's loudest watch alarm went off during the prayers, causing an epidemic of uncontrolled giggling from the infants.

The traditional school Christmas dinner passed off without too much incident a few days later, but when we entered the final week of term and the day of the class parties, the children's excitement rose like an approaching blizzard. Val looked more depressed than ever as I passed her in the office on Monday morning. She put down the phone next to Eileen, who was typing at speed.

'What's up, Val?' I enquired.

'Santa's got diarrhoea, that's what's up.'

'Eh?'

'Oh, you won't know, will you? The infants always get a visit from Santa when it's their party and Arthur Fawcett's always done it, but he's just called to say he's down with the squits, so muggins here has to organise someone else – and the parties start in about three hours.'

'Oh.' I didn't know who to suggest.

'Have you tried the vicar, Val? I think he's done it before.' It was Eileen: she always seemed to know what to do in a crisis.

'Eileen, you are brilliant.' Val picked up the phone and made a call. A minute later, the veil of grimness had lifted from her completely.

'He'll do it. Excellent, that's another job done.' She sighed. 'At least we don't have the bloomin' reindeer going past the windows any more. Do you remember that, Eileen?'

She gave a quiet grin. 'I most certainly do, Val. You used to do an admirable job.'

'What was all that about then?' I asked, somewhat confused.

Val put down her cold coffee and almost smiled. 'It was at the old school with the high Victorian windows – just before the party, we used to sit all the infants in their classroom and tell them to watch at the windows very carefully to look out for Santa's reindeer going past. I used to sneak out with a couple of hunting trophies with big antlers and run past holding them up above my head. I must have been potty.'

'Oh, they used to love it though, Val,' said Eileen. 'You should have seen their little faces – it was the highlight of their year, you know.'

'So did you have to retire the sleigh when the school moved here?' I said, looking at Val.

'No, it actually stopped when we were still at the old school. One year Rudolph got a bit carried away and forgot that the anti-burglar thorn bushes outside the windows had grown rather a lot.'

'What happened?'

'Well there was a sudden loss of reindeer and several of the children started to wail, apparently – Hilda told me that one boy asked why Father Christmas was using bad words, so that was that. Santa just walks to Cragthwaite now.'

Once the parties were over, the end of my first term of teaching was in sight, and I was ready for it. Only one final event remained, but it was the big one: the Christmas performance, featuring the infants' nativity and our panto. *Jack and the Beanstalk* had been in rehearsal for several weeks now, and the whole cast were heartily sick of practising it. With this being Howard Raven's final show for the parents, however, I was determined that it wouldn't be yet another of my disasters, and so final preparations were meticulous.

After much agonising over parts, the cast had been allocated as follows:

Hugh as Jack the giant slayer
Carol as Jack's mother
Jack Raw as the Ogre
Eve as the Ogre's wife
Tracey Pratt and Penny Garsdale as Daisy the cow

Tracey had set her heart on Daisy, and nagged, cajoled and begged me until I gave in – despite severe misgivings.

'Me dad's a dairy farmer, tha knows, Mr Seed. Us Pratts knows all about cows we do,' she had declared. 'And I want to be the front too. No way am I going to be the bum.'

For Daisy's rear end I had carefully chosen Penny Garsdale, a quiet and extremely sensible girl, whom I felt could keep the reckless Tracey in check on the night if need be.

The whole class spent long hours during the week painting a wonderful set and making props and costumes. George had a brilliant idea for creating a beanstalk which would appear to grow too: we wrapped one of the hall climbing ropes in green crepe paper, tied on leaves, and attached a piece of fishing line to the end. The line was hooked over one of the rope pulleys fixed to the ceiling and threaded through the doorway to the classroom next door, where it was controlled by a small team of eager beanstalk pullers led by Malcolm Willoughby. This clever device worked surprisingly well and the fine nylon line was quite hard to see, giving quite a magical appearance to the tumultuous sprouting stem.

All of the children playing the main parts learnt their lines admirably, not least Jack, who played up his 'Fee-fi-fo-fum' motto with enormous vitality. Eve made him a suitably characterful wife, wielding a huge wooden spoon with more than a glint in her eye. Hugh made the perfect gallant hero: he was like a thirties film star with his thick black hair, dashing looks and willingness to take on any number of dangerous stunts whether called for by the script or not. Carol played his acerbic mother to perfection: she rewrote the part to enable her to give Jack an outrageous verbal assault for flogging poor Daisy for a handful of beans. I didn't argue.

Daisy herself was a classic pantomime cow: Emma, being the most artistic member of staff, had created a beautiful heifer mask for her, complete with a bulbous wet nose and great long black eyelashes. Tracey and Penny were draped in a huge black and white sheet, and the finishing touch was a bright pink flapping udder made from a washing up glove filled with water and set madly dangling from Penny's waist like a hand from a sunburnt corpse. Tracey was more than competent at steering, and usually managed to stay on cue with her moos.

All in all, despite my nervous exhaustion, I was really looking forward to the performance. The only hitch was the stage; we had to borrow a set of temporary staging from the secondary school in Ingleburn and they were using it until the day before our show.

The stage arrived at lunchtime on dress rehearsal day but it couldn't be assembled with all the dinner tables still in the hall. This was a blow, but we decided to run through the show in the afternoon without the stage anyway, and put it up after school. The children were disappointed about not being able to practise on stage, but in the event I was delighted with how things went, as were the infants who were allowed to see this preview. The actors delivered their lines confidently, the beanstalk rose into the air like magic, bringing a lovely 'aaahhh' from the watching little ones, and Daisy herself was a star, especially when she danced along to the song which had been specially written for her grand entrance.

At home I kept Barbara updated with the panto's progress through rehearsals and extolled the children's comical performances.

'Why don't you come and see the afternoon show? You could get the bus then I'll take us both home.'

'Oooh, can I? That would be fun. Would the Beak mind?'

'We won't ask him – I'll just reserve a seat at the front.' I felt confident that I could get away with this, having done ninety per cent of the work for the show myself.

The big day finally arrived, and with relief I took a full register, noting that none of the actors, singers or special effects people was absent. After lunch, the hall was transformed into a mini-theatre with every available chair being crammed in front of the impressive stage, now properly installed, and final adjustments made to the set. Everything was in place for the two performances, one in the afternoon and the second in the evening.

By half past one the hall was crowded: every inhabitant of Cragthwaite seemed to be there plus aunties, uncles and grannies from outlying farms and the usual melee of restless toddlers and noisy babies. Barbara had pride of place in the centre of the front row. She gave me a little wave as I checked, double-checked and treble-checked my class's costumes and props. I checked I had the script for prompting. Everything seemed to be in place so we could all sit and enjoy the infants' nativity play, which preceded the panto.

The play was a delight, starting with two children being visited by Santa on Christmas Eve and leading on to the story of how it all began, complete with angels, shepherds, Mary, Joseph and bonkey. There was only one hitch when one of Santa's Reception reindeer refused to join in the reindeer dance. I looked over to Val and smiled. Later on it was discovered that the little mite was merely confused by the big brown antlers strapped to his head: 'I thought I was a tree . . .' he wailed after the show.

And so, after a great rumble of applause for the infants, our turn finally came. Hilda, sitting at the piano with great importance, played the opening song, and Hugh and Carol climbed up the little portable block of steps and stood in front of the lights. I prayed for them with tremendous hope as the music faded, and they began their lines. Visually, at least, it was stunning – several parents had helped with costumes and the actors really did look splendid. I needn't have worried about Hugh and Carol either – they both had that natural acting ability which cannot be taught, and they carried off the opening scene with assurance. It was a good start and I was hugely enjoying it, not least when a few kind members of the audience laughed at some of the jokes I'd attempted to add to the script. Barbara certainly enjoyed them.

As the scene neared its end, and Jack's mother told him that he would have to sell their beloved cow Daisy, I glanced over to see if Tracey was waiting in the wings. With relief, I spotted the shiny black nose in the hall doorway, and so I nodded at the choir who launched into Daisy's entrance number.

Daisy, Daisy, give me your answer Moo;
I'm half crazy, tired of milking you,
You're running out of mileage,
I can't afford the silage,
But you'll look great,
Upon a plate,
As a nice little Irish stew.

The audience tittered at the song and then launched into spontaneous applause as the panto cow made her splendid entrance, swaggering across the front of the hall, her feet and udder miraculously swinging in time with the music. It was even better than I'd thought – the show was going like a dream.

Tracey was obviously enjoying her big moment, and lifted her cow mask high to snort out a huge 'moo!' at the end of the song. Then something most peculiar happened. Tracey was clearly having no problems steering Daisy, despite the huge costume, and Penny behind her was holding on steadfastly throughout each move. There was, however, an obstacle that none of us had considered: poor Daisy, coming into the hall at floor level had next to climb the little flight of steps about three feet up on to the stage.

The manoeuvre started well enough: Tracey found the first step and mounted it confidently. In no time at all she had bounded up to join Jack and his grumpy mother on the platform. The only trouble was that Tracey, in her enthusiasm, had left Penny behind. Poor Penny, like most cow's bottoms, lacked vision, and simply couldn't find the first step at all. To make matters worse, she must have let go of Tracey's waist as the front end of Daisy continued its ascent, and I heard a little desperate squeal of panic from inside the costume. Daisy's back suddenly developed an unhealthy looking droop. 'Surely Tracey will realise what's happened,' I thought. But the stage-struck head clearly had no notion of the disaster ensuing behind and, to my horror, continued across the set towards Jack, who she was scripted to snuggle up to.

The effect of this internal bovine breakdown was startling. Very quickly, Daisy began to grow longer. In fact, as Penny still groped around with her feet for the first step to her salvation, and as Tracey continued walking, Daisy became the longest cow in the world. The sheet we had used to cover the two girls was enormous and, behind me, screams of laughter from the audience drowned out all my attempts at remote assistance. I glanced at Barbara who was having convulsions and holding a tissue to her face.

Then lots of things happened: Carol, although crying with glee herself, stopped Tracey in her tracks and pushed her backwards. At the same time, Hilda jumped off her piano stool and picked up Penny, dropping her on to the second step. Daisy really looked in a bad way now. Tracey started to tread on the drooping sheet as she back-pedalled. Penny crawled on to the stage on her hands and knees, her udder flopping dejectedly up the steps beside her. When the cow's two halves finally re-connected they were at different levels. I, along with everyone else, could clearly hear Tracey Pratt say, 'Geroff, Penny – yer head's up me bum.'

I can't really recall the rest of the pantomime. In the end, Hilda and I had to rebuild Daisy on stage, and she never did quite recover her composure. I do remember the audience clapping long and hard with appreciation, despite the mishaps, however. And I also remember, at the end, seeing Tracey Pratt's beetroot-red face when she took off the cow mask change from a scowl to a broad beam as the parents gave her and Penny a huge cheer.

'That was the best day out I've had in years,' said Barbara, as we climbed into the car after school. 'Possibly ever.'

'I'm never working with cows again, that's for sure.' Inwardly I felt a considerable pride, despite the various on-stage calamities.

'What about your dynamic headmaster – did he enjoy it?'

I looked at her and smiled. 'Who cares?'

The next day there was a subdued staffroom gathering organised by the school governors to say goodbye to Howard Raven. Arthur Fawcett, in his role as Chairman, had discreetly approached each of the teachers a few days previously asking if anyone had any pertinent memories or humorous stories that he could share on the day.

'Well, er, there isn't an awful lot that springs to mind,' I said, dredging up only recollections of embarrassment and disapproval.

'Strange, but everyone's said that, more or less,' said Arthur, looking disappointed.

'But I've only been here a few months, as you know. Val's taught at this school for nearly twenty years. She must have plenty of good tales.'

'I've already asked Val.'

Neither of us knew what to say.

On the day itself everyone stood around after school, nibbling peanuts and sipping sherry. The governors made an attempt to be cheery but the staff were simply too tired to even put on an act. Our minds were looking forward, not back, thinking what Joyce Berry, our new head, was going to be like and wondering how much she would change the school.

Emma sidled up to me and whispered, 'This is fun.'

'I've got a feeling things are going to be different next term,' I murmured.

'I'll drink to that, except I can't stand sherry.'

After fifteen minutes of awkward waiting, Arthur Fawcett cleared his throat, waited for silence and did his best to thank Howard Raven for his dedicated service to the pupils of Cragthwaite over many years.

'He has been well respected by the community and has seen a great number of changes. I'm sure that he will keep himself busy in the years to come.'

Howard Raven was handed a painting of the village and in return spoke a few words of gratitude and said he was looking forward to retirement. A polite round of applause followed. There were no funny stories or cheers. After a few more minutes, one by one, people made their excuses and left. It was all rather sad.

So that was it, my first term. It ended like it began, with a near disaster, but tired as I was, I could hardly wait for the next one.

Chapter Nine

Wilf

Christmas was spent with our parents: a heady mixture of sleeping, eating and telling tales of school and village life in the Dales. After much travelling between Yorkshire, Cheshire and Essex, we returned to Swinnerdale in the New Year, looking forward to moving into our new house. On the way home, we stopped off at Ingleburn to visit the shops and stretch our legs.

Ingleburn was the lower dale's only town and a proud little place, set high up on a hillside looking down into the stretching valley it served. It was dominated by a sparse, broad marketplace, part cobbled, always windswept, and hemmed in by stout grey three-storey houses, many with sagging stone roofs. Although it could be grim at this time of year, the town certainly had character: there was a pub next to the chapel and a taxidermist next to the pet shop.

Gangs of waddling jackdaws surveyed us from the roof ridges as we made our way to the footpath up above the town. A couple of thumping quarry wagons boomed past on the main road and then we were out of the houses and on to the high ridge which commanded such wonderful views up the dale. A few snowdrops were peeking out of the earth but the wind was hard and cold in this exposed spot. I put my arm around Barbara and could feel her shivering.

Streaks of snow capped the higher hills and, over to the west, low clouds were moving in, darkening Spout Fell and veiling the upper dale in a cloak of impending dampness. Looking down into the valley several hundred feet below us, it was clear that there had been a great amount of rain while we'd been away. The River Swinner had in many places spilled into the brown slurry-sprayed fields around it, leaving huge pools of water that caught the light like a trail of toffee wrappers. Everything looked dark and wet. We headed back to the car.

Two days later, back in Applesett, it was still raining. This didn't help to raise our spirits which were already low having learnt that Mr Crockett hadn't yet signed the contract for Craven Bottoms, since the house he was hoping to buy had fallen through.

'At this rate we might not even get in there before the end of January,' I moaned.

'Never mind, at least we've got this place as long as we need it,' said Barbara.

'But it wasn't that long ago that you were worried about how much it was all costing.'

'True, but I've come to the conclusion that worrying never solved anything. It'll work out in the end.'

'Yes, but it might work out that we lose Craven Bottoms.'

'No, I've a good feeling about that. It'll work out.'

There had been a definite change in Barbara, which at first I thought was something to do with her pregnancy, but which I then came to realise was the result of her feeling settled in Applesett. Not knowing anyone except a few nodding acquaintances like Mrs Dent at the shop and the Helliwells in the pub, and after her less-than-successful introduction to the Mums and Tots group, she had taken the radical step of spying out who had young children in the village and then knocking on doors and introducing herself. At first, people were taken aback by this extraordinary show of social audacity but then, already knowing who she was and that she was 'expecting', doors were soon swung open and kettles were quickly filled.

A couple of people suggested joining the chapel across the green, still an important institution in village life, and so we started going along to services on Sunday mornings and through this met a number of other local families. One of these was called the Burtons and it didn't surprise me that Barbara announced that she was going round to Mary Burton's that afternoon for a cup of tea.

'Mrs Dent's giving me a lift,' she said.

'Shouldn't you call her by her first name by now?'

'You're right – I don't know what her first name is, though.'

We spent five giggly minutes making wild guesses before settling on Dolores.

Like Mrs Dent, Jacob and Mary Burton were Dales folk through and through: they were farmers from Buttergill, the small wild valley behind Applesett, and operated a milk round in the village from their Land Rover. They were also stalwarts of the chapel and held in great regard from one end of Swinnerdale to the other. Jacob was an immense balding man with dark skin and hands like snow shovels, while Mary was fair and petite. They had four great, hulking, handsome sons who worked on the farm, which was situated high up, clinging to one side of the steep gill about four miles from the village. There was something wonderfully reassuring about these people; they were so warm and old-fashioned, it was almost as if the family was a part of the landscape.

While Barbara set off for Buttergill, I decided to brave the rain and go for a walk; I'd spent most of the past fortnight indoors and was craving some fresh air. Outside, the stifling clouds hung just a few hundred feet above the houses, shrouding the top of Spout Fell and still discharging grey sheets of water, which the wind played into ghostly swaying drapes. There were several small twisting streams flowing down the main slope of the village, meeting up on the road that bisected the green. Where these waters met, there was virtually a small river, bordered with piles of stones, twigs and other debris from higher up. As I continued down the sodden green, a strange deep roaring sound became apparent. At first I was bewildered by this noise, but quickly realised that it must be the waterfall at the bottom of the village.

At Applesett Falls, the normally tranquil Buttergill Beck dropped over a shelf of hard stone into a beautiful glade before going on to meet the Swinner a mile or so downstream to the east. It was a favourite place of mine to walk to, but today its tranquillity was devastated. As I turned the corner to walk down to the falls, I was met by a phenomenal blast of raw power. The ground was shaking and the falls were nowhere to be seen. In their place was a swirling fog of spray, completely hiding the whole scene. Several villagers were standing by the little bridge shouting to each other above the booming holler of the water. I went over, and was quite taken aback when I saw the boiling torrent, which was usually a trickling beck just a few feet wide. Great surges of foaming brown water were forced between the sheer sides of the little gorge beneath the bridge, rising up and smashing into the trees and rocks below. Someone noticed my approach and turned around. It was John Weatherall.

'Byy, she's lively today, lad.'

'Is this just from the rain in the last couple of days?' I asked.

'No, it's been chuckin' it down on an' off for over a week here – the ground can't take any more in. But I reckon this is mainly because all the snow's melted reet quick off Spout and up Buttergill. I've lived here all me life and I've never seen it like this. There's trees coming down and I've seen two dead sheep in there in the last few minutes. Did you know the road's blocked 'n'all?'

'Where?'

'Down by the junction – go and 'ave a look.'

I had no idea all this was going on. I suddenly thought of Mrs Dent driving Barbara up Buttergill – would they be all right in her rusty old Morris on those high twisting roads? I decided to run down to see how bad the floods were, then go home and phone the Burtons to see if she'd arrived safely.

The only road in and out of Applesett was covered by a small lake. This was at the place where it was nearest the raging beck and normally only a few feet above it. The stream here was clearly at least six feet above its normal level and as I waded in along the road to test the water's depth it was clear that it was over two feet deep in the middle. Just around the bend in the road I could see several bewildered-looking people standing beside their cars, obviously wondering how they could get through. It occurred to me just then that we were cut off – this was the only way in and out of the village. The new school term was starting in three days too: was I going to be able to get there?

As I turned round to head back up the village, I heard the deep diesel chug of a tractor which then came into view. It was carrying about five people, all gleefully hanging off the sides, and it was driven by Jacob Burton, his great, red, weatherbeaten face unmistakable. I waved, whereupon he stopped the big red Zetor with a nod. He stuck his head out of the door and shouted down to me.

'Now then, Andrew. I've just met your wife and Mrs Dent on the track up Butt'gill. They've 'ad to turn back – there's a landslide blocked the road. I think she'll be at home now.'

'Thanks, Jacob, I'll head right back and see if she's OK. But how are you going to get home if the road's blocked?'

'Oh, no worries, I've got lads on t'job with a digger.' He nodded back towards the valley. 'They'll have it shifted in no time – 'twill give 'em something to do.'

I watched as he steered the tractor slowly across the flooded street, causing a wake like a large boat. Jacob was obviously operating some sort of voluntary ferry service, I thought to myself; the Burtons always seemed to be helping other people. They just seemed to get along with everyone. I made a mental note to try to be more like Jacob Burton, and then I rushed back to The Shippon to see if Barbara was all right.

Two days later, the water had gone and I was back at Cragthwaite School. It was early in the morning on the day before the new term and there was a large yellow skip outside in the car park. As I walked towards the front door, a figure wearing cords and a rainbow jumper came out backwards, wrestling with a large pair of stepladders. It was Joyce Berry, the new head, and she seemed very pleased to see me.

'Good morning, Andy, how are you? Raring to go for the new term, I hope!'

'I'm, er, well, yes. Are you well?'

'Excellent, thank you. I'm just having a light spring clean.' She moved her eyebrows towards the skip, which was about three-quarters full.

'Right. Can I give you a hand?'

'Oh, you are a dear – that would be wonderful.' She flashed me a huge smile and put her hand on my arm. I wasn't used to this.

Emma then appeared out of the front door holding a great floppy rubber plant in a pot.

'Happy New Year, Andy! Joyce, where did you say you wanted this plant?'

'What do you think, love? In the entrance hall?'

'It does need brightening up.'

'Stick it there then, Emma – we can always shift it later.' Joyce dashed inside while I held the door for Emma and asked how she was, even though it was clear from her eyes.

She glanced around and grinned. 'We're going to have displays in the corridors! She's already asked me to put up some of last term's artwork.'

'How's Hilda taken to, er, things?' I asked.

'I don't care,' said Emma, giggling, as she put down the heavy pot.

Inside, the building was in turmoil. Joyce, I was soon to discover, was not a person to do things by halves. She'd clearly decided to make some changes as the new headteacher, but it looked like she'd decided to make them all at once. There were boxes and files everywhere, tables and chairs were piled up outside the classrooms and several cupboards stood empty with doors open and their contents spewed over the floor. I just stood and stared at the carnage. Val stomped past me, muttering under her breath. She didn't even say hello. I was just wondering whether to go and check if my classroom had suffered the same fate, when I noticed something that I had never seen before. The stockroom door was open.

In Howard Raven's long rule over Cragthwaite Primary, the school's main stock cupboard was sacrosanct. I thought about the little green book that I'd handed in each week with my requests for pencils and exercise books. At first I'd thought it was all a joke, but soon realised that running out of paper was no laughing matter. No exceptions were allowed to this arcane system, and certainly no one was permitted in the stockroom, except the head and secretary. I recalled asking Val about it early in my first term.

'Have you ever been in there?'

'Just once,' she replied. 'I came into school one holiday to pick up some things, and Pat Rudds was there, cleaning the hall floor and whistling. I needed some paper clips, so I asked her if she had a key for the cupboard. She gave me a funny look, but she unlocked it. She was in a rare good mood that day.'

I was in awe. 'Well, what's in there?'

'What isn't in there, you mean? There's stuff on the shelves that's been there for decades. You wouldn't believe it: there's enough paper and supplies for about nine schools, but the Beak seemed to be terrified to let anyone use it.'

'Did you take anything, then?'

'Well, I took my paper clips, of course.' She winked rudely. I recalled the frustration of her refusing to divulge any more.

And now the door was open. I looked round and noticed that Joyce was still outside by the skip. I went in. It was dark and cramped inside, and quite a lot smaller than I'd imagined, but on every wall the deep shelves were full from floor to ceiling. On one side there were stacks of every conceivable type of exercise book, piled high, with fading covers and yellowing pages. Next to these were dusty boxes of paper: graph, sugar, cartridge, poster, card, plain, lined, squared, spotted, coloured, white, thick, thin, and in every size, all in brown paper packages torn open along one side.

On the opposite shelves were pens and pencils, crayons by the boxful and even ancient metal tins of pastels. I saw charcoal wrapped in tissue and neat rows of plasticine, next to great white tubs of unopened powder paints in various colours.

Further along, it was even more exciting: there were magnifying glasses, boxes of test tubes and wooden stands, scales, timers, spring balances and clusters of tall glass thermometers. I wanted to touch everything. Right at the end, away from the door, was a large, shallow tray full of brand-new, unused sports equipment: bands, tennis balls, a deflated leather football, shiny whistles, shuttlecocks, and, most tempting of all, four beautiful gold-embossed ruby cricket balls in a small box.

Something else caught my eye: a small, round object furry with fluff, tucked between two packages. At first I thought it was a large marble but when I picked it up it was rubbery to the touch: one of those child's bouncy 'superballs'. I wondered what it was doing here then it occurred to me it must have been confiscated. I stared at it for some time but my eyes were blank. They were seeing Cragthwaite's past children, generations who craved but were denied fun, passing dour days in grey classrooms and a cold, empty yard, whilst creativity was locked in here, gathering dust.

'Just take what you want, Andy. I'm going to chuck half of this stuff anyway – it's moth-eaten.' Joyce gave me a fright, but I recovered quickly. All of a sudden, I was really looking forward to the new term. Things were certainly going to be different.

Some kids get on your nerves, however hard you try to like them. Wilf Bainbridge was one of these. Wilf had many fine qualities: he was bright, alert, often funny, and a good sportsman. But he was cocky. It was the only word that fitted him, and no one in Class 3 would argue. Wilf believed he could do anything, and he frequently prevented other children from having a chance to try things on this basis. At playtimes, he always ran the games, deciding who could play and who couldn't. Whenever anybody brought something in to show the class, Wilf would ask a cheeky question, usually along the lines of how much did it cost? When it was story time, Wilf always declared the story boring, even before he'd heard it. I tried; I tried really hard to like him. I thought of Jacob Burton: I bet he would like him.

For some reason, when the new term began, Wilf came back to school cockier than ever. I always liked to start each week in the classroom with a short opportunity for the children to share their news and tell of anything exciting that they'd done. I felt this was a valuable time, helping to build individuals' confidence in talking in front of an audience and, as a teacher, it also gave me a fascinating insight into the personalities of the group. On this occasion, Wilf interrupted just about everybody with smart remarks, usually designed to put down whoever was speaking. He then went on to boast about all the expensive Christmas presents he'd been given. Whenever I suggested that he let someone else speak, he broke into a smirk and looked at his friends. He never really seemed to do anything seriously wrong, but he irritated me considerably.

By Friday, everyone at Cragthwaite had fallen back into the rhythm of the school week. Joyce, despite reorganising much of the storage and furniture, had quickly won over the staff with her warmth and enthusiasm, even Val. She was in the staffroom at lunchtime when I was despairing about Wilf.

'He just gets on my nerves, and he constantly says that everything is boring,' I moaned.

'Is Wilf the tall lad with the ginger hair and lots of freckles?' said Joyce.

'You've spotted him quickly.'

'There seems to be one like him in every school, in my experience. Have you tried giving him some responsibility, Andy?'

'What d'you mean?' It hadn't occurred to me.

'It's just something that I've noticed helps sometimes, when there's a child you're struggling to get along with. They often sense that you're unhappy with them and react in more negative ways.'

'What do you suggest I do?' The staffroom had suddenly gone quiet, as everyone listened in to Joyce's psychology.

'Just give him a few special jobs to do: it doesn't need to be much – maybe to take the dinner money to the office, or to hand out equipment in PE lessons, that kind of thing.'

'Oh, right.' I was slightly embarrassed: I'd always avoided giving Wilf jobs like these, thinking that he wasn't to be trusted. While I made a mental note to try out this idea, Joyce continued speaking.

'While everyone's here, can I just say a few things? First of all, thank you all so much for making me so welcome here – I feel completely at home already, and I cannot tell you what a joy it is to be working with such a great team. I must also apologise again for all the mess and disruption you've endured this week – hopefully it's all sorted now and things can settle down. I hope you've all had a chance to take everything you wanted from the main stock cupboard and put it in your classrooms.' I smiled sideways at Val: it had been like a bonanza in there, with Emma in particular carting huge quantities of art materials to her room with unremitting glee.

'Is it OK if I put some of the PE equipment that was in there in the hall with the rest?' I asked.

'Of course, no problem. You don't use a starting pistol for races, do any of you?' said Joyce, doubtfully. 'Believe it or not I found one in there when I first started checking the stock in the holidays. It's in my office now anyway, if one of you wants to hold up a Post Office on the way home.' As the laughter died down, she continued. 'There's just one last thing, everybody: have you all remembered that it's assembly at three this afternoon?'

* * *

When three o'clock arrived, everyone looked tired, and the children trailed into the hall with several yawns. The shock of returning to work after two weeks' break had taken its toll on both pupils and teachers alike. I had to concentrate hugely not to yawn myself as the assembly hymn music began at the front. After the singing, Joyce asked everyone to sit down, and proceeded to tell the children how wonderful they were and what a privilege it was to be their new headteacher.

'And now, girls and boys, I've a lovely story to read you.' Joyce picked up a large book entitled *Classic Stories for Infants,* and began to read in a suitably dramatic voice. The tale was an adaptation of one of Aesop's fables, and featured various animals trying to get the better of one another. I was astonished: Howard Raven had never once told a story which was specifically aimed at the younger children. The infants, arrayed in long rows at the front of the hall sat rapt. Wilf, meanwhile, who was sitting at the end of his row near to me, made a fingers-down-the-throat gesture to Barney beside him and whispered, 'How babyish is this?' I glanced at him briefly, but decided not to say anything this time: he had clearly made up his mind that the new head was just as boring as every other teacher, if not more so.

When the story was over, Joyce asked what lessons it taught and then put the book away.

She stood up and locked her long fingers together. 'Now then, children, I have a special announcement.' The rows shuffled and various infants stole wide-eyed glances at each other. 'I am going to be handing out a new award in assembly each week from now on. Isn't that exciting?' There were several nods. 'Each teacher in the school will pick one child from his or her class who has worked especially hard to receive a special sticker: the Headteacher's Award.' There was an immediate buzz in the hall: the children had never had anything like this before, and it stirred a small wave of excitement.

'Big deal,' I heard Wilf murmur. 'It's a stupid idea and I won't get one anyway.'

'Now, we're going to start the award next week, so everyone do your very best, and you might win one of these,' continued Joyce, who then started to scrabble through a pile of papers on top of the piano. 'Oh dearie me, I've left the stickers in my room.' She looked up. 'Wilf in Class Three.' He suddenly sat bolt upright and flushed a little upon unexpectedly hearing his name in assembly. 'Would you please be a dear and go to my office to fetch the Headteacher's Award stickers: they're either on my desk or in the second drawer.' I was amazed, and so was Wilf. He threw a grin at Barney and headed off towards the door, pushing it with a thump.

Joyce clapped her hands smartly to regain the children's attention, since 100 pairs of eyes had turned away to watch Wilf disappear on his mission. 'While we're waiting for the stickers, does anyone have any questions about the award?' Not one child raised a hand – they'd never been invited to ask questions before. Joyce waited a few seconds and then asked the children to suggest the types of good work or behaviour that could win the award. This time several hands did go up and a number of sensible suggestions were made. Just as a Reception child was explaining about 'even being kind to horrid people', I heard the hall door open very quietly at the back.

It was Wilf, and his face was the colour of cotton wool. He held a small packet of round purple stickers in his hand as he walked gingerly to the front of the hall, and handed it to Joyce.

'Thank you, Wilf, well done. Are you all right, love?' She bent her knees and looked into his eyes. Wilf tried to answer but just let out a muffled croak.

'Ye . . . mm . . . hm . . . yeh, yes, thank you.' It didn't sound like Wilf at all – I'd certainly never heard him say thank you before, or sound so placid. Joyce looked at him doubtfully for a moment then started to open the packet of stickers as he shuffled back to rejoin the class. Wilf really did look peculiar – it was as if all his usual cockiness was gone in an instant. I continued to watch him out of the corner of my eye as he sat down next to Barney, wondering if he was about to be spectacularly sick. As soon as he was sitting, he leaned over to his friend, with a hand cupped over his mouth. The whisper was clearly audible:

'She's got a gun!'

After this episode, Wilf Bainbridge was decidedly less cocky than before, and although over time his former confidence gradually reasserted itself, he never was quite as difficult to like as previously. As the term went on Wilf grew on me, and more than once I found myself smiling at a thought: perhaps at long last I was becoming just a little more like the legendary Jacob Burton from Buttergill. Anyway, how could anyone not like a boy who gave his headteacher such unparalleled respect?

Chapter Ten

Isaac

The sale of Craven Bottoms finally went through in late January. Mr Crockett had at long last signed the documents and moved out, and our protracted wait for a house of our own finally ended, although for me, there was just a little more waiting to be done. It was a Friday morning, and the keys were due to be handed over at midday. Unfortunately, I would be at school teaching so Barbara planned to take the bus into Ingleburn to collect the keys, then as soon as I returned to Applesett we would go and step inside our new home.

'I can drive into town at lunchtime if you don't want to get the bus,' I said, wolfing my cereal as usual.

'Remember, I've got to go in anyway for my antenatal appointment at the doctor's.'

'Oh yes, sorry, forgot about that – it's just a check-up, isn't it?'

She nodded as I gave her a kiss and went to look for my bag. 'Yes, same as usual.'

So my day of waiting began, and at this particular moment, I was also waiting for Isaac Outhwaite. I often seemed to be waiting for Isaac Outhwaite: he was the smallest boy in Class 3, a sinewy scrap of skin and bone, a farmer's lad from the isolated community of Millscar, high up the dale towards Kettleby. Poor Isaac, not only was he diminutive, but everything he did seemed to take twice as long as it took everyone else.

On this occasion he was getting changed after PE. The rest of the class was lined up ready to walk back to the classroom, but Isaac was still in his vest and pants. He had one sock on and was hopping around the cloakroom wearing a grimace and trying to strain the other sock on to his foot.

'I think it might be easier to do that if you sat down, Isaac.' I tried to sound patient. Isaac grunted and sat down. He never spoke if a grunt would do, and for Isaac a grunt did do most of the time. 'Please try to be a bit quicker – the rest of the class is waiting.' I went over to the line of children, which showed signs of restlessness. Most of them had endured three or four years of waiting in lines for Isaac twice a week, and there were occasional resentful comments. Malcolm, in particular, looked very fed up.

'Why do we 'ave to wait for 'im, Mr Seed?'

'Malcolm, you know we can't leave him here on his own and go back to the classroom.'

'Well why don't you stay with him and we'll all go back, then?'

'He's trying his best – it's just that some people need a bit more time to do things than others.' I turned round. 'Are you ready yet, Isaac? We really need to get back to the classroom.'

Isaac stood up. He was not ready: he had his school jumper on, but it was back to front. His shoes were also on the wrong feet, making him look like Charlie Chaplin, but this was nothing compared to his trousers. Somehow, he had managed to put them on inside out. He was bent forward with a puzzled look on his face, wondering what had happened to the pockets, which now dangled at the sides of his skinny thighs like a pair of cowboy holsters. This was Isaac Outhwaite's other problem: everything the unfortunate boy did was back to front.

I clearly recall the first time I noticed this: it was the beginning of term and I had asked everyone in the class to write a paragraph about themselves. As I wandered between the tables I noticed Isaac, sitting hunched over his paper, carefully writing in large left-handed script, his nose only about an inch from the desktop. There was something most peculiar about his writing: the letters were upside down. His name was upside down and so was the date, even though the letters were in the right order. I watched him for a moment – was he some kind of a joker, playing a trick on the new teacher? But Isaac, even though he knew I was there, never even looked up. There was something rather grave about his face too, with its deep-set eyes and ruddy complexion. This boy was certainly no comedian.

I asked Val about him the next day.

'Oh, you've spotted an Outhwaite, have you?' She smiled to herself. 'Don't worry, they've all done that – his big brother and his two sisters before him. They all wrote upside down.'

'But, what causes it then? Is it some kind of rare congenital learning disorder?'

'Learning disorder? Ha!' This time she laughed. 'It's not a disorder, it's their bloomin' mother. She's a lovely, kind woman, Mrs Outhwaite, and how she ever makes ends meet in that tiny house in the back of beyond I'll never know, but she taught all of her children to read across the kitchen table.'

'What do you mean – what's wrong with that?'

'She didn't sit next to them, like anyone else. She sat opposite them, and she had the book facing towards her. All four of them learned to read upside down. She couldn't see the problem; it was only when they came to school and started writing that we noticed that something was up. The trouble was, it took years before we realised what was going on – it was only when Isaac got to Hilda's class that we found out. She spotted Mrs Outhwaite in the book corner with the poor lad.'

'Are you having me on?'

'You go and ask Hilda about it.' Val didn't look like she was making it up.

'But why does he still write upside down? I presume that you stopped her?'

'Oh aye, we stopped her, and all his brothers and sisters eventually got their reading and writing sorted, but Isaac . . .' She stopped and shook her head.

'What?' I said.

'Oh, you'll see.'

And now here was Isaac, standing with his trousers inside out and everything else back to front. I saw all right, but I couldn't wait for him any longer – we had already lost ten minutes of the following maths lesson. He would just have to manage as he was, despite the titters from the waiting class.

'Right, come on then, Isaac, join the line.' I was just turning away when he spoke, in his deep semi-grunt.

'I need toilet.'

I very nearly joined in the elongated groans from the class.

'Well, be very quick please, we're really late.' As he disappeared through the adjacent door, I turned round again to quieten the straggly line of waiting children. Several of them had slumped down against the wall, or were leaning on their friends like exhausted drifters in a bread queue. I decided to try some of the tactics I'd heard Hilda using with her class, starting with a brisk bark and a clap of the hands.

'Right, enough!' Several of them looked startled. They'd never heard me address them like that before. 'Everyone stop talking. Malcolm and Barney – off the wall, and no one is to lean on the person in front or behind. I want to see everyone standing straight with their arms folded, in silence.'

Amazingly, it worked. The queue suddenly stiffened and hushed. I was so pleased that the forbiddingly stern face I was holding nearly cracked.

'That's better. Now, I do not want to hear another noise until we are all back in the classroom.' There followed about six seconds of blissful silence, and then an eerie sound arose from behind the wall along which the class was lined.

'Ooohh . . . oww . . . owww . . . oooh.' The eyes of several children widened distinctly. 'Ooohh . . . oww . . . owww . . . oooh.' This was followed by the stamping of feet against a hard floor, and another series of 'Oohs' and 'Owws'. I went into the boys' toilet.

Isaac Outhwaite stood in the centre of a pale green lake. His ruddy face was now plum-coloured and he was jiggling up and down with obvious consternation. Both hands were scrabbling at the flies of his dark-stained trousers. In a flash, it became clear what had happened. Poor, poor Isaac. His zip fastener was on the inside of his trousers and he was clearly baffled as to where it had gone. Nature had called but the door was locked. I suddenly felt great compassion for this bedraggled, rural urchin of a boy. I would have gone over and put an arm on his shoulder but I couldn't reach him across the sea of wee.

'I made a mess,' he croaked.

'Don't worry about it, Isaac. You can wear your PE kit,' I said, inwardly despairing at the contemplation of him getting changed once more.

At lunchtime, I found myself outside on cold playground duty amongst the flying footballs and gangs of scuttling, shouting children. I wondered if Barbara had managed to pick up the keys for Craven Bottoms, and tried to console myself with the thought of our new house and all the exciting plans we had for it. My moment of peace didn't last long; a small, fair-headed infant with ketchupy lips was tugging severely at my arm, causing my cup of tea to dribble.

'Quick, Mister, Adam's felled over!' she wailed.

'Careful, please – where is Adam?'

'He's over there!' She waggled an arm indiscriminately. I walked in the general direction, past girls playing at ponies, and games of Kiss, Cuddle and Torture, nearly stepping on a decapitated Sindy doll along the way. Eventually I found Adam, but he had already found a dinner lady and was being soothed while he picked the grit from his palms.

I looked at my watch: ten to one. Normally I enjoyed playground duty and the opportunity it brought to meet children from the other classes, but the bitter dampness of the wind today made me feel distinctly unsociable. Just then I felt a whack on the back of my shoulder. The shock didn't improve my mood, and I spun round swiftly ready to reprimand the culprit. Amongst a group of smiling onlookers was a small boy in huge grey shorts picking up a tennis ball. It was Isaac and he was laughing; I opened my mouth to tell him off, but the recollection of his earlier trouser calamity in the toilets cut me off.

'Never felt a thing.'

After a slow afternoon I rushed home, my mind full of anticipation about our new house. I wondered if Barbara had resisted the temptation to go into Craven Bottoms already.

I pushed open the door of The Shippon and saw her in the kitchen.

'I got the keys,' she said in a thin voice before I could ask about the doctor's appointment. Her face was red and covered in large blotches. My mind raced back to the mums and tots episode but this was evidently more serious.

'Barbara, are you all right? What's the matter?' I held her close as a sudden panic about the baby flooded through me.

'I'm OK, really, I'm fine. Don't worry.' She attempted to smile but her mouth didn't seem to be working.

'Is everything all right with the baby? What did the doctor say?' I tried not to sound frightened but I was gabbling. She looked at me and nodded. There were tears pouring from her eyes. I held her again, knowing that for some reason she couldn't speak. I started to cry too.

We held each other tight then I felt her release a little. We both sat down and found tissues.

'It was the baby's heartbeat,' she croaked.

'What do you mean?'

She blew her nose twice and looked at me through bruised eyes. 'Doctor Fearn was testing for the baby's heartbeat and couldn't hear it. I just went into a panic – I thought we'd lost it. I'm sorry.'

'You don't need to be sorry about anything. She must have found the heartbeat eventually, did she?' Even though I sounded calm I was shaking.

Barbara held my hand and nodded. 'It just took so long and I kept asking questions and that made it harder to hear. She said it happened all the time and I really had no need to worry, but everything had been going so well and I couldn't face the thought of losing our baby so suddenly.'

'You poor thing.' I passed her another tissue and took one for myself. 'Did Doctor Fearn say anything else?'

'She found the heartbeat eventually but said that we had one of the biggest wrigglers she's ever known.'

'But everything's normal?'

Barbara managed a weak smile. 'Everything's normal with the baby – it's just me that's the problem. I'm an overemotional blubberhead.'

'Don't be daft: any mother would be worried under those circumstances.'

'Will you forgive me for scaring you?'

'Barb, there's nothing to forgive, really.' I gave her another hug.

She looked up. 'It's a good job I've got you.'

We stayed in each other's arms for a minute then remembered that our new house was waiting for us across the green.

'It'll save you a few bob if you take the plaster off yerselves, of course.' John Weatherall tapped one of the walls of the kitchen with a screwdriver. It was Saturday, and we were in Craven Bottoms at long last, and ready to get to work on some of the most urgent jobs that needed carrying out. The survey had confirmed what we had feared about rising damp in the small musty kitchen at the back of the house, and John had agreed to do the work, which delighted us since so many people in the village had recommended him.

'Aye, all the plaster and rendering needs to come off up to about three feet, and then we can drill the walls and inject your damp-proofing silicon. These old stone houses are all the same: full o' damp.'

'So we can do that, can we, John?' said Barbara. Much to my relief she sounded like her old self again, now that the heartbeat drama was behind us.

'Oh, aye, no problem. You just need a couple of chisels and she'll be off in no time. Have you got any chisels, lad?'

'Erm, only wood chisels, but I've got a hammer and a mallet,' I said, desperately trying to think where they were among all the boxes still piled up at The Shippon. John disappeared into his van and came back with two cold chisels the size of rolling pins.

'There, them'll see it off. Give us a call when you've done, and I'll send someone to sort yer drillin'.' He waved and returned to his van.

I looked at Barbara. 'Are you OK to do some of this? It's going to be heavy work.'

'I can manage a bit. Anyway, it'll take you ages on your own.' She reached for a chisel. 'Good grief!'

Two hours later, I was standing in a nearly empty, dust-filled kitchen, having ripped out all of the ancient cupboards and shelves along the wall. A great pile of twisted wood now filled the back yard, and the walls were at last ready to be tackled. Taking out the old cupboards had been unexpectedly easy, and I judged that removing the plaster and cement from the walls would be a straightforward undertaking too.

It wasn't. As soon as I gave the chisel a whack, and a lump of plaster fell away, great billows of choking dust enveloped me. Barbara returned from a sit-down to see how it was going. She insisted on having a go. Within a few minutes we were both coughing and our hair was white. Hankies around the mouth helped, as did opening the window, but our next problem was aching arms: John's monster chisels and the big hammers required to hit them were causing us to wilt. Added to this, the ancient plaster on the walls was mixed with tough horse-hair, which markedly increased its reluctance to leave the wall. After twenty minutes we stopped, exhausted.

'I need a break,' said Barbara, shaking dust from her thick brown hair. 'Want a cup of tea?'

'I want a gallon of tea. Do you really think you should be doing this heavy stuff?' In addition to looking like an ancient bandit, she suddenly looked shattered.

'Well, it is a bit of a strain, but I'll be all right if I have a rest.' I wasn't convinced.

'Barbara, I really think you should go back to The Shippon and lie down. I'll make the tea, and then come back here and finish this.' She didn't argue, and I was relieved.

The tea refreshed me, and returning to the dusty kitchen alone, I resolved to give the job my all and try to hack off all the plaster before the end of the day, so I could cheer Barbara up with some progress. I soon found that whacking the walls with a club hammer first weakened the plaster and made it easier to loosen with the chisel. Very soon I had removed a large area of plaster and was feeling rather pleased with myself. I looked at the rough wall underneath – was that cement or stone? I gave it a mighty clout with a chisel and watched, to my dismay, a chunk of mortar about two inches thick fall to the floor. I'd taken off a lot of plaster, but I was still nowhere near the stonework: it was going to be impossible to manage the job on my own in one day.

After a short bout of depression and a rest, I reassessed my target and decided to aim to clear one wall – surely I could manage that. I took up John's mighty chisel and the big hammer and stared at the enemy before me.

Several hours later I was on my knees in the bottom far corner of the wall, loosely slapping at the last obdurate lumps of cement with lifeless arms. I had just about done it. The wall was a rough, ugly bare stone surface, but it was clean of rendering and plaster. I lurched outside into the back yard for some air. My clothes were thick with grey powder and my hair alone must have held about half a pound of dust. I went back into the kitchen – it looked worse than ever with great piles of hairy rubble all over the floor. Even though I had finished the wall, the sight would hardly cheer Barbara up; I would have to clear away the mess too.

I returned to The Shippon for a brush and some boxes, and told Barbara that she should come over to look at the kitchen in about half an hour. I just about had the energy to scrape the great piles of plaster and cement into the boxes and heave them out into the yard, and then to sweep the floor. At least it was tidy now.

While I was waiting for Barbara, I weighed up what we needed for the kitchen: damp proofing, new plaster, paint, new floor covering, new sink, new cupboards, tiles maybe, new electrics probably too; it was going to be expensive, without a doubt. The only part I hadn't thought about was the ceiling. I looked up. It was possibly even more depressing than the rest of the room. The ceiling was covered in sheets of aged yellowing fibreboard, each one sagging wearily and joined with ugly pieces of painted tape, twisted and peeling. Those would have to go, for sure. I wondered what was behind the fibreboard: there must be something – after all, it was only really thick cardboard, hardly structural.

It then occurred to me that there was no better time than now to find out what was behind this grotty ceiling covering: there might even be some lovely old wooden beams. Now, if I discovered that, wouldn't Barbara be cheered? I reached for the long broom and gave one of the boards a poke with the handle. It sounded very hollow. I gave another one a poke. It moved – in fact, it seemed to be more or less loose. I took a firm grip of the handle and gave it a really hard push, then immediately regretted it.

The board was like a taut belly squeezed by a belt. For a second or two, it took the upward strain, but then suddenly creased and snapped in two. Something awful rained down on me from above: it was mainly sawdust, but there were dark bits in it, and larger objects. A lot of it went down my neck and some in my eyes. I managed to open my eyes in time to see the board next to the one I had poked descend in sympathy, sliding into the kitchen and pouring more mysterious gunk down on to my newly swept floor. What *was* this stuff? There was a huge amount of sawdust, peppered with wood shavings, scraps of newspaper, pieces of stone, and disconcerting quantities of mouse droppings. There was a dead mouse too. I could feel my flesh crawl, and I shook my head violently to remove as much as possible of the poo which I felt certain was nestling in there with the powdered plaster and sawdust. Next I took off my shirt and jumper and shook out more bits. There were plenty.

Once the dust had settled a little, I looked up into the mammoth hole in the ceiling to see what my disaster had actually revealed. It was too dark to see clearly, but there was definitely some sort of long shape up there. I needed a closer look, but there was nothing to stand on. I glanced around the rest of the house, but Mr Crockett had been most conscientious in clearing everything out. I tried outside – there was only the pile of wood and the boxes of plaster rubble. I stood on top of one of the boxes, which took my weight. I dragged it back into the kitchen and placed it below the hole.

The box raised me about a foot, and I could now touch the edge of the hole quite easily, although it was still difficult to see what the long thing was. Since I had already obliterated the kitchen floor again, I decided that a bit more disorder wouldn't really make much difference. I pulled at the fibreboard next to my head and heard a sickly cracking sound as the thin wooden framework on which the boards were nailed gave way. There was a spectacular crashing roar as the whole ceiling collapsed, discharging untold measures of sawdust and mouse muck into our dream kitchen. I then wobbled as my handhold disappeared, causing the box beneath me to collapse, returning the plaster to the floor from which I'd earlier cleared it.

At least there was now nothing to restrict my view of what was above. And what was above was part of a brick wall – the upper half of an unsupported load-bearing brick wall. Then Barbara walked in.

'I made a mess,' I croaked, forgiving Isaac Outhwaite everything he had ever done.

Two hours later John Weatherall was back in the kitchen. He looked up and swore. It was the only time I'd ever heard him swear.

'We need an RSJ under that right away.' He looked at the sawdust and explained that it was probably put there for insulation. He then looked at the wall and nearly said, 'Is that all you've done?' He didn't though; instead he said, 'Don't swallow any plaster dust, will you? They sometimes used to put arsenic in it, y'know.'

It was our first day in our new house.

Chapter Eleven

Rose

It was now February and, incredibly for me, nearly halfway through the school year. This was the first time that I began to feel that I really knew my class properly, and consequently, I had become extremely attached to the twenty-four-strong enthusiastic rabble with whom I spent most of my day.

I was fascinated by the social chemistry of the class, with its dominating characters, comedians, workers, carers, poets, athletes and trudgers. There were unlikely friendships, long-established cliques forged in the early infants, and strange geographical loyalties founded in outlying villages, hamlets and farms from where over half of the children were bussed to school daily. Along with alliance, of course, there is always enmity, and I was frequently saddened to see that certain children avoided each other as far as possible, some even subconsciously.

There was one child in Class 3 whom no one avoided. Rose Alderson was imbued with that mysterious aura which no amount of psychology, learned or amateur, can ever really quantify. Her popularity amongst the children was all the more surprising because it had no basis in a strong personality or physical charisma. Rose was a quiet girl, and although she had clear features and long shining hair, she was rarely labelled as pretty or beautiful. Her eyes, however, were striking, and almost seemed to glow with intense gold-green warmth.

Rose was followed wherever she went, and most intriguing of all, she was admired equally by both boys and girls. Whenever a boy was paired with a girl for a classroom or PE partner, it was usually the signal for moans of protestation, but not when the girl was Rose – this produced only sighs of envy.

Some children liked to profit from their regard in the class, but Rose was never one of these: she was on friendly terms with everyone, and never once sought to gain any advantage by being so well liked. She was also an excellent worker, and possessed a particular talent for writing stories, something I greatly admired, and could take very little credit for sharpening. There was one occasion when Rose surpassed herself in respect of this gift.

I had stayed up late the previous evening sanding window frames in Craven Bottoms and had left insufficient time for planning the following day's work in detail. Slumping down into my favourite chair in The Shippon, I made a rapid decision to abandon the English lesson on spelling I had intended to teach, and decided to let the class write a long story. All I needed was a good title. I looked around the room for inspiration and saw a five-pound note on the mantelpiece, neatly folded under a dusty carriage clock. 'The Day I Found Five Pounds' would do nicely.

I was delighted to see that the children were inspired themselves the next morning, and the quiet atmosphere of scuttling pens that followed my brief discussion about ideas and planning was a more-than-welcome surprise. As usual, I toured the room while the children wrote, giving spellings, reading paragraphs and making suggestions for improvement. After twenty minutes, even Jack and Isaac, two of the planet's most reluctant writers, had ground out passable beginnings, as dreams of spending this unimaginable sum gripped them.

When break arrived I was astonished to hear groans from some of the class.

'Aww, I want to finish my story, it's got everything has this plot,' said Eve.

'Well, as you've worked so wonderfully well this morning,' I said, 'I'll let you all carry on for a while after break and we'll miss a bit of maths – how does that sound?' There were gleeful cheers followed by a rush for the door, as stiff limbs were unshackled from the desks. When everybody else had left the room, I noticed Rose still sitting at her table at the far side of the room, writing furiously.

'Aren't you going out to play, Rose?'

'Oh Mr Seed, I can't stop now, I'm just in a really important part of the story – I want to write my ideas down now so I don't forget them. Can I stay in and carry on?' She made the 'pleeease' smile peculiar to girls of that age, but it was her eyes that gave me no choice.

'Of course you can, Rose.' I felt rather uneasy, knowing perfectly well that I would have refused some others.

I spent my lunch hour in the staffroom reading through the finished stories. As always on these occasions, I was caught between black despair at the children's grammatical limitations and jovial admiration at their unbridled imaginations and charmingly simple view of the world. The stories were certainly better than usual this time, and I put three or four aside, including Jack's and Isaac's crumpled efforts, reminding myself to give their authors special praise when I returned to the classroom. Then I came across Rose's story: it was nine pages long and entitled 'A Note of Caution'. For the work of a nine-year-old, it was utterly compelling.

I spent the last fifteen minutes thinking of superlatives to share with the class about this piece of work. The plot was simple enough: Rose finds a five-pound note outside and surreptitiously spends it on sweets, only to find that her mother had lost the money herself, having earmarked it for a treat for Rose for being so kind and honest. Not only was this tale fluently written with impressive vocabulary and great accuracy, but the characters seemed real, and Rose's use of dialogue and descriptive asides was mature beyond belief. I was desperate to show the story to Joyce or Val, but there was no time – it was one o'clock and I could already hear two infants clanking the little hand bell up the path to the playground.

Barney was the first to appear in the classroom, having raced up the path as usual.

'Have you read us stories then, Mr Seed?'

'I have, Barney, and they are fantastic.'

'Can I read mine out to the class then?'

I was staggered; he had never asked to do this before. Several other children, now arriving back from the playground, overheard and asked if they too could read their efforts. I waited until everyone was back inside and the register was completed.

'Class Three, you are amazing. I've read your stories over lunch-time and they are just su-*perb*.' Five or six children straightened their backs and folded their arms. 'I know a lot of you would like to read them to the class, but we haven't got time for everyone this afternoon so what I'll do is pick three or four and we'll hear them for story time, last thing, and then we can have some more tomorrow, OK?' There was more sitting up straight and tightening of lips, and two or three hands shot up before shooting back down again.

At three o'clock, the atlases from a rather dull geography lesson were hurriedly collected and desks were cleared ready for story time. I had chosen Jack's story, along with Barney's – although this was virtually incomprehensible in parts – and, of course, Rose's masterpiece. Jack leapt up in ecstasy when his name was called, and he puffed out his barrel chest prodigiously for the reading, which was carried out in his familiar booming staccato mode. Jack had managed to chisel out three-quarters of a page in a thick pitchy script, the equivalent of *War and Peace* in his terms, and the class gave him thunderous applause when he reached the somewhat incredible conclusion, the five pounds having been planted by an alien who abducted Jack away for unnamed, nefarious purposes.

Barney read his story at 5000 mph and laughed so much at the funny bits he had included that none of us had a clue what was going on. In the end we applauded him anyway – he had, after all, shown undoubted enthusiasm. A bow was given to the class as he sat down, with a typical flourish.

'Now, we've time for just one more story today,' I announced, 'and this one is something very special. When I read this at lunchtime, I was flabbergasted at how good it is. Rose, it's your story; will you read it to the class, please?'

Rose looked at me and shook her head. There was a swift chorus of, 'Go on Rose!' but she didn't move from her chair. I was astonished.

'Rose, this is the best work you've done all year! It's exceptional. Don't you want to share it with the class?' Jack grabbed the clutch of paper I was proffering and took it over to Rose.

'I don't like reading things out loud, Mr Seed.' Her voice was stifled and thin.

'Will you read just part of it then?' She shook her head again, which brought more calls from all quarters of the class, but she didn't move. After a few seconds, where it was clear that there would be no change of mind, I chose another story, and Eve was only too glad to stand up and share what she had written. Just after Eve had finished, the bell rang and the children started their customary chair scraping.

'Well done again, everybody,' I called. 'Could I please have the stories back?' Jack, Eve and Barney came over, and returned their work with satisfied smiles. Rose hung back; she waited for everyone else to put up their chairs and leave the room then she came over holding her story. She looked at me: there were huge tears in her eyes. She said nothing, and left the room.

That day I discovered that Rose, for all her ability and popularity, was a painfully shy person. The tears which blurred her vibrant eyes haunted me for some time, and I waited for a quiet moment to apologise, and promise that I wouldn't pressure her in such a way again. It was a hard lesson for both of us, but clearly I still had a lot to learn both about teaching and about the children of Class 3.

Val noticed that I was subdued when I passed her in the corridor after the end of school.

'What's up? Bad day in the mobile?'

Something told me that she probably wouldn't be the most understanding person to talk to about the situation. 'No, just, er, a lot to think about.'

'Well, thinking's clearly a strain for you, so take it easy.'

I headed for Joyce's office and showed her some of the stories. She read a few lines and gave an amplified gasp.

'Andy, these are fabulous. You must get them on display in the entrance hall.' She looked up. 'Is everything OK? Barbara all right?'

I decided against mentioning Rose but told her about our fright over the baby's heartbeat.

'Oh, how absolutely dreadful for you both. I would have been just the same as Barbara – sick with worry. My two are grown up now but I'll never forget the first time I was expecting, it's all ups and downs.'

It occurred to me that I knew virtually nothing about Joyce's home life. Before I could say anything she took the rest of the stories off me and said, 'I'll put these on display. You go home and take care of your wife – I don't want you working too hard at school.'

'But there's so much to do.'

'Nonsense, I'm your boss. Go on, skedaddle.'

The following weekend Barbara and I were back at Craven Bottoms, ready to resume the attack on our rogue kitchen. Weatheralls had finally managed to install the RSJ under our hanging wall, and thereby made the room safe. We were finishing off our plaster hacking when there was a loud noise outside, followed by the sound of a familiar voice.

'That's the job – drop her there, Bill!'

We wandered outside to see what was going on, glad of some fresh air and a chance to stretch our backs. John Weatherall was back again, this time hurling large stones off a pickup parked next to the house.

'Now then, Andrew,' he called. 'Yer ceilin's holding up all right?'

'Yes, it looks really good, thanks. Er, what are you up to then, John?'

'Building a garage, lad, for your neighbours. Have you met Ralph and Wanda yet?'

'No, we haven't; do they own the cottage at the back of our house then?'

'That's them. They only visit the village about three times a year.'

'Oh, it's a second home then, is it, not a holiday cottage?' asked Barbara.

'Aye, that's right. They bought it a couple of years ago and they've been doing the place up bit by bit. Not short of a few bob, those two.'

John never missed the opportunity to share his phenomenal knowledge of all people and things local, and went on to explain in vivid detail about the different jobs he'd been asked to do on the cottage to get it 'just perfect' for Wanda. Walls had been knocked down, a new stone roof supplied, elaborate stoves and fireplaces had been installed and, most recently of all, a plush new bathroom suite had been fitted at great expense.

'Aye, it's the garage next – got to be matching stone, and they want an arch above the doors, but I'm not complaining – it's more work for me, and I need it. Oh, and don't forget we've a darts match next Thursday: away at Skirbridge.'

'Oh I won't forget, John, but we'd better get back to our kitchen, it's cold out here,' I said.

'And shout if you want a cup of tea,' added Barbara. John waved a hand and went back to his pile of stones.

A few hours later, Barbara had gone for a much-deserved lie down, and I had finally reached the alcove in the corner of the kitchen with my chiselling. I stepped back and considered this strange hollow in the thick wall: it would certainly be a fine place to fit shelves or make a recessed cupboard, but why was it there? I tapped the back of the alcove, and was surprised to hear a rather hollow sound, quite distinct from the dull resistance of the other walls. I chipped a little piece of plaster away from the place where I'd knocked, and noticed that it was quite thin. A little more scratching with the chisel revealed a strange surface beneath this top layer – like a series of wooden strips. I cleared a larger area, then went out to ask John Weatherall to have a look.

'Them's laths, wooden laths, lad. Must be a partition, this – once a doorway, I would guess, into next door.' John gave the laths a tap to confirm his speculation.

'Why would there be a doorway here into another house?'

'These houses are older than you might think, Andrew. They've all seen a lot o' changes. I would guess that this room belonged to the cottage next door at some stage. It was prob'ly sold and blocked off, but at least a hundred years ago I would say, looking at this.' He picked up a piece of plaster off the floor and peeled away a thick dusty layer of paper from it and passed it to me. It was a scrap of ancient-looking wallpaper, most likely Victorian.

'You've got a few layers there, eh?' said John. I peeled away the delicate hand-painted paper skins – there were eight layers.

The following evening, I called in at John Weatherall's. We had finally undressed the kitchen of its obstinate coats of plaster and cement, and the damp proofing could go ahead at long last.

'Right, well done Andrew,' said John. 'RSJ's in, and the walls are ready. I'll send one of me lads around next week to do your drillin' and injectin'. We're bangin' on wi' a few jobs at moment, so I don't know exactly when it'll be, but we'll get it done, don't you worry.'

'OK, John, well you've got a key anyway. Just let us know when it's finished.' I tried not to sound too disappointed, even though everything seemed to happen so slowly here. I contented myself that this was just the way of the Dales as I walked back to Barbara and her wonderful, wriggling, tummy bump in The Shippon.

A pair of arctic weekends passed before any more progress was made on the house. There was a knock on the door of The Shippon early the next Saturday morning. It was a greasy young man of about seventeen, with the signature grimed overalls of the building trade.

'Mr Seed? Am frum W'thrulls.'

'Pardon?' I said, trying not to crease up my face too far.

'Av done yer walls – damp-proofin.' He nodded towards the dim misted shape of Craven Bottoms across the green.

'Oh, right, sorry – you're one of John's lads.'

'Aye. Well, fust job's done, an Mister W'thrull ses he'll send plasterer round when she's ready.' He nodded and walked over to a battered van parked on the road.

After breakfast, Barbara and I walked across the crispy village grass to see the kitchen, and to continue with our decorating upstairs, which was now rapidly transforming the once musty bedrooms. To our disappointment, the kitchen looked exactly as we had left it a fortnight earlier, except that there was a neat line of holes all the way round the walls a few inches above the floor. I don't really know what we had expected to see, but at least something had been done. There was also an enormous masonry drill bit in one corner, about eighteen inches long.

'Oh, the young lad of John's must have left this,' I said. 'I'll drop it off at the smithy later.'

We traipsed upstairs towards the cold bedrooms and contented ourselves with the thought that at least we would be able to sleep well enough in the house, if not actually eat in it for some time. Another thing which always gave us heart was the elevated view from each of the two main bedrooms upstairs: the front bedroom presented a fine panorama of the village and Swinnerdale beyond, over to Castle Heywood; the back bedroom looked directly up the spectacular flanks of Spout Fell, stretching to the fragmented crags of its higher reaches.

I put my arms round Barbara's midriff. 'Everything OK with junior and you?'

'Everything's fine. I still feel bad about scaring you that day in The Shippon with the heartbeat thing.'

'Let's forget about that now. Doctor Fearn's given you the thumbs up and, well, you look great.'

'I feel so much better.' We hugged and I said a silent prayer of thanks. Deep inside was the warm feeling that we had turned a corner in the last few weeks.

At about midday there was a sharp rap on the front door.

'It'll probably be John asking if the kettle's on,' said Barbara. I went to see. There was a tall woman in a silk paisley scarf standing outside. As I opened the door I thought she looked rather grim.

'Morning, can I help you?' I proffered.

'I'm your next-door neighbour, Wanda Holt.'

'Oh, hello, it's very nice to meet you at last.'

'No, it's not. I'd like you to come and have a look at this.' It sounded bad. I called up to Barbara and we followed our sombre new acquaintance outside, past a large blue Mercedes, and along the path running alongside our house to the cottage at the back. Wanda opened the door and we both instinctively gave our feet several extra wipes on the thick mat before stepping into a lustrous kitchen straight from the pages of a coffee-table magazine. We barely had a chance to cast covetous glances at the elegant wooden cupboards, tiled floor or handsome new appliances before we were whisked through two more doors and into the bathroom.

The bathroom was just as impressive as the kitchen. Everything in there was colour-coordinated and expensive looking – a feast of cool golds, greens and whites. The Holts certainly had fine taste and none of the budgetary problems that held us so firmly in check.

'Please look at my new bath.' The edge in Wanda's voice made us obey instantly. The bath, like everything else in the cottage, was beautiful, except at this particular moment it had five neat, round holes in its far side. I didn't dare turn round, but I distinctly heard Barbara trying to stifle an embarrassed snigger. Wanda, however, was clearly not amused. I don't think my next comment helped either.

'Well, it's a good job you weren't having a soak at the time.'

So we'd finally met our neighbours. When John found out that his young apprentice had drilled through the thin partition wall and into next door's new bathroom suite, he laughed long and hard, insisting that his insurance would cover a replacement bath, however posh it was. It was all right for him, he didn't have to live next to Wanda.

Chapter Twelve

Barney

Joyce Berry was a remarkable person. She loved people, and from the first day I met her I cannot recall a time when Joyce wasn't talking to someone. Joyce's sociability, and the warmth which emanated from her presence, seemed to set everyone around her at ease, so that anyone passing would always stop to talk to her – or more likely she would stop herself; children, parents, school staff, visitors, advisers, inspectors, postmen, cleaners, dinner ladies, and, most of all, other headteachers. Joyce had time for them all.

It was a constant wonder to me how Joyce ever managed to keep on top of the administrative mountain allotted to primary school headteachers in those days, not least as she insisted on teaching each class for a long period at least once a week. Joyce thrived, however, because she was never content to carry out one task at a time: an ever-open office door frequently revealed snapshots of her opening the morning mail while interviewing a five-year-old about playdough in the urinals, and a walk down the corridor might disclose her taking a maths lesson whilst simultaneously placing a telephone order for scraperfoil and pipe cleaners from Arnold's.

Joyce's enthusiasm and love of the job enabled her to win over the children of Cragthwaite School in a trice: she hugged her way into the infants' affections and charmed the older boys by using their nicknames at carefully judged moments. The parents too were swiftly persuaded of the new head's worth by unexpectedly being made welcome, and by the many positive changes that quickly became apparent.

I noticed there was one person who appreciated Joyce more than any other in the head's first term. Eileen Marsett had been the school secretary at Cragthwaite Primary for ten years and had only ever known one boss: the ghoulish Howard Raven. She was an efficient, conscientious and capable administrator but her sensitive, diffident nature made her an easy target for the school's intimidating former head.

I had become used to Eileen's drawn, long-suffering look when I passed her in the office during the autumn but Joyce's arrival had brought about a transformation in her that lifted the spirits of everyone. I greeted her early one miserable February day.

She beamed. 'A very good morning to you, Andy.'

I couldn't help remarking, 'It's good to see you happy, Eileen.'

She drew closer through the office hatch and spoke in a hush. 'You know, I can't tell you what it feels like to be appreciated after all these years.'

I told her she deserved it and headed for the classroom with a bounce in my step.

No headteacher can really become a success without the full backing of the teaching staff, of course, and one of Joyce's greatest triumphs was to make the school a better place in which to work. We quickly realised, even the forceful and wary Val, that here was a person we could trust, and one who understood the intricacies of trying to beget wisdom into the young, distracted and wisdomless.

The only person who remained unconvinced about Joyce was Mrs Hyde, the school's grim dinner lady.

'At least Mr Raven kept the brats quiet at lunchtimes,' she said when I saw her in the hall during dinner. 'Mrs Berry seems to *encourage* them to talk.' I was just about to reply when Mrs Hyde screeched at an infant for spilling his water. I retreated; she was not the kind of person to reason with.

All in all, it took Joyce very little time to completely transform the school: in addition to fostering warm relationships with those around her, she made sure that the classrooms were properly resourced, a dull dusty building was suitably brightened and that a number of creative activities which had been sadly neglected under Howard Raven's regime were reinstated, such as art, craft and music. This is not to say that everything during Joyce Berry's first term at Cragthwaite went swimmingly well. For a start, I discovered that there was one aspect of school life about which she was somewhat less than ardent, and second, that Joyce's enthusiasm for change, coupled with her manic approach to reorganisation, would lead to a rather fretful mid-February.

The first time I heard a grouse amongst the teachers about Joyce that term concerned her passion for arranging school activities left, right and centre, perhaps in the mistaken belief that all of us could manage to juggle five things at once in the same way that she was able. It transpired that in a single week she had organised for all of the children's photographs to be taken, the school nurse to visit, a fund-raising event for a local charity and, most worryingly of all, a new parents' evening. In previous years, appointments for parents had only ever been made following written reports in July, at the end of the school year. Joyce, however, believed that parents should also be given mid-year feedback on offspring progress and so, despite a barrage of grumbling, mainly from Val, a Thursday evening was set aside. The week was particularly busy for me, as I had also arranged a football match on the Friday. This game was a significant event too, being the annual confrontation with great local rivals, Kettleby Juniors.

At Monday's staff meeting, Joyce was checking that everyone was in tune with the week's events.

'Right, busy week, so let's go through the diary. Tomorrow the photographer's here and he'll need the hall all morning, so PE is cancelled. I thought we might have a staff photo taken – what do you think?'

'Do we have to smile?' said a mock-sour Val. Everyone else nodded in agreement – it was another first for Joyce, who scribbled a note and then continued through the diary.

'OK then, Wednesday: the nurse will be doing the head lice check in Eileen's office after assembly in the morning – Reception first. I'm going to talk about raising money for Ingleburn Hall Care Home in assembly, and rather than the traditional sponsored thing that Val tells me usually happens, I thought it would be more fun to have a penny trail in the hall.'

'What's a penny trail?' asked Hilda.

'Oh, it's very simple; the children bring loose change and arrange it in a long line around the hall floor. I used to do them at my last school – they're great fun and less bother than collecting sponsor forms.' Once more, there were nods of concurrence from the staff.

After a long discussion about the plan of attack for Thursday's parents' evening, Joyce dropped in a last item, which wasn't on the agenda.

'There's one more thing I wanted to mention: football at playtimes. I've noticed how crowded the playground is in winter and also how many accidents seem to be caused by the bigger boys rushing around playing football. They do seem to take up a disproportionate amount of the yard.'

'Ooh, there'll be trouble if you stop them playing football at break.' Val shook her head. 'I saw it done once before and they just started playing rougher games instead: British Bulldog, mock fights and the like.'

'Well, I didn't actually mention stopping them playing, but I did want to hear your views on whether we should consider it,' said Joyce.

'I feel quite strongly about this.' It was the first time I'd spoken in the meeting. 'Most of the boys are very keen on the game and it gives them an extra chance to practise – there's a big match on Friday, and they need every opportunity they can get to improve.'

'But don't you have football training after school for that?' said Joyce.

'Well, yes, but some of the boys have transport problems and can't stay behind.'

'Oh, I see.' She didn't seem convinced. Then Emma spoke up.

'How about this for an idea: my little ones are often knocked over by the footballers at playtime, so why don't we restrict the game to one half of the yard and the infants can play in the other half?'

'What an excellent idea!' said Joyce, enthusiastically. 'What do you all think?' Val and Hilda added their approval, and everyone looked at me. I knew there would be trouble from the boys over this, but I could hardly argue against the consensus, and it was clearly a good idea.

'Yes, OK then, we'll only find out if it works by trying it, I suppose,' I mumbled.

Joyce looked pleased. 'Good. Right, that's it. We'll start the new playground system tomorrow – and we'll end the meeting there.'

'But it's *useless* playing on only half the yard – we can't do anything.' The thick-set nine-year-old boy threw the football into his bag with disgust. It was Barney Teasdale. 'Why can't the infants play on the grass, Mr Seed, or stay inside?' It was the end of playtime on Tuesday and crowds of steaming children were piling into the warm cloakroom.

'It's too muddy on the field, Barney, you know that.'

'But it's the match on Friday – we'll get 'ammered by Kettleby if we don't get some decent games in this week.'

'I'm sorry Barney, there's nothing I can do about it.' He looked distraught: football was Barney's life, and he had been talking about the impending match against Kettleby for weeks – suggesting positions for his team-mates, quizzing me about the opposition's best players and giving advice, in his own magnificently blunt style, to each of the other boys on how they could improve.

'Anyway, I haven't got time to talk about the match now; we're going into the hall.' I called over to the class. 'Everyone line up, please! It's our turn for photographs.' Several children produced combs and assaulted their hair. It was also noticeable that a number of girls were wearing smart dresses, and that Hugh was trying to hide a yellow bow tie, which he had surreptitiously produced from his coat pocket.

'Well, am ready,' said Barney, pulling the back of his hand across his nostrils, and distributing a smudge of green slime along one cheek. I looked at his clothes. The shoes were falling apart, the trousers were torn at the knees and mud-caked, and the pale blue shirt he always wore, even outside on sub-zero February days like this, was hanging out in sympathy. I was just about to ask him to at least blow his nose when Joyce appeared.

'Mr Seed – before your class goes into the hall, could you just quickly come along for the staff photo? It'll only take a minute.' She dashed down the corridor before I could ask what I was supposed to do with my waiting class. I quickly addressed them.

'Listen, Class Three, I'm just going into the hall for a minute. Stay in your line quietly and be good.'

In the hall, a short, bearded man was orchestrating the school staff into his preferred design for the picture. I joined in the arrangement, wondering if anybody at all was supervising the 100 children we had abandoned.

'Ah, you must be Mr Seed,' said the photographer. 'Tall, so we'd better have you in the centre at the back.' I moved accordingly. 'Now, the headmistress should be at the front, in the middle, course.' He flourished towards Joyce, who quickly sat and practised smiling. 'Now, who should we have next to the boss?' He winked playfully at Joyce. Val sat down purposefully in the next chair, without being asked. The bearded man considered questioning the move, but decided against it, instead smiling towards Eileen, Hilda and Emma, who were then fussed into exactly the position and pose required. He took a few paces back, shook his head, and made several changes, swapping people round and shifting chairs nearer together by millimetres. I could hear ominous noises from the other side of the wall behind us.

To everyone's relief the photographer finally retired to his camera, looking pleased with the composition. He spent a few more seconds fiddling with light meters and flashguns then finally took two pictures after imploring us to smile. The grins we reluctantly produced featured clenched teeth, however: our minds were all fixed on returning to our classes to quell the inevitable.

Being young and reasonably fit, I managed to reach the hall door first. When I opened it, I immediately heard what I feared most: a great cacophony blowing down the corridor from the cloakroom. I turned the corner just in time to see Barney launching himself across a line of coats towards an airborne football for a diving header. The ball slammed into the girls' toilet door to a tumultuous cheer from half the class, which died abruptly as I came into view and bawled for quiet.

'Whose idea was it to have a game of football in the cloakroom?' It was a stupid question. Twenty extended fingers targeted a sprawling Barney who, to my disbelief, smiled and said, 'Sorry, Mr Seed – good goal though, wannit?'

* * *

The following day's normality was destroyed by the arrival of Nurse Michaelis, and the head lice inspection. This time, Joyce decided not to interfere with what was clearly a well-ordered routine, run by Eileen and the bustling, efficient nurse. In what I later recognised as an established ritual, all of the children in my class began scratching their heads when they heard the 'nit lady' was here, and accusing each other of being infested with the familiar parasites. At lunchtime I also found out that there were indeed a few cases of head lice in school, although none this time in Class 3. I was sitting in the staffroom along with the other staff when Nurse Michaelis appeared.

'Right, we've five children with lice in Classes One and Two, I'm afraid – here's the list and a letter for the parents. Before I go would any of you like me to check your hair?' Joyce stepped forward and took the letters.

'Thanks for organising this morning so well. Actually, would you mind giving me a quick check – I have been feeling a bit itchy recently.' Along with the others, I tried incredibly hard not to stare as the nurse went over to her bag and produced the special comb. Joyce seemed quite matter of fact about having her head inspected in front of the assembled teachers, and Nurse Michaelis was clearly used to it too. She parked Joyce on a chair and began teasing out strands of wavy fair hair.

'Do you have much close contact with the children then, Mrs Berry?' asked the nurse. I heard Val cough.

'Well, I do enjoy giving the little ones a hug now and again, don't I, Emma?'

'You do, and they love you for it,' said Emma.

Nurse Michaelis continued her wary combing. 'Well, when you do it in future, you'd best keep your hair clear of theirs – I'm afraid you're crawling with our little friends.' There was a momentary silence, when I wondered if Joyce was going to screech. She didn't, of course.

'Do you know, that's the fourth time I've had head lice since I've been teaching. Have you any of that lovely shampoo for it?'

On Wednesday during assembly, Joyce had also announced her plans to raise money for Ingleburn Hall Care Home by creating a penny trail in the hall. The children seemed very excited by the idea and, the following day, a surprising number arrived early with loose change to lay around the hall floor in a giant circle. I stood with Val, watching the trail of coins grow.

'What's going to happen at lunchtime then, when the tables and chairs are put out?' she grumbled. 'And I'm supposed to have games in here this afternoon.' These things hadn't occurred to me; they obviously hadn't occurred to Joyce either. By nine o'clock the circle was, amazingly, three-quarters complete. I noticed Barney standing with his friends at the far side of the arc.

'Come on boys, the bell's gone,' I called. Barney came over.

'Someone's put 50p in the line, Mr Seed. I thought we were only supposed to bring coppers.' He didn't miss a thing.

'Well just leave it, Barney – I'll sort it out later.' I rushed back to the classroom, in fear of being late following Tuesday's debacle.

At break I returned to the hall to pick up the 50p coin – it clearly wasn't a good idea to leave it there. The coin was gone, so

I went to see if Joyce had picked it up. She hadn't, but said that she would ask the other staff if they'd done so.

Ten minutes later I was back in the classroom teaching maths. There was a knock at the door and a top junior girl from Class 4 walked in with a note from Joyce that read, 'All classes please meet in hall at 11 a.m. to sort out missing coin.'

Amidst groaning from my class, we returned to the hall once more. I deflected questions about why they were there and told the children to step over the coins carefully and sit down. We were the first class to arrive.

'Do we sit on the coins or not, Mr Seed?' It was Eve.

'No, sit in your usual lines but leave a gap for the coins,' I said, turning to everyone.

Class 4 came in next and sat on the coins. Eve looked at me sternly. Class 2 followed, and Hilda decided to sit them around the outside of the circle of money. There was then a long wait for the youngest children, during which time the three seated classes found it impossible to keep their hands off the large ring of cash, despite several threats from Val. A 2p coin rolled gracefully across the front of the hall as Joyce entered. She looked surprisingly grim. Joyce was just about to address the children when Class 1 finally appeared, a flustered-looking Emma shooing them through the doors. The first child, a freckly ginger gnome, was confused about where to sit, since Class 2 weren't in their usual places. He saw Hilda pointing to where he should go, but he didn't see the line of coins that every other child had carefully stepped over. Now moving purposefully, he kicked a spray of shiny pennies into the children of Class 3, which caused huge amusement to everyone who saw it. Amazingly, the next Reception child did precisely the same thing, flicking money in all directions. Inevitably, Barney Teasdale jumped up and began collecting the loose money. Several others followed him, and for a second there was an anarchy of sliding children before Joyce bellowed, 'SIT DOWN AND KEEP STILL!'

They did. I did too.

After the scattered coins were returned, Joyce lectured the whole school about honesty and about the heinousness of taking money intended for an old people's home. She certainly showed another side to her character that none of us had seen before. The children listened in silence. Joyce finished by demanding that the 50p reappear by the next day. It was Thursday morning, and we still had parents' evening to come.

The afternoon passed uneventfully, the children clearly subdued by the righteous force of Joyce's lecture. Unfortunately, this meant that I had more time to think, and worry, about the impending parents' appointments beginning at five o'clock. At the end of school I scurried round the classroom in a dash of nervous tidying. I had an hour and a half to smarten the displays, set out the children's work on their desks and read through my notes and records before the first parents arrived. I was quietly terrified. At half past four the door of my classroom opened and Val walked in.

'You all right?' I could tell that she knew I wasn't.

'Fine.'

'Liar. Never mind, you'll not have any problems – these are good parents in this part of the dale, well mostly. Just tell them what nice kids they've got and that they've improved since September.'

'Is that what you do then, Val?'

'Well, not exactly – but I've been around just a bit longer than you. Anyhow, better go now – I need a fag before we start. Have fun.' She disappeared, leaving me thinking how much I'd like to see her do things.

When the mothers and fathers did finally arrive and I began talking to them, my anxieties quickly evaporated and I found that I actually enjoyed meeting them. For a start, it was great fun trying to identify which parents belonged to which child from the ones I hadn't already met, and secondly, it soon became evident that most of them were far more nervous about parents' evening than I was. The fact that they actually listened to me intently and believed what I was saying put me further at ease, and soon I was able to relax and watch a pattern emerge as each new couple arrived in the classroom.

The first thing I noticed was that the mums invariably took the lead: they keenly rifled through their child's work while the husbands often drifted around the room looking at the displays or chuckling at the stories on offer. The mums also tended to do most of the talking: this was particularly noticeable amongst the farming families, where the wife would usually fire a number of insightful questions while the customarily huge husband sat awkwardly in his best jacket, twiddling giant thumbs and wondering if the tiny plastic chair beneath him would support his weight for much longer.

The parents also, unsurprisingly, shared with abundance the characteristics of their children: Jack's dad was as wide as a bed,

Terry's mum was unmistakably timid, Eve's mum was a friendly gabbler, and Rose's parents both captivating – perhaps it was their lilting Irish accents. Hugh's mother was so posh that I almost found myself unable to speak to her, for fear of mispronouncing my words; worst of all, when I did talk, I began involuntarily employing the most absurd sub-aristocratic accent, which went totally against my principles. Mrs Richmond, however, had a familiar twinkle in her eye that quickly set me at ease, and soon we were both laughing at some of Hugh's quirkier adventures in the class.

The final appointment of the evening was at eight o'clock, with Mr and Mrs Teasdale, Barney's parents. Mr Teasdale, being about six foot five, seemingly in both directions, decided to forgo the classroom chairs altogether and parked his tremendous bottom on a table, while Mrs Teasdale drew up close. Her slightly furrowed brow set the tone.

'I've been looking at Barney's books, Mr Seed, and, well, they're 'orrible.' She held up two decrepit exercise books, all folds, tears, smudges and crossings out. 'I know he's always found it 'ard to concentrate, Mr Seed, but I 'oped that when he mebbe reached this age, he'd start knuckling down a bit . . . you know.' Her eyes wore a pleading but resigned look.

'Well, Barney is a nice lad, of course, and he, er, has certainly improved since September.'

'How's his English, then?'

'Well, it's not his best subject, but he can read quite well, and he can write well too, if he concentrates.'

'Concentrates? Mr Seed, you know as well as I do that Barney Teasdale has never concentrated on anything in his life except football.' Mr Teasdale shifted a little on the table behind, but remained quiet. 'What about maths?'

'Maths. Well, he understands things all right but he doesn't get a lot written down in lesson times.'

'Don't tell me – he's too busy nosing off what everyone else is doing?'

'I'm afraid so, Mrs Teasdale.'

'Well, is he good at anything then?'

'Of course. He's very good at football.' The anguished expression on her face told me swiftly that this wasn't what she wanted to hear, but Mr Teasdale suddenly became quite animated.

'In centre midfield for the big game tomorrow then, is he, Mr Seed?'

'Er, yes, Barney's been talking about it for weeks,' I replied, noticing that Mrs Teasdale was already rising from her chair, with elevated eyes; she gave a sideways nod towards her husband.

'Aye, and so has he, 'n' all.'

The following morning was Friday. I was quite late arriving at school, but decided to have a quick look in the hall to see if the missing 50p coin had reappeared. The previously decimated circle of money had been roughly repaired, and now formed an impressive ring right around the room. I quickly scanned the coins for silver. There were a number of francs and pesetas, and an almost complete set of Esso World Cup tokens, but there was no 50p. Joyce would be furious. What punishment would she inflict on the children? Staying in at playtimes? That would have the boys wailing again with the big football match coming up after school. I couldn't bear the thought. I reached into my pocket. Among the change was a 50p coin. I knew it was a stupid idea but it would save a load of bother. I knelt down and slipped the coin into the circle. Unexpectedly, I heard the hall door move but looked up to see it close again without the sign of a person. I grunted in frustration – it was bound to have been the miscreant trying to return the money.

Kettleby was a proud, thriving little town situated high at the top of Swinnerdale. It was always heaving with visitors in summer and it was always freezing cold in winter – just like today, as I stood at the side of the madly sloping football pitch near the river. Kettleby Junior School was slightly larger than Cragthwaite but it was positioned right in the middle of the town, and had no playing field of its own. I had been told by Ron Troop, the deputy and football coach, that the ground was near the river but it had taken me a long while to find it among the twisting lanes outside the town, and we were now quite late. Despite the biting wind coming off gaunt Bleabrough Fell to the north, there was a sizable turnout of parents for the match. This was purely on account of the great historical rivalry between the two teams. I supposed it was because this was probably the only meaningful match that either team played all year, the upper dale's other educational establishments being too small to put together more than a couple of keen infants and a dog. Ron came out of the huddle of Kettleby players who were busy waving their arms to keep warm, and jogged over to me.

'Bit late, aren't you?' He was always rather abrupt.

'Hello Ron, yes, sorry. We got a bit lost, my fault.'

'Well, we better get started right away – I'll have to make it twenty minutes each way or it'll be getting dark.' I was just about to say that our lads could do with a warm-up when he turned away and blew his whistle.

After a few panics over laces, the Cragthwaite boys were ready, and took their positions, conspicuous in their awful shrunken yellow-grey nylon kit. The team consisted of the best players from Class 4 along with Barney, Wilf and Cameron from my class. Ron blew his referee's whistle once more and we were under way. The six or seven parents, including Mr Teasdale, who had transported the children from Cragthwaite, shouted their cheers into the wind, which swallowed them easily before continuing its assault on our ears.

Barney was immediately in the thick of the action; he wasn't the captain, and was over a year younger than some of the players on the pitch, but he was a born leader on a football field, and immediately started barking orders and encouragement to his team-mates. He also used the ball exceedingly well, and after just four minutes he played a long pass through the middle to Ian Scott, who slipped it around the last defender before calmly slotting a low shot into the Kettleby net. One–nil! The Cragthwaite parents bounced with delight on the touchline and I hollered my congratulations to the team. After that, things got even better. Wilf won a free kick outside the opposition penalty area and Barney floated in a great cross, which was looped into the goal by Penny Garsdale's brother, Stephen. Ron Troop reluctantly gave a little 'pip' on his whistle and pointed towards the centre circle before muttering something disparaging to his poor goalkeeper. We were now well in control of the game, and to make matters worse for Kettleby, their players started arguing amongst themselves, hurling accusations about the lack of marking and tackling.

Two minutes later it was 3–0. Barney was involved once more: he played another exquisite chipped pass to Ian Scott who beat two defenders before crossing for Cameron to tap in the ball at the far post. I couldn't believe it – this was the best football that Cragthwaite had played all season, perhaps ever. I looked over at Mr Teasdale who was virtually dancing a jig by the halfway line. A few seconds after the restart of the game Ron blew the whistle for half time. I looked at my watch: he had only played seventeen minutes. He immediately marched over to the far corner of the ground away from all of the spectators, and stabbed his finger down at the pitch along with a snarl for his players to join him, pronto.

I spent the half-time interval telling the boys what a wonderful job they were doing and trying to stop Barney interrupting me with more suggestions for new tactics to further extend our advantage in the match. After a quick drink they ran back out on to the pitch slapping each other on the back, eager to start the second half. The Kettleby players, meanwhile, stayed in a tight knot at the far side of the pitch for several more minutes. Everyone could hear the low growl of Ron Troop's voice rattling out orders to his beleaguered boys; he was clearly not happy. I could see that my team were getting cold while this was happening, and several of them looked over to me to do something, not least Barney, who threw his hands up in despair – he was never good at waiting at the best of times. I told them to jump up and down.

Eventually the Kettleby players ran back on to the pitch to restart the game. Several of them had clenched fists and there was a lot of shouting and clapping from the older boys. It didn't take long to see that they really meant business in this half. Wilf played the ball to Ian Scott as we kicked off and immediately a stocky Kettleby defender came sliding in and smashed Ian's legs from under him.

'Foul!' screeched Mr Teasdale from a few yards away.

'Play on!' snarled Ron, waving his arms, even though Ian was still down. Kettleby had the ball, and they weren't going to give it away cheaply. This pattern continued for the next five minutes: every time a Cragthwaite player received a pass, the opposition launched themselves in like missiles. Several of my players were bruised and battered in this onslaught, but each time Ron ignored the challenges, crying out, 'Good strong tackles, Kettleby,' or 'Get up lad, you're all right,' to the latest victim. Worse was to come: Kettleby won a corner and there was a huge muddy scrum as the ball dropped in front of our keeper. A leg shot out and the ball was in the net. Suddenly, the large watching crowd of Kettleby parents came to life. There was a great roar of encouragement and the home players raced back to their own half, eager to keep up the pressure. Overhead, thick clouds rolled off the fells, increasing the gloom as dusk approached.

For the first time, I could detect doubt creeping into the minds of the Cragthwaite boys. They looked nervous, and their passes began to go astray. Kettleby, aided by some discreet coaching from the referee, saw that they were back in the game. Somehow, with desperate defending, we held out for another five minutes, but shots were now raining in on our goal. I shouted encouragement, as did Mr Teasdale from further down touchline, and his son on the pitch, who was battling as valiantly as ever. A minute later, however, it was 3–2. A long shot from a Kettleby player hit a defender and stuck in the small black swamp that had now developed in the penalty area. It was whacked into the net by one of their players, to an explosion of delight from the upperdale spectators. I looked at Mr Teasdale. All the colour had drained from his face.

'There's only six more minutes to go,' I said, hopefully. 'We may be able to hang on.' With Barney hurling himself around the pitch tackling, heading, passing, blocking and running, we survived the next three minutes. They hit the post, and another minute passed. Two left. Our keeper made a great save and another minute had gone. One left, but we were under siege. Barney cleared a header off the line, and my watch showed that twenty minutes had passed, although it was now hard to see the hands as the gloom of twilight began to cloak Swinnerdale. It looked like we had made it, but Ron Troop clearly had no intention of blowing the whistle with his side so clearly on top and in dire need of an equaliser.

Another minute went by, then two. Kettleby continued to attack. Darkness continued to fall. It was now hard to make out the colours of the kits at the far end of the pitch. We were into the fourth minute of 'extra time' when the referee awarded a mysterious penalty to Kettleby.

'Handball!' he confidently shouted from the halfway line.

'Byyy – I wish I had eyes like that,' said one of the Cragthwaite mothers on the touchline.

The penalty was scored, once again to roars of delight from the home players and supporters. 3–3: I was so disappointed for our boys.

'Well, at least he can blow for full time now and we can go home,' I said to Mr Teasdale, who now had his hands permanently over his face.

'I wouldn't count on it, lad,' he replied through his fingers. 'He's carrying on.'

To everyone's utter astonishment, he put the ball on the centre spot and shouted, 'Right, a couple of minutes left, lads.' My watch showed that thirty-two minutes had been played in the second half. He was obviously determined to win this game at all cost. Another period of Kettleby pressure passed. I now could only see the ball when it came near me, and the lights of the farmhouses on the surrounding hills began to speckle the scene, like fallen stars. Mr Teasdale was now really losing patience.

'Come on ref, it's nearly my bedtime!' he wailed. But the whistle stayed in Ron's hand and Kettleby kept pressing. A winning goal was inevitable. And then it came. Out of the thick murk in our mudbath goal area, a shadow picked up the ball, put his head down and ran. He beat two tired players and continued his remarkable surge. The ball was under tight control, as feints and swerves took the boy clear of more lunging silhouettes. It was Barney, and he was heading for the Kettleby goal with one last heroic burst. Somehow, with a kind deflection, he was past the last defender with only the goalie to beat. It was now dark, very dark. Barney pulled back his leg to shoot, Ron picked up his whistle to blow. I couldn't see a thing; I just looked towards the hazy figure of Ron, expecting him to blow the final whistle, but with a possibly supernatural attack of conscience, he kept his lips together. There was a yelp from the far side of the pitch and out of the night, Barney Teasdale came running and jumping, his arms in the air. He had scored, and it was clearly the greatest moment of his life. His dad, unable to contain himself, ran on to the pitch and out of somewhere a shrill whistle blew.

I was still tingling with excitement when I got home at half past six and that evening I recalled the whole match to Barbara in great detail. 'You should have seen our parents at the end – they went crackers.'

'I bet they did.' She stifled a yawn.

'I know you're not really interested in football but everyone in Cragthwaite will be talking about beating Kettleby for years.'

'Well done you.'

'You're not really listening, are you? I'd better start again from the beginning.'

She threw a cushion at me.

At the following Monday's assembly, Joyce addressed the school.

'Last week was a very busy one, and probably not the best week I've had at the school. But I have to say that it ended very well. Something very exciting happened at the end of last week that a lot of you don't know about and I'd like Barney Teasdale to come out to the front and tell everyone about it.' There was raucous clapping and cheering as Barney rose up and edged his way along the sitting line of Class 3 children. As he passed me by I gave him a pat on the shoulder. He leant over and whispered, 'Don't worry, Mr Seed, I won't mention that you nicked the 50p.'

Chapter Thirteen

Anita

The arrival of March saw us finally move out of The Shippon, and across the green into Craven Bottoms. Barbara, now sporting an impressive abdominal bump, was particularly excited. The much-renovated kitchen looked beautiful, with delicious blue tiles, smart pine cupboards, a shiny new cooker, and a safe-looking ceiling. John Weatherall had made a splendid set of solid wood shelves to fill the infamous alcove too, but it was to be some time before I could look at them without seeing Wanda Holt's face, or for that matter, a vision of a bath full of holes. We hadn't seen Wanda or Ralph since our unfortunate first introduction, but we vowed to try and make a better impression on them the next time they visited the village.

'Have you remembered that I'm out this morning?' said Barbara, as I dumped the last of the boxes from The Shippon.

'Yes, you're going to see Iris again.'

'Don't sound like that – it's important for me to make new friends in the village.'

'But do you really need to go today when we've got all this to unpack?'

'I won't be long – I'll be able to help this afternoon.'

I exhaled in irritation. 'We've got all the months ahead of us to get to know people in the village, don't you think we should get the house sorted first?'

'We'll get there, don't worry. There's no need to get so . . . irked. Anyway, Iris is a lovely person and she's really interesting to talk to.'

I tried to think of something smart to say but inside I knew how essential a proper social life was to Barbara. How would I feel being at home most of the time in a village? And I couldn't disagree about Iris.

Iris and Don Falconer were incomers, like ourselves, who lived in a vast former farmhouse at the top of the village. Don was a workaholic financial consultant and often away for long periods, leaving Iris, unable to drive, at home with their toddler son Stewart. Iris was a cuddly, generous person, forever inviting people around for coffee.

She introduced herself at chapel one Sunday and that afternoon welcomed us into her lavish home. The carpets were so thick that my feet disappeared, and everywhere there was leather, polished oak and dainty ornaments in glass cabinets. But for me the most memorable thing about Iris Falconer's home was her choice of biscuits. She always produced a huge plate of Marks and Spencers Luxury Selection, the type with quarter of an inch of chocolate on top, and the type that we could never afford. That first afternoon I ate six and Iris kept pushing more towards me. Recalling this, I looked at Barbara.

'So, will Iris have her biccies out?'

'She always has her biccies out.'

'Can you smuggle some out for me?'

'Don't be silly – she knows I don't even like chocolate biscuits.'

'But I do, especially hers.'

'Well then, you'll have to come round and chat or play trains with Stewart.'

'Then the house will never get done . . .'

She gave me a look of despair and changed the subject. 'Don't forget that my mum and dad are visiting next weekend.' This I had forgotten.

'Oh right, yes, but where are they going to sleep? We just can't afford to buy beds.' It was a strange situation having three bedrooms but only one bed.

'I've arranged to borrow two camp beds from Mary Burton.'

'Oh, well done. While we're on beds we need to think about a cot for the baby.'

'I've sorted that.'

'Oh, do you know someone who's got one? I thought you'd set your heart on a new one.'

'We're getting a new one.'

'How are we going to afford that?'

'We're not. My parents have bought us one.'

'Fantastic. Maybe they could bring it up on Saturday?'

Barbara chuckled. '*What* a good idea, I never would have thought of that.'

I ignored her tone. 'Anyway, it's lucky that they're coming up now the kitchen's finished.'

'Yes, I'm often lucky like that.'

I decided not to say any more.

* * *

Now that the rooms of the house were finally decorated and habitable, I was also able to spend a little time thinking about making a workshop in the garage, something which I'd been looking forward to for some time. Up to this point, the garage had been used as a storage space for all of our junk, along with the boxes from the various moves we'd made over the last few months. I now began clearing out a space and thinking about making a proper workbench, as well as finding places to hang all of my tools. This was something I particularly enjoyed, especially as I began to imagine what I might use the workbench for when it was finished.

Strangely enough an opportunity to make something exciting soon arose but rather than being at home, it was with the children in my class at Cragthwaite Primary School.

Back in the autumn term the school received some unexpected help from the RAF at the nearby Hauxton airbase, when the set for the Christmas panto was being constructed. One of the girls in Val's class had a father who was a squadron leader there, and was always tremendously eager to assist the school in any way he could. He arranged for a number of huge sheets of amazingly strong triple-thickness corrugated card to be delivered to help with the production. In the event, only two of the sheets were used, but I immediately saw a number of tantalising possibilities with this material and carried the remaining sheets off to my classroom, knowing that we didn't have room to store them elsewhere.

The child who volunteered to help me carry the sheets was Anita Thwaite. Anita Thwaite was a phenomenon: probably the most practical and helpful person I have ever met. She cleaned the blackboard, washed the paint pots, sharpened the pencils, tidied my desk, sorted the bookshelves and did numerous other tedious tasks, often without being asked. Anita just saw what needed to be done and did it, without fuss: she was a teacher's dream. Unfortunately, the second half of the spring term produced an occasion when Anita was just a little too helpful.

This half term began with another new initiative: a whole-school project on the theme of 'Water'. Joyce got the ball rolling by suggesting that we all visit the local sewage works with our classes. The staff thought she was joking, but a few weeks later we found ourselves chugging along the Twissham Road in one of Ripley's ancient buses to find out all about drains, sludge and settling tanks. The children were delighted, of course, and all along the journey feverishly competed with each other to provide the most unsavoury descriptions of what we would see there.

As it happened, the sewage works was a quite fascinating place to visit, not least because we were given an excellent talk by one the technicians, a Mr Temple, which included full details of all the bizarre things that people flush down their toilets. Among the objects picked up by the various filters and screens were hundreds of hairbrushes and toothbrushes, false teeth, wigs, and a number of glass eyes. His most amazing discovery, however, was a live snake: several of the children gave involuntary shudders at the thought of sitting on the loo while a black mamba came looking for its way back home. After the talk we toured the works and were given a full explanation of the various processes that removed the lumps and nasty bits from the water. I was inspired: there were tanks, filters, pipes, pumps, rotating sprayers, gravel beds and more – the possibilities for building classroom models were endless.

That night I set about making some plans for representations of the various pieces of machinery we had seen. The whole place was a giant system all linked together with pipes, to produce clean water. It suddenly occurred to me that for once we weren't short of raw materials to make things with at school, as we could use the huge sheets of RAF card. So why not go for the big one and make a complete working model of the entire sewage works? Only a crazy fool would even contemplate taking on such a task with nine-year-old children: well, I was ready.

Back at school, small groups of children were set to work and soon the monster construction began to take shape. It looked like a giant closed box in the shape of a staircase; every stage had to be at a different level to get the water to flow down through the system. On each step were tanks made from biscuit tins, connected by plastic tubes. The lowest level featured a superb rotating sprayer, made by George and Malcolm, which was designed to trickle water into a final collecting jar at the base of the colossal model. It took about three weeks to finish, and everybody in the class was involved at some stage. Tubes of Copydex were expended to seal all the leaks, and by the end of the month it was finished. There was tremendous excitement in the room when I told the class that the huge model was ready to be tested, and that everyone could gather round to see. The class were adamant that it was all going to work properly and therefore that we needed really dirty water to replicate raw sewage.

'Have I to go out and get some muck, Mr Seed?' It was, of course, Anita.

'Well, we do need something to make the water going in

realistic,' I replied. 'OK Anita, you and Carol can go outside with a basin and add a bit of soil to some water.' Anita grabbed a plastic bowl from the sink, half-filled it from the tap, and disappeared with Carol at pace.

After about ten minutes, I sent George out to find them, as they hadn't returned, and everyone was becoming impatient waiting for our mini sewage works to perform. Following a further five minutes' wait, I sent Martha out to see what had happened to George. Another two minutes later, all four returned, each holding a corner of the basin and looking like they had been on a jungle camouflage course. Their faces, clothes and hands were smeared with every conceivable kind of dark stain, and a few that could not be conceived. Anita, grinning wildly, announced,'Well, Mr Seed, you won't get water muckier'n *that*!'

I looked, and didn't dispute her claim. There was mud, sticks, leaves, stones, sand, straw, grass, oily globules, and what looked suspiciously like small clods of dried cow dung floating on the surface. The rest of the class seemed satisfied that the criteria had been attained, and so Anita carefully poured a jugful of the slime into the top tank of the cardboard refinery. I was just about to explain that we now needed to leave this dirty water to settle for a day before letting it through to the next stage when I looked up and caught a picture of exhilaration and anticipation on the faces of the class clustered round the invention. They were pressing in, eagerly waiting for the next stage, and some of them, no doubt, were expecting crystal-clear, mountain-spring-like water to appear at any moment. I couldn't disappoint them so I decided to let the water right through the system, filthy or not.

Anita clearly felt that she was in a senior position of responsibility with the project at this point, and demanded, with a booming 'SHHHH!' that everyone was completely silent. It suddenly occurred to me that there was going to be a great disappointment right then: the stones and bits of muck were bound to block the narrow pipes to the next tank and barely a dribble would emerge. But I was wrong, and the following moment will always stay with me as one of the most magical in my whole teaching career.

I gently turned the little tap, filched from a winemaking kit, which opened the tubing from the first tank, and asked George to switch on the motor of his rotating sprinkler. The children watched in hushed awe as dribbles of grey liquid seeped through the first clear tube and filled up the second tank. Once this was half-full, the water continued its journey down, through the various filters and biscuit tins until it reached the sprinkler. Clusters of pink forefingers traced its deliberate progress all the way. Would the sprinklers work? Would the whole system finally clog up with silt and gunge before it reached the end? Anita kept on feeding the first tank with jugs of sewage to keep up the pressure. And then, remarkably, droplets of water began to emerge from the sprinkler, and in a few seconds it was spraying fine beads of surprisingly clean-looking water on to the gravel beneath; the class broke out into a spontaneous bout of applause. It was a wonderful moment.

Anita quickly realised that water would soon be coming out of the final tank and spilling on to the floor, as I'd forgotten to put down a collecting container. She dashed away, returning with a yoghurt pot, and we all cheered again as it began to gradually fill.

Jack asked if we should get Mrs Berry to witness this historic moment.

'Well, it's not every day that you get to see a working model of a sewage farm,' I smirked. 'I'm sure she won't mind being disturbed for this.' A few moments later Jack opened the classroom door to let Joyce in. The class was bursting to tell her all about how the model worked, how dirty the water was, and about several other major claims regarding the contraption. Joyce was flabbergasted, and spent quite a while looking over the workings and asking for explanations. It felt like a real moment of triumph for me – she was as impressed as I was proud.

'This is truly marvellous, Class Three – I can't believe you made it all yourselves!' I thought back to Howard Raven's sour-faced visits to my room; it could hardly be more different. Joyce continued to ask questions.

'And the water's gone right through and it's fairly clean?' she said, disbelievingly. 'Can I see it then?' We all looked to Anita who was still positioned by the yoghurt pot, no doubt making sure that it didn't overflow.

'Er, the pot's empty, Mr Seed,' she said, flushing a delicate vermillion.

'Oh, what happened, Anita – did it spill?'

'No. I drank it.'

That evening, Barbara and I found ourselves sitting on one of Iris Falconer's plush leather sofas. I recounted the story of Anita and the 'sewage' in full, gruesome detail, much to the amazement of Iris. I was determined to earn my chocolate biscuits. Not surprisingly, Anita wasn't at school the next day. Although it was hard not to join in the laughter at her inexplicable swig, I did worry whether she might have contracted something horrible, remembering the foul concoction that had been added to the water that passed through the model. As soon as it was morning break I phoned her brusque mother.

'Oh, don't fret, Mr Seed – she'll be right.'

'I was just wondering why she was off school. Is it a tummy ache?'

'No, it's not that.'

'Have you taken her to the surgery? Maybe your doctor suggested staying off as a precaution?'

'She doesn't need a doctor; Anita's eaten far wus things.'

'Well, maybe you should get her checked out, Mrs Thwaite, just to be sure?'

'She'll be back tomorrow, it's nothing.'

'But she could have acute blood poisoning.'

'Acute blood poisoning? Don't be daft. It's acute embarrassment, that's what it is. You'll see her tomorrow.'

And I did. Anita was as helpful as ever from that day on, but never quite so passionate about volunteering.

Chapter Fourteen

Lucinda

After a draining day in the classroom, I would often go for an early evening walk around the village and let the therapeutic Dales air and scenery tend some refreshment to my numbed psyche. There were many delicious walks to choose from, but one spot had emerged as my favourite: the waterfall. Now that spring was here and the floods of winter had subsided, Applesett Force was a magical and surprisingly calm place, hidden as it was in a quiet corner of the village. This was where I headed one Friday in late March.

I walked past the burly stone mill, which had supplied the village's electricity before the war, and down towards the beautiful little packhorse bridge, sturdily built to withstand the rages of winter torrents, and now painted with lichen and patches of quivering toadflax. I stopped on the bridge and followed the beck up towards the fall, set in its own dramatic cleft, with great overhangs of jutting rocks sprouting huge trees and creating a canopy for the small caves and stone ledges beneath.

The whole place possessed that singular atmosphere that is created by the sound of falling, rushing water and rich dampness set in a natural green echo chamber of rock, and I dearly loved it from the first time I went there. I clearly recall almost bursting with excitement when I'd discovered the waterfall and hurrying to the phone box to tell Barbara: 'It's beautiful, and it's virtually right in the village – I can't wait for you to see it!' Then, of course, there were the great floods of January, when the gentle falls became a booming surge, hidden behind cloaks of spray.

It was at the waterfall that I first noticed a peculiar optical effect, which was later to become a favourite game with visiting children – although Barbara and I enjoyed it just as much. I learnt that if you stood or sat still, and stared at the falling water for about a minute then looked quickly at another object, it seemed to mysteriously rise; this worked best, we later discovered, if you looked at the ragged stone cliff right next to the waterfall afterwards. It was a most weird sensation, but always great fun.

Dusk was now stealing away the last of the light, so I headed back to the house. As soon as I opened the door, Barbara called to me from the kitchen.

'Andy – come and look at this.' I walked up the sloping hallway and found her kneeling down beside the new shelves in the alcove.

'What's up?'

'We've got mice.' She pointed to a small pile of droppings underneath the bottom shelf. 'That's the last thing I want in my lovely new kitchen – how do you think they could have got in?'

'They must have come in from another room – all the holes were cemented up when we did the walls. I'll check around the house tomorrow.'

Barbara strained to get up, rubbing her lower spine hard. 'My back aches like heck.'

I helped her up. 'Is there anything I can do to ease it?'

'Yes – promise me we won't have another baby right away.'

Was that serious? Somehow, I felt this wasn't the best time to ask.

I spent most of Saturday morning looking in cupboards and in the numerous dark and musty crevices in which Craven Bottoms seemed to specialise. I didn't like what I found: there were mice droppings in several places including under the stairs, in the garage, and in the spare bedroom on top of a pile of LPs. My worst discovery, however, was in the large pink-walled cupboard that we called Mrs Tiplady's bathroom. It was in here that I kept all my boxes of notes from college, old letters, and various folders for school work as well as collections of interesting objects that might come in handy for art lessons. It was a scene of rodent devastation.

The mice had clearly regarded this collection of important boxes as a kind of choice buffet: everything had been nibbled – paper, cardboard boxes, bags, letters, folders, plastic containers – they had sampled the lot. My college notes, now full of holes and yellow stains, had been a particular target, and the whole place reeked intensely. Until then, I'd been fairly ambivalent about mice, but at that moment I declared war.

Barbara went into Ingleburn and bought a whole range of poisons and traps, which we positioned around the house wherever there was a concentration of droppings. I felt certain that this would do the trick, but over the following week, there was no evidence that the mice were going to be easily beaten. On Wednesday, Barbara walked into the kitchen and saw a mouse sitting on the worktop: it dived behind the fridge and somehow escaped. The following evening I heard scrabbling noises coming from the roof space above our bedroom. And things got worse.

I went round the house and checked all the traps and the poison. We had managed to catch one mouse, but the poison looked like it had hardly been touched and there were fresh droppings everywhere. I waited another week, but the population of mice seemed to be thriving more than ever, and what's more, they were becoming cheeky.

It was Saturday night and I'd decided to watch *Match of the Day* and treat myself to a hot chocolate. Barbara couldn't keep her eyes open and had gone to bed. I was just enjoying a replay of a fine goal when a small movement caught my eye near the door at the side of the room. I turned around and watched a nut-brown mouse squeeze itself under the door of the living room and casually amble along the side of the skirting board towards the fireplace. It stopped for a moment, as if to sniff at a crumb on the carpet. I couldn't believe it. I thought about hurling a cushion at this impudent intruder but decided it would be better to watch and see where it went. The mouse then continued to trot over to the fireplace. It hopped on to the hearth, scrambled up the grate, and to my astonishment, shot right up the chimney.

This was too much. I wanted to wake Barbara right away and describe the contemptuous effrontery of this diminutive pest, but I restrained myself and waited until the morning.

'We've got to get rid of them, Barb; we can't have our baby being trampled by mice in the night.'

'You're right, they're not exactly hygienic, are they? But are you sure that this one went up the chimney last night?'

'I watched it clearly – it just disappeared up there in a flash.'

'What if there's a whole nest of them up there?'

'Let's have a fire – that'll sort them out.'

'I'm not sure about that, Andy, we've never used the fire before: what if the chimney needs sweeping?'

'Oh don't worry, I'll just give them a quick blast of smoke: they won't like that.'

Barbara didn't look at all convinced, but I went in search of some sticks and paper with boyish enthusiasm for my new plan. Five minutes later, I'd cleared the grate and made what I considered to be a textbook wigwam of scrunched-up newspaper and split sticks. Barbara continued to mutter her doubts as I applied a match.

'Goodbye meece.'

The chimney obviously had a good draw of air, and within seconds a smart crackling fire was sending long shots of flame into the black opening above.

'Haven't you made it a bit fierce? I thought you were just going to smoke them out,' said Barbara, taking a pace backwards.

'Oh, it'll die down in a minute, no problem.' I stepped back myself to admire my work: I did like a good fire.

'Why is it making that funny noise?'

It was making a strange sound, a kind of hushed, distant roar, as if a lot of air was being blown or sucked somewhere.

'I don't know.' And I also didn't know why small pieces of something dark were now falling down the chimney into the fire.

'Andy—' Barbara's words were then interrupted by a sharp *crack!* from the chimney breast. The chimney was on fire. The plaster above the fireplace had just split with the tremendous heat being generated behind it. I was in the process of deciding how best not to panic when a hefty tangle of scorched sticks landed on the fire, bursting a cloud of ash and smoke into the room.

'I know what's happened! It's the jackdaws – they've been trying to make a nest on the chimney.' But Barbara was gone. She was dialling 999.

The fire engine arrived much faster than I thought, considering that it had to travel eight miles up the dale from Ingleburn, and that it was manned by part-time volunteers. In the intervening period I threw some water on the fire, assured Barbara without any conviction that our new house wasn't going to burn down, and tried to think how to block the fireplace so that the fire couldn't feed itself with more air. In the event, after a few frightening minutes of howling roars and smoke and cracking plaster, it became clear that the fall of burnt jackdaw nest sticks had smothered the fire in the grate and that the chimney, now empty of fuel, had stopped burning.

One of the essential charms of Applesett is the design of the village green, a great stretched circle of grass framed with houses. I'd always considered it a lovely feature, the way all the homes faced inwards, keeping a watchful eye on one another. This layout certainly lent the place a comforting sense of community, but not, as I quickly discovered that day, without a price. As I ran outside to look up at the chimneystack, it soon became apparent that I wasn't alone. Several front doors were open, and there was a broken ring of people staring and pointing at the thick, black pall of smoke gushing upwards from the rooftop of Craven Bottoms. It wasn't something you could hide. Nor was the large red fire engine wailing and flashing its way up the village to stop outside our house. Within seconds, the remaining front doors swung open, and to my dismay, the throng of spectators enjoying the spectacle was rapidly enlarged.

With impressive speed, a fireman was up a ladder and on to the roof. Several others jumped into the living room and, after a crackle of radios, it was confirmed that the fire was out.

'Jackdaws, mate. You need a wire cage up on yer pots.' I nodded a lot.

It seemed that the chimney was not only a solid and well-built stone construction, but that it was relatively free of soot, otherwise the fire could have been much worse. The firemen, needing to get back to their full-time jobs down the dale, quickly disappeared, then the gawping villagers slowly dispersed too, and I finally sat down and tried to comfort Barbara. We were both shaking.

'You pinhead.' She was right. 'We've taken an eternity to buy and renovate and decorate this house and just when it's finished you decide to burn it down.'

'Sorry.'

'Next time, listen to me before you do something like that.'

Once again, I nodded. 'At least we got that mouse.'

She didn't laugh. I didn't laugh either: I was thinking about something else. I recognised one of the firefighters – he was the father of a girl in my class.

As I drove to school on Monday, dreading the idea of having to tell the tale of what happened countless times, I consoled myself with the thought that a situation like this is never as bad as you expect.

And it wasn't: it was worse.

Eileen was first. As soon as I stepped through the front door she was out of her office like a torpedo. I'd never seen her move so fast.

'Are you OK? I heard about the fire. Is the house damaged then? It can be awful, I know – happened to my friend's sister two years ago and the room was ruined. Do you want a cup of tea?' I had only answered the first question when Joyce appeared. She repeated Eileen's questions then drew me into her office.

'I really am sorry, Andy, and we've another very busy week in school, I'm afraid.' As usual, she was standing very close, and her potent perfume almost made my eyes water. I wondered whether anyone could see in through the window. 'Anyway, I've some good news for you – which is just as well, I suppose. I was so impressed with your magnificent sewage works model that I've decided to get some money together for you to buy new Design and Technology resources. I know you're always struggling with what there is. How does £60 sound?'

'That's wonderful, Joyce, thanks. I'll be able to get all sorts of things that I've been wanting.'

'Excellent, I thought you'd be pleased, and you can order things right away – Eileen's doing an order tomorrow.' She flickered her long black eyelashes and smiled.

'OK, I'll put together a list today after school.' I glanced at my watch. 'Right, I'd better get into my classroom.'

'There's just one more thing, Andy. Next week, on Friday, we have a group of visitors coming from County Hall to look around the school.'

'Oh right, who is it?'

Joyce looked just a little agitated.

'It's a group of councillors, advisers, and education officials. They want to see a small rural school in action. Er, make sure you've got plenty for them to see won't you, love?'

I nearly made it to my classroom unspotted, but was intercepted by Val in the cloakrooms. She looked at me and took pity.

'Yes, I've heard about it, and no, don't worry, I won't go on about it.' I tried a weak smile. 'Much.'

The rest of the day was one of the worst in my first year at Cragthwaite. Every child had heard about the fire. Nearly every child asked me if my house had burnt down. Several wanted to know where I was going to live. Jack asked if it had been caused by a bomb. I decided against saying, 'No, it was a mouse.' Worst of all, the continuous humiliation put me into a bad mood and I snapped at a number of blameless children, which then added guilt to my shame. The thought of going home to Barbara's righteous indignation didn't help either.

Just about the only child who didn't mention the fire was Lucinda Bentham. This was strange indeed, because it was her father who was the part-time fireman. Lucinda was a striking child, a classic English rose. She was quiet, softly spoken and wonderfully polite: qualities that weren't greatly in abundance in Class 3, it has to be said. Lucinda was regarded by some of the other children as being a bit dainty, or posh. She certainly loved horses, and she was always immaculately turned out in floral dresses, but Lucinda was not posh. In fact, she possessed one of the dirtiest giggles I'd ever heard, and certainly wasn't averse to telling rude jokes, even to the boys. Lucinda's other quality was sensitivity and she seemed to recognise that I was having a hard time over the chimney fire on this particular day. So, despite her father being directly involved, she kept schtum, and rose even further in my estimation as a result.

I felt a huge relief at half past three when the children went home. I stayed in the classroom and avoided parents by keeping low and tidying out the cupboards. When everyone had gone I sat at my desk and breathed deeply. Then I remembered Joyce's money.

The next hour was a real pleasure, and a wonderful escape from the mania of the last two days. I sat with a catalogue and ordered materials and equipment – something I'd never done before. It was clear that Joyce wanted to impress these visitors next week, and also that she wanted me to put on a good display of Design and Technology work as my part of the deal. I needed something that would bring quick results, as we only had two weeks. Then I spotted the answer. While at teacher training college I'd spent an excellent science session working with needleless syringes and plastic tubing to experiment with hydraulics. The catalogue had a set of 100 syringes for only £8. I wrote down the reference number and began to think of what we might do with them.

A week later the new technology resources had arrived at school and I was busy showing the class how to join two syringes together with a length of plastic tubing. I pressed one of the plungers in gently and smiled to myself at the gasps of amazement from many of the children as they watched the other plunger move out slowly, as if by magic. At college, the syringes had been filled with water, but this seemed to me like a recipe for disaster and so we just settled for air – they worked almost as well.

'What are we going to do with these things then, Mr Seed?' asked Eve, as usual speaking while putting up her hand rather than after.

'Well, you hold one syringe and push it or pull it to operate the other one, which can move something – it's a kind of simple remote control system.'

'So what are we allowed to make?'

'Right, this is where I want you all to think really hard. You need to come up with an idea for a model where a syringe can move something. It can move something up and down, or in and out. If you're clever, you can use a simple hinge and the syringe will make something swing. When I was at college, one of the other students made a tipper truck using that idea.' There was lots of excited whispering and turning round amongst the class after this, and I gave them twenty minutes to come up with a sketch of a design.

They were inspired. Tracey brought me a delightful drawing of a whale, with the syringe used to make its water spout pop upwards. Fergus thought of a jack-in-the-box, and Rose produced a beautifully detailed plan to make a flower spring up out of a plant pot. Running true to form, Barney wanted to make a gory hand slither out of a coffin, and Wilf a 'cheeky pig' who would peep out from behind a sty. There were many other excellent ideas including a huge crocodile with opening jaws, a spacecraft lifting off, a man with a growing bump on the head and, from Anita, a clever joke machine that delivered a pop-up punchline. For once, there didn't seem to be a single child who was stumped for ideas: no one emerged with the dread line, 'I don't know what to do.' I was just becoming really excited that the class was going to produce a brilliant display of Design and Technology work for the forthcoming visitors when I realised that I hadn't seen everyone's design.

Lucinda was sitting at her table and drawing quietly. I had asked everyone to bring their work to me for checking before proceeding, but Lucinda hadn't appeared. It wasn't at all like her not to follow an instruction; I walked over to her. She was rubbing out part of a rather messy sketch of a lorry.

'Have you decided what to make then, Lucinda?' She looked a little uneasy.

'Er, not really. I thought about a lorry but I didn't want to copy the idea you mentioned about the tipper truck.'

'Usually you have lots of ideas – have you thought of another model you'd like to do?' She squirmed a little in her chair, and didn't look up.

'Er, well, I did think of one, but I . . . it's not very good. I think I should do something else.'

'Well, have you drawn a design for your first idea, Lucinda? I'd like to see it – perhaps I can give you a bit of help with it?'

'No, I don't think it's very good at all, Mr Seed.' She was acting very oddly. I reached down and picked up her piece of paper. Lucinda squirmed again. I turned it over. There, drawn in bold outline, labelled, well proportioned and eminently workable, was a picture of a fire engine.

My initial reaction was one of depression: quips and questions about the chimney fire, both in Applesett and at school, had only just died down, and this was bound to revive the topic, at least in the classroom. Lucinda was still staring down at her table; I looked closely at the picture. It was a superb drawing: she obviously knew a lot about fire engines and every detail was convincing. I could see, too, that she intended to use a syringe to raise the main rescue ladder upwards – it was a fine piece of work.

'Lucinda, this is excellent.' For the first time, she raised her eyes. 'Did you copy this from a book?'

'No, I just did it from memory.'

'Well, I think this will be much better than the lorry. Why don't you start making it now?' Her lips suggested the faintest hint of a half-smile. She moved her chair back, stood up and went over to the boxes of resources to look for parts. It was pointless, but I turned the drawing of the fire engine face down again.

Cragthwaite Primary School was looking magnificent: It had been spruced up with rampant vigour by Joyce and all of the staff for the important visitors from County Hall, and now that they were here, we all felt confident that they couldn't fail to be impressed. In the sagging old mobile classroom, Class 3 had worked wonders with their syringe models, and the display of work made me as proud as it did the children. Everyone had produced an admirable-looking model, and to my amazement, most of them worked, too. There was the fearsome crocodile, the grisly hand, a deliriously happy whale, a dazzling jack-in-the-box and a hilarious effort from Jack featuring a boy sticking his tongue out. The models were carefully arranged on a large hessian drape, everything neatly labelled and exhibited at different heights to create a really eye-catching display. The centrepiece of the show, however, was undoubtedly Lucinda's fire engine.

The design had been realised quite wonderfully: the bodywork was made from small boxes glued together and fitted on to a strong wooden chassis to which carefully painted plywood wheels had been attached. The syringe, cunningly hidden inside one of the boxes, was fixed to a splendid ladder made from dowelling and matchsticks. The whole thing was tidily finished off in bright red, with a blue light on top crafted from an egg box and sweet wrappers. I could hardly believe that Lucinda had made it unaided, especially as it worked so well: a quick squeeze of the remote syringe and the yellow ladder rose smoothly and resplendently to the vertical. The rest of the class were as full of admiration as I was.

It was late afternoon when Joyce and the councillors, advisers and officials finally reached our classroom. They all looked a little weary, probably in need of a cup of tea after a long day being shown countless exercise books and being introduced to endless staff and children.

'I hope you don't mind if we have a quick look around, Mr Seed,' said Joyce in a hearty voice from across the room. She was remarkably jolly. I noticed one of the entourage, a large dark-suited chap with a distinguished ashen beard move over to the Design and Technology display straight away. He was clearly very interested in the models and peered closely at the labels. He also seemed a little unsure as to whether he was allowed to actually touch them or not, so I moved over towards him.

'I'm particularly pleased with this work,' I said, suddenly feeling and sounding at least as jolly as Joyce.

'They're fascinating – I've been in quite a few schools, but I've never seen models like this before.'

'Would you like me to ask one of the children to show you how they work?'

'Yes please, I'd be most interested.' The choice was easy – I waggled a beckoning finger at Lucinda, and she rose from her chair and came over.

'Lucinda, would you give this gentleman a demonstration of how your model works, please?'

She mumbled a slightly embarrassed, 'Yes,' and reached for the syringe. One of the other visitors came across and asked me about reading books, but I stayed within earshot of Lucinda and the bearded chap, desperate to hear his reaction to the demonstration. Out of the corner of my eye I could see the yellow ladder slowly rising upwards as Lucinda operated the syringe, and I could also hear a response from the man.

'Fascinating, fascinating . . .' he was saying. 'And you made this yourself?' Lucinda nodded.

'So, it's pneumatic then, is it?' he asked.

'No, it's a fire engine.'

Back at Craven Bottoms, mice activity ceased for a couple of weeks, as though word had passed around that the owners of the house were rather more dangerous than the rodent population had at first surmised. We didn't see them in the kitchen or living room for some time but they gradually crept back into the ancient cupboards and the rooms attached to the garage. We tried a range of strategies to evict them over the rest of the year, without success, but setting fire to the house wasn't one of them.

Chapter Fifteen

Charlie

'I've never been in a house this big,' said Barbara, as we tramped up several flights of stairs in the great, rambling, Victorian pile. We were in Hauxton, the nearest sizable town to Swinnerdale, and it was the first evening meeting of our antenatal classes. Barbara had been keen to go to the NHS course at the health clinic in Ingleburn but a friend of ours from York had insisted that it was essential for us to book sessions run by the Natural Childbirth Centre. This meant not only paying but having to travel fifteen miles to a stranger's house.

At least the house was impressive. We entered a cavernous attic room and were told to make ourselves comfortable among a sea of giant floor cushions by our leader, Olivia. There were no chairs. Olivia herself was tall with red hair that reached to her waist. She wore a fiercely patterned cheesecloth dress and enough beads to start a market stall. We glanced around. There were three other smiley, bohemian-looking couples amongst the cushions, with each woman clearly pregnant.

They're *very* fondue and stripped pine, I thought as we lowered ourselves on to the carpet. Barbara lifted her eyebrows towards me as Olivia opened her hands.

'Well, it's delightful to have you all here this evening. Welcome to The Limes, and over the next eight weeks I'd like you to feel at home here as we all journey together towards parenthood. As you can see we only have four couples on this course and you're all first-timers so it'll be cosy and we'll all be able to nurture each other.'

Barbara wriggled among the cushions, muttering, 'Well it's not very cosy so far.'

Unaware of my wife's quiet disdain, Olivia carried on. 'Let's start with introductions then. Why don't we all tell everyone our names? Shall we start here?' She pointed to a tanned couple who hadn't stopped beaming since we arrived. They were called Hugo and Tamsin. Next to them were Rufus and Emilie, then Giles and Fleur.

'I'm Andy and this is Barbara,' I said. 'A and B.'

Barbara dug me in the ribs and whispered, 'Why did you say that bit?'

'I don't know, sorry.' Evidently I hadn't managed to switch off my helpful teaching mode.

'That's lovely!' said Olivia, not for the first time. 'What I'd like to do next is explain briefly the NCC's philosophy, which underpins these sessions. We believe that antenatal classes are more than practical instruction in preparing for a baby's birth. Our aim is to give you the opportunity to explore your feelings, to understand your personal needs and to enable you to make plans for a wonderful, natural experience that reflects your own cultural values.'

'Sounds really woolly to me,' murmured Barbara, who was still fiddling with a pile of pillows in her efforts to get comfortable. 'I just want to know how to stop it hurting.'

'Behave,' I mouthed.

Olivia then went on to outline what each of the sessions would cover. She talked for some time about bodily changes, labour, pain relief, exercising, massage, foot rubs and water births. 'We're very big on breastfeeding too,' she said. 'Any questions at this point?'

I was going to ask about chairs and maybe a cup of tea when Hugo enquired if we would be addressing the topic of music at the birth. Barbara glanced at me. 'I hope you've booked a string quartet,' she murmured.

A few minutes later Olivia had us all sitting crossed-legged in a circle. 'One of the most important aspects of this course is learning relaxation techniques. I like to start with these so that we can practise them through the weeks. Partners should join in, too.'

A minute later everyone was deep breathing with eyes closed. All except me: I seemed to be deep wheezing. I also had my eyes open to see if anyone had noticed it was me. They hadn't – they were all drifting off into some kind of meditative daze, although I suspected that my partner was pretending.

Next, Olivia announced that we needed to learn to let everything out.

'I think mine's already out,' said Barbara. 'It hasn't been in for weeks.'

Unfortunately that started me giggling. Barbara managed to keep a straight face until we had to practise sighing. Then we both lost it, especially as Hugo's sighs were so loud that it sounded as if he'd been wounded at the Somme. At least they masked our guffaws.

In the car on the way home we accused each other of not taking the class seriously.

'You started it, with that woolly comment,' I said.

'But it was woolly. Olivia was woolly, her house was woolly, Hugo and Tamsin were woolly. It's a moth's paradise.'

'Well it sure is different from Applesett . . . So don't you think it's worth coming here?'

'No, I do really. She did say plenty of sensible things and the deep breathing was good. I think we'll actually learn a lot when we get used to the Aga types.'

'And stop behaving like little kids . . .'

'Arty-farty or not, they're all really friendly and it does us good to get away from Swinnerdale once in a while.'

'OK, but when we get home I'm throwing the settee away. It's giant cushions or nothing from now on.'

'Why do I put up with you?' she said, squirming slightly as the baby gave her a kick.

As we pulled into the village I yawned, suddenly feeling very tired and glad that the following day was Friday.

Friday was always a special day at Cragthwaite School: winding down the afternoon with sharing assembly; Joyce encouraging everyone to go home early; and, of course, the promise of a weekend lie-in ahead. This Friday was extra special too – it was the last day of term, and the Easter break was ahead. In many ways it had been a remarkable day, and at the end of school I wanted to get away as quickly as possible to tell Barbara all about it, but first I decided to drive down the dale into Ingleburn because it was market day.

Ingleburn market was a treat. The town was always thick with cars, vans and Land Rovers as the dale's folk made the most of their opportunity to buy fish or pick up cheap tools and clothes. It always amazed me that a place could be so profoundly transformed in a single day: the town's broad, normally empty, wind-blasted marketplace became a throng of long-skirted ladies dragging trolleys around the flapping stalls and stopping to chat with farmers and neighbours. There were long tables of wobbly cut-price china, racks of slippers, Hoover bags and aged cassettes between spades, hardy perennials and countless cakes. The fresh vegetable and fish stalls were always thronging, but my own favourite was the Cheese Van with its sagging bow window full of giant slabs of creamy farmhouse Lancashire and free samples of the local Wherndale, pale and sweet.

My reason for visiting the market was to pick up a plastic baby bath – there was a stall that sold all kinds of household goods at implausible prices, and we were busy preparing the baby's room at Applesett. I soon found a bright yellow tub and headed back to the car, eagerly anticipating the journey home.

The road from Ingleburn turned a corner and dropped away into the mouth of the dale, revealing a glorious panorama. The great, shelved bulk of Spout Fell was resplendent, its crooked shoulders rising from the wooded valley floor hundreds of feet below. I loved this view. The ragged peat hags, deep-shadowed bare crags and heather-topped gritstone heights of the hill warned me that I was leaving behind the cosseted rolling farmland of safe fields and fat, comfortable farms, and entering a wilder, higher land – a place of rock and rushing water, of steep rawness and scouring winds, but also of glorious views, pure refreshing air and space. It was here that fence gave way to wall, oak to ash, clay to limestone and corn to sheep.

Spout Fell was truly a grand guardian of the dale: a giant gatepost, at times a frightening sentinel, but to me, always welcoming, and none more so than today as I headed to Applesett to see Barbara and to tell her the magnificent story of Charlie Capstick.

As I drove home I tried to think back: how had it all started? I think it began with school dinners. Cragthwaite School had its own kitchen, attached to the hall, but no dinners had been cooked in it for years. Instead, 'hot' dinners were brought in from Kettleby by van, in large metal containers every morning. These were supposedly kept warm by Mrs Harker in the kitchen, a woman we all referred to as Cook, despite her true role being simply as a disher-up of the lukewarm slops that passed for food. The meals were truly appalling, worse even than the jokes of old: typically grey fritters, heaps of chronically stewed cabbage and blocks of yellow stodge that passed for pudding. I ate it because it was free, but even then the price seemed high. For me the worst thing about the food was that it was cold – it had, after all, spent at least an hour touring upper Swinnerdale, calling in at a number of tiny schools, before being left out for several minutes in our kitchen to cool further, coagulate and shrivel, while it was served to its unfortunate victims.

Usually, I ate in the hall with the children, but if I was particularly busy I would carry my tray out to the mobile classroom so I could read plans or write notes while eating. In winter, this journey of a few yards outside would inevitably extract the last few degrees of warmth from the hoary potato and gravy, rendering it completely cold and solid. The final insult came one bitter February day when a howling gale blew all the peas off my plate.

Some children simply couldn't endure these school dinners, and this meant that an increasing number of them brought packed lunches from home to eat in the hall, sometimes even when they were entitled to free meals. One of these children was from my own class: Charlie Capstick.

Each week I sat on a different table in the hall in order to talk to children from the various classes, and on this particular day I was looking amongst the packed lunches. A chair was invitingly pulled out for me.

'Come an' sit 'ere, Mr Seed – you 'ant sat wi' us before.'

Picture the child: matted mousy hair, a small pale face, dull eyes and grimy clothes. This was Charlie. He lived alone with his mother in a council house on the edge of Cragthwaite and he was, I suppose, as close as anyone in the village came to being poor. I sat down and said hello to the younger ones around the table whom I didn't know too well. Charlie, always cheerful, introduced me to everyone.

'That's David and Gavin from Miss Torrington's, that's Mary and Lisa from Mrs Percival's, and I think you know the older ones from Class Four.'

As usual, I talked to the little ones first and asked them what they were having for lunch. Their plastic boxes were overflowing with bread rolls, scotch eggs, packets of crisps, biscuits, chocolate bars, fruit, yoghurts, and cake. It was always a mystery to me why parents gave them so much to eat – they never seemed to finish it all, especially the younger children. I glanced next to me at Charlie, and was just about to ask him what he was having when

I noticed that there was only a small margarine tub in front of him, with the top still on. He lifted one end of the lid and pulled out a small floppy jam sandwich, quickly closing the container. He turned and smiled at me, but I said nothing. Charlie produced no more food from his lunch box, and I wondered whether there was anything else in it. He simply leaned forward and folded his arms, waiting for permission from the roving Mrs Hyde to leave the table.

The following morning I went alone into the hall at morning break and looked through the pile of lunch boxes on the table in the corner. I found Charlie's grubby margarine tub. Inside there were just two jam sandwiches.

There was great excitement in assembly next morning. At the back of the hall standing high up on top of the vaulting horse were four enormous chocolate Easter eggs. The decorated egg competition had been another of Joyce's new ideas and now she was reminding the children that entries must be brought in on Friday, the last day of term, and that there was a chocolate egg prize for the best entry in each class.

'Now then, who can remind me of the rules?' said Joyce. A line of hands shot up from the Reception children at the front. Joyce raised her eyebrows at a diminutive pigtailed girl. 'Susie?'

'Does everyone get a prize?'

'No, Susie, just one person from each class. But what do you have to do to win the prize? Hands up.' This time she tried a boy with one hand in the air and the other down the back of his trousers. 'Do you know, Gareth?'

'Yes.'

'Well what do you have to do?'

He looked up for inspiration. 'I don't know.'

Gareth went back to scratching his bottom. Joyce persisted.

'Let's have one more try from Class One. Sally, do you know?' This chubby horde of freckles looked very confident.

'You have to decorate a egg. And it should be hardly boiled.'

'That's very good, Sally. You can decorate a boiled egg any way you like and it can be part of a big scene too if you prefer. Are there any questions?' There were. A girl from Class 4 asked who would be judging the competition.

'The teachers will decide the winners for each class.'

A boy from Class 2 asked if he should put his name on his entry.

'That's a good question,' said Joyce. 'Please do not put names on the eggs – we don't want to know who made each one until the winners are announced. Now, one more quick question from Class One: Eddie.'

'My rabbit died last night.'

The decorated egg competition was a new concept for Cragthwaite, and throughout the rest of the week all the talk amongst the children in my class was about the various spectacular creations they were making and about who they thought was going to win the coveted prize. I asked who was going to enter. Every hand gleefully went up in the air.

On Friday morning, before the start of school, there was mayhem in the hall. The children had been instructed to bring their eggs before nine o'clock, and put them on the table marked for each class. It quickly became apparent that a single table provided nowhere near enough space for the entries. The children were pouring into the hall with huge cardboard boxes, some lugged by parents, containing giant complex scenes. Like the other teachers, I had expected there to be a collection of mainly painted eggs in egg cups, but the children had thought very differently.

Val called me into the hall to help her put out some more tables. As I did this, I couldn't help noticing the incredible entries. There were snow scenes with egg skiers, moonscapes with egg UFOs, egg cowboys in sculptured deserts, and eggs disguised as every conceivable animal, most ensconced in junk-crafted habitats: penguins, owls, pigs, monkeys, pandas, mice and bloated cats were everywhere. I looked at Val who raised her eyebrows to the sky.

'I'll stay here to make sure no one touches them. Don't forget we've all got to be here at break to do the judging.' As usual, Val sounded less than thrilled by the prospect of yet another of Joyce's initiatives but I was really looking forward to it. As I opened the hall door to leave, another child was coming through. It was Charlie. He was smiling, as usual, and holding a small, tatty-looking egg, covered with scraps of red paper.

When playtime arrived, I grabbed a cup of tea and hurried back to the hall to join the other staff. Joyce told us to only look at our own class's entries to save time, and to choose a winner as quickly as possible. The two tables marked *Class 3* were crowded with an incredible array of work. I could scarcely believe the quality of it: nearly every entry was elaborate, witty, and decorated or assembled with extreme care, and there was hardly a misplaced blob of paint among them. This really was very strange: I had taught the class for over six months now, and they had never produced anything like this – it was astounding. I just didn't know where to start looking for a winner. I turned around and saw Emma shaking her head.

'There's no way my class has done these,' she said. 'This is all parents' work. What's the point of that?'

I looked back at Class 3's decorated eggs again. Emma was clearly right – now that she'd said it, it looked like scarcely any of them were actually made by children at all. A glance around the hall confirmed that this was true for every class. I thought back to the assembly. Joyce had never actually explained that the eggs should be the child's own work.

'What are we going to do then, Joyce?' I asked. 'Just pick the best anyway?'

'No, I don't think you should. Choose one that at least looks like the child has helped a bit. I think that's fairer.'

There were three or four entries that came into this category, but they still looked like the makers had been given lots of help. And then I saw Charlie's egg. He had made a small stand for it from the end of a toilet roll tube, but otherwise it was just a single egg – no background, no scenery, no visual wit. Charlie had decorated the egg with scraps of coloured paper, torn from magazines and glued on in a kind of feathered effect. He had used just reds, purples and a few blue pieces. It was simple and tatty, but I liked it. It was also the only egg that I could be sure had been made unaided. What was I going to do? There would probably be a furore if I chose this tiny dishevelled entry above the other card-board and foil masterpieces on show. I just couldn't do it. The bell rang for the end of break.

Back in the hall, at lunchtime, the noise was ferocious. The children were bouncing around with excitement, pointing at the entries and constantly asking me if I had chosen a winner yet. I said that I hadn't, which was true. Along with the children I looked back at my class's entries and wondered what to do. As if reading my mind, Charlie walked past.

'Hello, Mr Seed.' He wasn't as excited as the other children, just his usual serene self. He sat at the next table and put down his margarine box. As always, out came the floppy white jam sandwich.

This was impossible: after lunch I went to see Joyce to ask her what to do. She wasn't in her office.

'I saw her go out in her car,' called Eileen from across the corridor. Oh, wonderful.

I tried Val. 'I'm just choosing the best one,' she said. 'Can't be doing with daft parents making a stupid fuss over Easter eggs.' She was no help.

Busyness snatched away the afternoon's remaining time, and well before I was ready for it, the assembly was under way and the school hall was crammed with parents and eager children. I still hadn't chosen a Class 3 winner. The hymn and story passed in a blur, then I heard Joyce say that the competition winners would now be announced. She asked the teachers to go over to the eggs and hold up the winner from each class when called. I wandered over, the tremendous weight of responsibility almost crushing me. Emma held up a good entry, which gave some impression that a child had helped a little. Joyce asked whose it was and there were whoops of delight from a couple of adults at the back when a little girl stood up and wobbled forward to collect her egg. The same happened with Hilda's choice.

'Right, Class Three next, Mr Seed. Which one have you chosen?' I wavered for another second, then chickened out and held up a farmyard scene with two smiling pigs. It was Isaac's. He trod on several younger pupils in his rush to reach the front of the hall and grasp the chocolate reward for something I was sure his mother or older sisters must have created.

Val's class went through the same rigmarole and it seemed like it had all finally ended. I felt almost ashamed that I didn't have the courage to pick Charlie's egg. I looked for him. He was sitting very still, his grubby face impassive amongst a sea of disgusted and ignominious-looking children who also hadn't won. Joyce interrupted my depression.

'There's just one more thing. The standard of entries was so unbelievably high for this competition, that I decided to buy some more prizes for runners-up, including some little eggs for everyone.' From behind the piano she produced four more giant boxed Easter eggs and a colossal bag of mini chocolate eggs. There was a great cheer from the children. And from me.

When I held up Charlie's egg as the winner of the second prize, there was no whoop from the parents; instead there was a completely unexpected roar of delight from my class, with cries of, 'It's Charlie!'

He stood up as slowly as an old man, in a state of complete disbelief. When he walked out to the front towards Joyce, carefully sidestepping the other children, realisation had replaced shock, and he wore a grin that nearly split his face asunder. Joyce ruffled his matted hair. I surreptitiously lifted a finger to intercept the welling tears that were blurring my eyes. It was such a little, little thing, but I honestly believe that it was the greatest day of Charlie Capstick's life.

Chapter Sixteen

Cameron

The Easter holidays came, and March passed into April, witnessing a milky sun draw daffodils out of the green at Applesett. Barbara and I found ourselves sitting amongst a line of people in the high-ceilinged village hall, being welcomed on to the hall committee by Mrs Dent, from the shop. We weren't really sure how it had happened; Mrs Dent had simply assumed that we would want to join this esteemed company, and had detailed the meeting almost as if it were compulsory. We decided that it would be a good way to become involved in the life of the village and so, once the introductions were over, found ourselves sitting and listening to Major Asquith inside what seemed to be a former church.

'Well, there's only one item on the agenda, and that's fund-raising. I'd like to propose that we continue serving cream teas to visitors throughout spring and summer, as usual. Is everyone in agreement?' I looked along the line. John Weatherall, Mary Burton and Mrs Dent were all nodding in accord, along with everyone else.

'That's splendid,' continued the Major. 'So we just need to establish a rota – now what have I done with my pen?'

'How do the cream teas work then, exactly?' Good old Barbara:

she asked the question I was thinking about asking. Mrs Dent stepped in.

'Oh, it's very simple – we all take turns to serve tea and scones in here on Saturdays. We do our own baking and provide the tea and milk. You can do cakes too if you like. Everything else is here: crockery, cutlery, teapots and so on. You need to set a few tables and chairs out, and put up the price list and that's about it really. I think we charge 20p for tea and 30p for a scone with jam and cream. Mary'll fetch you some cream from t'farm, won't you love?' Mary nodded and Mrs Dent continued. 'We get a lot of walkers here when the weather picks up and there's no café, so it's a good way of making a few bob for the hall, like.'

It all sounded great fun, although it made me a little nervous when Barbara suggested that we go first, since the baby would make the work harder as the season went on.

We spent the next few days planning how we would set up our temporary tea shop. Barbara seemed extraordinarily excited by the prospect.

'I thought you were going to make some more Christmas decorations this week,' I said.

'I did quite a few last week. Anyway, I always wanted to run a café when I was young.'

'I didn't.'

She ignored me. 'I'll do plain scones, fruit scones and cheese scones, and that special lemon cake, and lots of buns. What do you think?'

'Well, don't overdo it, Barb. If the weather's bad there might not be anyone around.'

'Yes, but we can always eat the leftovers ourselves, and give some away. Now, which type of scones do you think will be most popular?'

'I can't see the point of doing three types – no one'll want cheese scones, surely. It's traditional to have plain or fruit scones for a cream tea, isn't it?'

'But it's no bother to do a batch of cheese scones as well, really.'

'Well I wouldn't bother to do many, Barb. Go mainly for the others.'

Easter Saturday was misty, but dry. At ten o'clock we were up at the village hall, setting out tables and chairs, arranging the frightful green tablecloths and piling up cups and plates. Barbara found half of an old stable door with CREAM TEAS painted in classic dribbly farmer's enamel. This was propped outside and the doors were opened. Inside were three large trays of scones and cakes, next to the bubbling urn. We hung around the door, not sure what to do with ourselves.

Our first patrons arrived at quarter to eleven. A fit-looking middle-aged couple smiled, exchanged 'good mornings' and wandered inside. They looked around for five seconds, whispered something to each other and wandered out again. Not a good start.

'Perhaps we should have a cuppa and a cake – it might look like we're customers,' I said. We did. Then a large family appeared. They looked at the little chalk-board menu and then sat down.

'Tea for two and four glasses of squash for starters, please,' said the man, with a jaunty north-eastern lilt. We sprang into action with a clatter of china. 'The scones look lovely – did you make them, pet?' said the woman, grappling with two toddlers.

'All home made,' beamed Barbara.

'Can I 'ave a cheese scone, mam?' said the oldest child, a girl of about twelve.

'I want one too,' added a smaller boy. After a little deliberation they went for three cheese scones and two slices of lemon cake. Barbara gave me a 'told you so' look and served them efficiently.

An elderly couple wandered in and ordered two cream teas with plain scones. I mentally marked myself a score. Two more walkers then appeared. I was now losing track of the orders, and hadn't asked for any money at all. The latest customers asked for cheese scones. The Geordie family asked if they could buy four more cheese scones to take away with them.

'They're gorgeous,' said one of the kids. Barbara thrust me a dark glance as I swept past with more teas. I could hear her muttering.

'There's only one cheese scone left now, and it's not even lunch time.'

By the end of the afternoon I had managed to take some money. We had made over 100 cups of tea and had to apologise for the lack of cheese scones about forty times. I did the washing-up.

'I don't know why I ever listen to you,' she said when we were back at home. 'Next time we'll just do what I think.'

'But it was only a few scones.' I immediately regretted saying it.

'WHAT DO YOU MEAN ONLY A FEW SCONES? I can barely walk with this great lump I'm carrying. I'm shattered; I spent all day yesterday baking the wrong things and now after messing around all day serving fussy ramblers you're telling me it doesn't matter?'

I decided that opening my mouth to say anything other than 'sorry' would be dangerous. I retreated sheepishly and made a mental note to be much more accommodating to expectant mothers in general and this one in particular.

The rest of the Easter break passed in a blur and I soon found myself back at school: it was now the summer term. On the first Monday in the classroom I was approached by Cameron Dent.

'Mr Seed, it's lambin' time on our farm and ma dad says it might be an interestin' time for you to bring the class over for a visit, just maybe for an hour or so.' This was a major speech for the retiring, fair-haired lad, one of those it had taken a while to get to know.

'That would be great, Cameron. Maybe we could go on Thursday – your farm's just outside the village, isn't it?'

'Aye, it's just ten minutes' walk from the school. Thursday'll be fine – I'll give the class a talk about sheep if yer like.'

'Yes please, Cameron. I'm sure I'd learn a lot too.'

I was amazed by this offer: Cameron was a popular boy in Class 3, not least among the girls, and was an excellent sports player, but very rarely did he contribute to discussion or answer questions – to hear him offer to give a talk was staggering. I went off to see Joyce to check if the farm visit was OK, wondering if he could really do it.

There was something warm and comforting about the Dents' farm. The straggle of stone buildings, the padding cats, heaps of muck in the yard next to bits of pipe, tractors, trailers, muck-spreaders, crates, railway sleepers, oil tanks and fertiliser bags. Behind the empty black silage clamp, feeding troughs, shovels, stakes and wire were spread in a scattered tangle. The rusty skeleton of an old horse-drawn raking machine was pressed against a roofless barn. Churned-up mud was everywhere.

As we turned out of the yard and towards the open fields, the children's attention was immediately arrested by the sound of worried bleatings drifting in on the breeze. Smooth-fleeced lambs hopped and scurried round the hillside while their mothers chewed nervously, their scraggy grey wool clarted with droppings. Several of the children ran over to get a better view of the newest tiny Swaledale lambs cowering by their mothers near the wall. Cameron disappeared to tell his father that we'd arrived.

The farm was situated on the hillside behind Cragthwaite, two or three hundred feet above the village. The view from here was spectacular, and the signs of spring's grip on the year were all around: thick tufts of new grass stippled with celandines; sharp green shoots of sweet cicely, racing with garlic mustard, meadowsweet and cranesbill. In the field a spindly lamb butted its head under its mother and suckled fiercely, its bottom in the air and tail twitching with glee. Cameron approached, accompanied by a broad old man wearing a battered jacket tied at the waist with string.

'Dad says we best go over to the big shed so everyone can sit down out of the wind. This is me grandad.' The old man grunted indecipherably.

The children enjoyed arranging themselves on the bales of straw inside the cold barn, and took a while to settle down. Cameron, his confidence clearly boosted by being on home turf, stood up and quickly took charge.

'Right, we have a few beasts here, but it's mainly sheep on this farm and I'm going to tell you about the jobs we have to do with 'em through the year.' Grandad grunted again.

'The new flock is established in October. Dad goes to the sheep sales and buys in his new sheep. Early November is tuppin' time. We 'ave one tup for every fifty sheep and we 'ave to gather the sheep every day for the tups to serve. We produce Swaledale sheep only. In the New Year we 'ave to feed the sheep with hay and silage, and then from March we give them sugar beet nuts as well.' The whole class was now still and listening intently; Cameron's authority was completely absorbing.

'A lot of farms in the dale cross Swardles – that's Swaledales – with Bluefaced Leicesters to produce mules. The Leicester gives lots of lambs and good milk. The Swardle is a rubbish mother but it's very hardy and can survive on the hills round 'ere. In spring we keep feeding 'em until the grass starts growing again like it is now. Me dad says that later someone from the class can feed 'em some nuts.' In an instant almost every child's hand shot up in the air.

'We'll decide that later,' I said. 'Let's hear the rest of Cameron's talk first.' Grandad stood up at this point and grunted again before saying, 'Sorry lad, I just need the nessy.' He ambled over to the door and disappeared. Cameron smiled and then continued.

'Right, lambing starts in mid-March and it's the busiest time of the year. Every sheep needs to be checked three times a day at least and giving birth is very stressful for them. We spend a lot of time looking after new lambs – they die really easily so it's important to get them on the tit right away.' At this point there was sniggering from the boys around Barney. None of the local children were laughing – it seemed to be just the incomers; Cameron ignored them and continued with his excellent talk.

'We have to keep the right lambs with the right mothers, especially the twins. Sometimes a sheep will pinch a lamb from another and sometimes the mother dies and we get orphans or pet lambs. There are two in a pen over there which me mum feeds with a baby's bottle.' Every head turned towards the far corner of the barn where two speckled grey faces peeked between a metal grate.

'Lambin' takes about a month and we 'ave to put the twins on the lower pasture where there's better grass.' The door crashed shut and Grandad reappeared, muttering, 'Aye, a lot of them gets the grass staggers wi' twins.' We looked at Cameron for a translation.

'He means that a lot of the mothers have an illness where they need calcium.'

'Aye – grass staggers, or shakes, or tremlins.' Grandad was now coming to life. 'And thes foot rot – stinks does that, byyyy.'

Cameron jumped in quickly before Grandad took over. 'In May we push the sheep and single lambs on to the higher fells. In summer we worm them every four weeks and in June we do the clippin' or shearing. The hogs are clipped first – they're last year's lambs. We get contractors in to do it now, and the wool is wrapped in big sheets and Dad says we don't get much money for it. We also count the flock at this time and every sheep and lamb is re-marked using a wooden stick. Our mark is a red stripe on the shoulder. In August the sheep are dipped to stop sheep scab and stuff like maggots which eat into the skin.' There was a collective 'Eeeuuurrrghhh!' from the class that made Grandad smile. Cameron took the chance to glance at his notes, which he had hardly used.

'In September the lambs are taken away from their mothers and put on better ground.'

Grandad came to life again at this point. 'Aye, best be fogged up f'the job.' Cameron decided to ignore him and press on.

'The lambs and mothers make an awful noise for three or four days then – I can hardly sleep. We keep them apart as far as possible cos they sometimes escape and try to get back together. Then it's time to prepare for the autumn sales again – the gimmers are sold first, at Kettleby, and then fat lambs and yows. Right, that's it.' There was a tumult of applause from the children for Cameron, and I felt strangely proud – it had been a quite overwhelmingly good talk.

'OK, Class Three, you can ask questions now,' I said. Barney sprang up immediately.

'My dad says sheep are daft. What daft things do your sheep do?' Cameron was unperturbed.

'Well, they are daft a lot of the time. They're always gettin' their heads stuck in wire and jumping on walls or trying to jump over the river. At lambing times sometimes the yows will butt you, and I've even seen them chase dogs.' Grandad stood up at this point, clearly determined to make a contribution.

'The main trouble wi' sheep is that thes always tryin' to die. It's an endless battle o' wits on a farm – they try to die and the farmer tries to keep 'em alive. I should know, I've spent sixty years fighting the beggars.' At the back of the bales, Barney starting laughing again and dug Wilf in the ribs while pretending to hold a machine gun. I pulled a disapproving face at him and tried to encourage Grandad.

'Er, have things changed much with sheep farming over the last sixty years then?'

'Well, we never had quad bikes for rounding up, like this youth 'as today. When I started there were three shepherds working here. Mind, the dogs were better then – and the men were better with the dogs.' For a moment I feared that I had unleashed him on a nostalgic journey that would never end, but then he paused and looked up. 'But, apart from the quads, it's not really changed – t'owd Swardle yows are the same as in ma day.' I saw Cameron breathe a sigh of relief.

'Right, time for one last quick question,' I said. This time no hands went up. Then Barney blurted out, 'What's the nessy?' He looked at Grandad, but Cameron answered.

'It's short for the necessary – you can work that one out for yourselves.'

Back outside, the sky was darkening and a low curtain of fuzzy cloud topped the higher fells and seemed to envelop the whole dale with the threat of rain. Cameron shouted over to me through the cold wind. 'I've got a bag of sugar beet nuts here, Mr Seed, for someone to feed the sheep before we go back.' Again, almost every hand in the class went up. Before I could choose, Cameron made a suggestion.

'Mr Seed, I think Barney should have a go first.' He seemed very certain, so I nodded, despite being a little bemused. Barney took the bag with his usual swagger and headed over towards the gate.

'What do I do then, Cam?'

'Just go into the field and rattle the bag, then tip out a long line of the nuts.'

Barney gave a thumbs-up then opened the gate and casually strutted into the large field. The class leant against the wall to watch. He went about fifty yards then rattled the thick plastic bag hard. Within seconds an immense gang of ragged bleating sheep came charging up the hill towards him. Others hurtled in from the sides with tremendous speed and noise, with Barney now looking decidedly panicky. It was clear that he wanted to drop the bag and escape. The sheep now completely surrounded him, twenty or thirty thick on every side, and he began to hop up and down and wail for help. They were tugging at the bag and making it impossible for him to distribute the food. The class was in hysterics. Cameron quickly climbed the gate and ran over to rescue the beleaguered boy who now seemed to be drowning in a sea of grubby wool. Within seconds the bag was emptied, and both boys were back behind the gate, one looking decidedly cooler than the other. I did my best to look concerned for poor Barney.

The farm visit ended with a special treat. Cameron's mother invited everyone into her cavernous farmhouse kitchen for a drink of warm, creamy milk, fresh from the cow.

'Would you prefer a cup of tea, Mr Seed?' she asked. I couldn't have wished for anything else. It had been a truly wonderful day. Cameron's mother brought the tea, along with a small plate. 'Would you like a scone, too? I've got cheese and plain.' I didn't blame her for giving me a funny look as I laughed at the question.

Chapter Seventeen

Martha

It seemed to me that nothing could surpass the beauty of the dale in May, but then June arrived. After a showery interlude of a few days, the first weekend of the month was clear and fine, and I was aching to go for a walk. Now that summer was upon us, my classroom felt almost claustrophobic and the release of a good stride on the hills gave a particular joy. Barbara, now nearly eight months pregnant, decided that she probably wouldn't get too far.

'I'll only hold you up, Andy. Go on, you go on your own – you'll be able to stretch your legs. It'll do you good.'

'But won't a bit of fresh air do you good, too? And, er, you'll be by yourself again.' I was desperately trying to detect if I was supposed to read the opposite meaning into her words. In the last few months the need for this had become increasingly evident.

'I'll do a little gardening at the front, then I can sit down when I need to. Or I might pop round and see Iris.'

It seemed safe but I decided to minimise the risk anyway. 'OK then – I'll go on my favourite short walk behind the village and around to the waterfall, then I won't be gone long.'

A few minutes later I was up the Buttergill Road and through the first stile, which was no more than a cleft in the heavy stone wall. Butterflies swerved among the feast of purple cranesbill in the verges and the air was busy with the flicker of dancing flies. A curlew played behind, sailing past on the wind with its great bowed bill, calling with that eerie liquid warble, which for me, along with the running water of the becks, the call of the rising lark and the bleat of new lambs, was among the most evocative music of the Dales.

I was only a few minutes from the village, but I was in a different world. Here, on the hillside, the breeze was gentle and warm – so different from the winter blast I'd often met in the same spot earlier in the year. Higher up the view opened further, revealing a mist hanging over the distant valleys, marking out the folds of land in a silver relief. I looked back at Applesett. The village was enclosed by thick trees, resting quietly on the flat sloping ridge between Hubberdale and Buttergill, its doll's-house cottages straggling along the edge of the long green. I could make out the maypole, the sturdy chapel topped with slate and the white-fronted pub near the stone cross. I still couldn't believe that we lived there. I thought of Barbara on her own and began to descend.

Back at school on Monday, there was great excitement in the classroom when Eve pointed out that it was exactly two weeks until we set off on the residential trip to Oswalfarne in Northumberland. Along with Val, who was going to lead the week-long visit, I had been making preparations for some time, but had tried to keep everything as low-key as possible for fear of upsetting Martha. The girl's mother, Mrs Micklegate, had not relented in her determined stand that she should not have to pay for any school activity, and that Martha should therefore not be allowed to go on the trip. To me, and to all of Martha's friends, it was a cruel tragedy that threatened to spoil what should have been the highlight of the school year. Martha herself, with admirable stoicism, seemed to have accepted the situation, but I was still desperate to find a way for her to go. Barbara and I had talked for many hours about possible solutions, and deeply regretted that with the baby on the way, we could not afford to pay for her ourselves. At lunchtime, I went to see Joyce.

'Even if you had the money, Andy, Mrs Micklegate wouldn't accept it I'm sure. I've already offered her the suggestion that the school would subsidise half of the cost, but she didn't even listen to me. The trouble is, she just won't sign the permission form whatever happens now – with her it's just a matter of principle.'

'Yes, but it's Martha who's paying for those wonderful principles.' Part of me was seething that someone could deprive a child in this way. 'All her friends are going and now they're excitedly talking about it all the time. It's just not fair, Joyce.'

'You're right, Andy, but I'm afraid there's nothing we can do about it.'

'And what are we going to do with Martha that week?'

'Oh, don't worry about that – I have a plan for her. You'll be busy enough with all your preparations for the trip right now, and so will Val. I'm going to take her class while you're both away, and I have a few special things lined up for Martha. In fact, when the bell goes, can you please send her to see me and I'll explain to her what's going to happen.'

Good old Joyce. I left her office feeling a lot better about the situation, but deep down I still longed that there would somehow be a last-minute reprieve and that Martha would make it to Oswalfarne. I had no idea how it would happen, and the thought of once more appealing to Mrs Micklegate was certainly too grim a prospect – the woman frightened me to death. Perhaps she would relent and bring in the permission letter at the last minute. All I could do was hope, and pray.

The next two weeks in school were almost entirely made up of planning and preparing for the trip. My class, with fevered enthusiasm, painted large watercolour maps of Oswalfarne Island, showing all the important landmarks, the most significant of which was considered to be the small hotel where we would stay. We talked about the island's tumultuous history: the early Celtic monks who came over from Ireland, the building of a great abbey and its destruction by piratical Vikings, and the legendary miracles performed by the great St Oswald, the place's iconic hermit. We looked at slides and pictures of the abbey ruins, castle, limekilns and harbour then discussed the wonders of the notorious causeway that flooded at high tide, the towering sand dunes and the wave-battered cliffs.

The children were particularly interested in the area's wildlife: the seabirds, rock-pool creatures and, most of all, the seals that I promised they would see. I had hoped to visit the island with Barbara at Easter but babies and new houses had conspired to keep us in the dale, and consequently nearly all the information I passed on to the class was gleaned from books. I did think it was a good idea, however, that the children should be able to ask questions to someone who had been there before and experienced the lodgings, and so I arranged for Val to talk to the class for half an hour one afternoon. Val did scare my class considerably with her stocky frame, stern appearance and abrupt manner, and when she stood in front of them, they all seem to melt with dread.

'Right,' she bellowed. 'Oswalfarne. Who has a question, then?'

There was silence, accompanied by almost perfect stillness. She folded her arms and waited. I'd hoped that she would give a brief talk first, but Val liked to do things her own way.

'Well, I might as well return to my class, and let Mrs Berry get back to her office work,' she grumbled. 'Mr Seed told me you'd have loads of questions.' There was another wait.

'Come on, Class Three,' I said. 'Miss Croker doesn't bite, you know.' They didn't believe me. After another ten seconds of embarrassing silence, Hugh slowly raised an arm. Val raised an eyebrow at him. He cleared his throat.

'Er, what . . . er, what's the food like in the hotel?'

Val replied that it was very good and went on to describe some of the meals that Mrs Snook, the landlady, traditionally provided for visiting school parties. Now that Hugh had made the breakthrough, the questions came thick and fast, and Val seemed to enjoy answering them. With about ten minutes to go, I asked her if there was anything else that she felt the children needed to know about the island before the trip.

'Oh yes, there is one thing that you all need to know about – the hairy caterpillars.' The children looked at her, unsure whether she was serious or not.

'When we go out walking among the sand dunes, which we'll do a lot, you'll be passing through a lot of tall spiky plants called marram grass. The grass itself isn't too bad, although it can give you a bit of a prick, but you have to beware of the hairy caterpillars that live on it. They're about as long as your thumb, and dark brown with thick, furry bodies. In fact, they look very cute and harmless, but six years ago I found out that they're not as innocent as they seem.' The class ogled her, rapt. 'It was another trip from this school and there were two girls who were having their lunch on top of one of the dunes. They found several of these hairy caterpillars and let them crawl on to their hands and arms. Well, about an hour after lunch, when we were all walking along the beach, these two began to complain that they felt dizzy. We sat them down and they went a right funny colour and started to groan. In the end I had to take them back to the hotel and Mrs Snook drove them to the doctor's on the mainland. He looked at them and asked if they'd been touching caterpillars on the island. It turns out that they had a kind of sleeping sickness.'

I looked at my class once more – several of them were frozen with horror. 'We found out that the two girls had actually been stroking the caterpillars and the doctor said that each time they did this, tiny amounts of poison were injected into their skin from the long hairs: it had built up and made them very queasy.'

Suddenly Barney, with quaking solemnity, croaked from the back of the room, 'Did they survive?' Val, playing the saga with increasing relish, kept a straight face and delayed a moment.

'Of course they survived, you crackpot. They were fine. The doctor gave them a bit of medicine and by tea time they were running around with the others.' Barney just stared at her, seemingly convinced that not only had they perished but that the whole thing was a conspiracy. Val continued.

'So what lesson can we learn from what happened to those two girls, then?'

Terry raised his hand. 'Keep yer coat and gloves on all day, Miss?' Val looked at me in disbelief.

'I think the lesson is, don't touch the hairy caterpillars, Terry,' I said.

'Byyy – there's no danger o' that,' he replied. Everyone laughed, including Martha.

I visited Val in her classroom after school, to finalise the plans for the week away.

'Is that story true, Val?'

'You're not sure, are you? Well, yes, it did happen all right – best to avoid a recurrence, eh?'

'Well, they certainly won't touch any caterpillars now – they'll probably all have nightmares, though.'

'Oh don't be soft – anyway, let's see what you've planned for the trip.' I passed her my notes and went over the details of each day. She grunted a few times, which I optimistically took to be a sign of approval.

'They're OK, but we need a lot more walks, and physical games every evening.'

'But I have planned quite a lot of walking,' I protested.

'Look, Andy, the plan is simple: we wear them out during the day as much as possible.'

'Why?'

'Why? So the buggers get more than half an hour's sleep, that's why.'

'Oh.'

That evening I revised the itinerary and added further expeditions, and games of beach rounders, football and cricket each day, in addition to the numerous other activities like the worksheets, treasure hunt, museum visits, boat trip and talent show. It was certainly a full programme now. I showed it to Barbara.

'It sounds like fun, but you'll be dead on your feet,' she said.

'And what about you, and the baby?' I said, smoothing my hand over her bloated abdomen. I wondered about the strain that such a weight must be putting on her body. 'Are you sure you're all right about me going away with only a month to go?'

'I'll be fine – your mum's coming over for a couple of days and you're only three hours from here as long as Mrs Snook can drive you to the station if it all starts to happen.'

'Mum said she'd stay as long as you needed her, anyway.'

'And Mary and Iris will be popping in, so don't worry.' Her face beamed with that wonderful lustrous skin which seems to attend childbearing.

We talked again about what it would be like to have our own little baby and tried to imagine how it would change our lives. Our anticipation had been mounting as we'd attended antenatal classes in Hauxton and had enjoyed learning together about what to expect with the arrival of a new infant. Being new to everything, it seemed such a big adventure.

Barbara struggled off the settee to go to bed, and saw my Oswalfarne notes lying on the floor.

'What about Martha? I don't suppose there's any good news?' I shook my head. There was less than a week to go.

The next few days passed in a blur of manic preparation and anticipation in the class. Each morning I hoped to see Mrs Micklegate approach the classroom, but she never came. Martha, however, was in remarkably good spirits. All of her classmates, and the girls in particular, had rallied round her quite magnificently during this period, and I also noticed that Martha had been hugely buoyed by going to see Joyce in her office earlier in the month. I felt like asking her what had passed at that meeting, but instinctively felt that it was somehow special and private.

It was half past four in the morning, but my alarm was insistent. It was the day of the trip and I had to rise early, along with everyone else who was going, to make sure that we set off from Swinnerdale in time to beat the tide on the Northumberland coast and pass safely over to the island across the treacherous causeway. I kissed Barbara quietly on the cheek and crept out of the house, marvelling at the village's dawn serenity. At school, a few drowsy children were already congregating outside the front doors, with apprehensive parents lugging suitcases and giant lunch boxes. Fergus struggled through the gate with a bag the size and shape of a dead cow. His hair was frizzed up riotously and he was grinning with glee. The pitch of conversation rose steadily as more travellers arrived, and a small mound of luggage began to materialise along the path.

With vain hope I still watched for Martha and her mother, but I knew, like everyone else, that they would not appear.

After twenty minutes of checks and ticklists and counting, a jubilant cheer rent the June sky as a long white coach appeared at the end of the drive. Following an agonising wait for it to reverse, there were hugs and warnings from the parents and a wild scrap between Wilf, Malcolm and Barney to secure the back seat. Eve and Carol demanded that I reserve it for the girls on the return journey. I agreed. The colossal stack of suitcases was then packed into the coach by the driver and several of the parents, none of whom could quite believe the size and weight of Fergus's monster bag.

'What's he got in here – his family?' said one. It just about went in. Val climbed on board, along with Mr Towler, one of the school governors, who was our additional adult helper. I heard the commotion quickly subside as Val announced her usual threats, and then I too stepped on to the bus, carrying out a final head count before looking outside of the door to say goodbye to the gathered parents. The driver slipped into first gear and we rumbled slowly up the drive, with frantic waving all around. It was half past seven and we were off. As we passed the school gate, a spontaneous screech erupted from some of the girls near the front of the coach. There was Martha, waving us goodbye and smiling. Joyce stood behind her, with one arm round Martha's waist, and the other wiping away a tear.

Chapter Eighteen

Clive

'There you go.' The coach driver turned his head back to me and thrust out his arm towards the sea. From our elevated position on the long coast road, I could just make out a thin spike of sand jutting away from the coast. A tight cluster of low buildings was visible at one end of the island, and the faint green of ragged dunes.

'Look to the right, everyone!' I shouted through the grind of the engine and the faint hum of singing from the rear of the coach. 'That's Oswalfarne.' A cheer went up, and the children leaned over for a better view.

After three and a half hours of steady northward trundling, the bus finally turned off the coast road, and swayed down the narrow track to the causeway that crossed the stretching sand and mudflats, now bared in the tide's absence. I was delighted that right away my class began to recognise landmarks that we'd talked about in class.

'There's the wooden posts.'

'Look – the refuge box.'

'Is there anyone in it?'

'Don't be daft.'

'What's that big castle place?'

'That's the castle.'

'Oh.'

'Hey, I can see the beach.'

'Can we go on it now?'

'Where's the sea?'

'The tide's out, you nutter.'

'What if it comes back while we're on this road?'

'Then we're doomed.'

The excitement was immense, and this babble continued as we edged around the island's shaggy dunes, finally reaching a crescendo as we entered the little village and pulled up. With a hiss from the doors and another cheer, everyone finally left the coach and lined up outside the Oswalfarne Hotel. It was a friendly faced, respectable red-brick building at one end of the island's only community, and the children were desperate to get inside and find their rooms. With a little effort I managed to calm them down and remind everyone that our first plan was to drop off the luggage and then head out for a walk around the island right away. Mrs Snook, the hotel owner, came out to greet us and quickly organised a place to stow our pile of bags. The coach driver then appeared with a pile of jumpers, hats, sandwich boxes and games that had been left on the bus. Most of them belonged to Fergus. I ticked him off with a smile while Val told everyone to find a partner for the walk.

'Er, there's just one more jumper here.' It was the driver again. 'It's a big one.'

I held it up. 'Right, who came with a dark blue sweatshirt?'

'Isn't that yours, Mr Seed?' said Eve. My blush was profound.

Val laughed as much as the children and then waved her arms for quiet.

'Right, you lot, listen to me and listen carefully. We've all had a long journey and now we're all going on a long walk. I just want to remind you about the rules. Stay together, no running, and no going off ahead or anywhere out of the teachers' sight without permission. Is that understood?' There was a long choral acknowledgement, and we set off towards the castle.

A muscular salt-breeze welcomed us on to the narrow path which wound out of the village and over to the diminutive harbour. A squadron of agile herring gulls swooped down to assess our presence, obviously aware that long lines of children usually meant sandwiches and other delights. We needed to make at least a mile or so before lunch, however, and the birds rapidly lost interest. The children were disappointed, but were soon diverted by our arrival at the harbour's small pebble beach. Within seconds, the neat line of pairs of children disintegrated as Barney and Wilf spontaneously charged on to the shore. I looked at Val, half expecting a roar of disapproval, but none came: she seemed much more relaxed now that we were out of school.

'Just remember, don't go anywhere near the water,' I called, recalling that this was my own class now running wild. The children quickly split into two factions: one group immediately began scouring for interesting pebbles or shells (I had earlier announced a prize for the best beach find), while the other grabbed clutches of small stones and started skimming them into the low waves lapping the shoreline. It was wonderful to see my class having this kind of freedom to enjoy themselves in a different and adventurous environment. I also took a moment to admire the view.

The harbour itself was just a tiny rounded bay, guarded by a small rocky headland from which a short but robust stone and concrete pier projected. There were two weary-looking fishing cobles tied to its sides, and the water was full of bobbing rowing boats and tatty dinghies. At the foot of the pier was a huddle of dilapidated sheds amidst heaps of lobster pots, coils of rope and rusty trailers. Apart from the children, there was not a soul to be seen. The other side of the bay stretched off towards square black rocks and the lofty, puckered crag that bore the island's fierce little castle. I was just about to remark to John Towler what a tremendous view it was when I noticed Val striding down the beach towards the group of skimmers. I then saw a stone fly from a hand and land with a sharp wooden crack in one of the rowing boats nearby.

'Oi! Clive Lambert – come here!' Val had seen it too.

Clive Lambert. Poor old Clive. If I hadn't seen who had thrown the stone I could have guessed. Trouble and Clive Lambert were just magnetically attracted to each other. His talent for exploring the boundaries of the permissible was legendary in Cragthwaite, both in the village and at home, and now it was clear that the tall pasty-cheeked boy was anxious to allow this peaceful North Sea island to benefit from the full range of his capabilities. He had actually been admirably quiet on the bus, mainly on account of his position in the seat in front of Val, perhaps, but it was worthy of credit, and I did try to praise him whenever he managed to behave well or even show restraint. Alas, however hard he tried,

Clive remained a stranger to self-control. This was demonstrated after lunch.

We had crossed an area of sand dunes where hundreds of grey rabbits scattered before us as we battled through the marram grass and dusty sand. The children found this very hard going and there were soon cries for a rest. Val spotted an area of tall mounds with a good view and we sat down. Most of the children, however, rather than resting, decided to try diving down the soft sides of the steep dunes, hurling themselves off overhanging tufts of grass and rolling down the cliffs of fine white sand. It seemed harmless enough and was obviously great fun, so Val and I let them carry on, keeping a wary eye all the same. Clive, along with Barney and Anita, was in his element here, demanding complete attention before launching himself off the highest tufts with flailing limbs and blood-curdling yells.

'At least we can see him,' said Val.

After a few minutes, the physical cost of climbing the crumbling dunes took its toll and all of the intrepid jumpers lay down and searched for drinks. I decided to wander round and count the children, just to be sure everyone was present. Halfway through, I heard a small wail and saw a girl running towards me. It was Tracey.

'Quick, Mr Seed, Sylvia found a hairy caterpillar and Clive came over and flicked it at her and it landed on Carol and Clive said it touched her and that she's probly gonna die.'

I walked over, assured Carol that she would live and reluctantly ordered Clive to stay with the teachers on the long walk back to the village. He muttered all the way.

* * *

It was good to be back inside the warmth and civilisation of the hotel, especially with the smell of home-cooked food drifting into the entrance from the kitchen. The children were exhausted after the long trek around the island, but they quickly revived when their rooms were allocated and they were able to lay claim to a bed and unpack their bags. Val had told them all to have a wash and get changed before the evening meal, and suggested that a time of quiet rest would be in order too. There was anything but quiet, however. The children were lodged in eight small rooms, scattered along corridors and on two different floors, and were desperate to see each other's accommodation.

I was alerted to what was going on by the sound of pounding footsteps and giggling outside my door. There were bodies rushing round everywhere, although they all scattered in an instant as I stepped out. I told Val what was going on then went round each of the boys' rooms telling them to stay inside, while Val did the same with the girls. I then went back to my room and left the door open a few inches. There followed a period of doors creaking open and lookouts whispering, but no actual footsteps until there was a sudden heavy burst of running followed by a resounding metallic boom. Someone had found the dinner gong.

After the evening meal and a game of cricket in the hotel garden, Val gave a stern lecture about staying in rooms and threatened personal confrontation if the gong was unofficially rung once more. No one owned up to striking it, of course, but several children gave furtive glances towards Clive when the question was asked.

When bedtime arrived, Val and I girded ourselves for a long night of patrolling. We weren't disappointed. There was a huge racket coming from one of the boys' rooms, so I opened the door without warning. Fergus, in striped pygamas, was bounding across the carpet on a pogo stick, while the others were hitting rugby balls with a cricket bat. Fergus's giant bag lay open across his bed. The room fell silent but I was so astonished that I didn't say anything for a moment. The delay broke the tension and the boys collapsed into spasms of laughter before I found myself joining in. I removed the sports equipment and ordered them into bed, shaking my head in disbelief.

After subsequent sessions of pillow fights, and more peeping out of doors, there began a period of wailing among the girls, brought on by tales that someone had seen the small coat of armour by the top of the stairs move. Eve, naturally, was involved and the rapidly spread rumours that the hotel was haunted brought back memories of Preston Blaise Hall. I was greatly relieved that Val was there to deal with it. She told them that ghosts were banned and that she would personally sit by 'the statue' as the children called the suit of armour, and give it a whack if it moved.

Lights out had been at ten and by the time the haunting episode had finished it was eleven thirty. Despite continuous whispering and sniggering from behind every bedroom door, it seemed that things were finally settling down: at least the children seemed to be staying in their beds now. Val suggested that we should now take it in turns to walk the beat along the corridors, so at least one of us could get a rest. Mr Towler agreed to stay on the second-floor landing while I surveyed the first floor, where the majority of children were sleeping. After about twenty minutes of relative calm I was beginning to think that tiredness was overcoming excitement with the majority of Class 3. Then, with a slow whine, a door opened and Hugh appeared. He was wearing silk pyjamas.

'Er, sorry to disturb you, Mr Seed, but I thought you ought to know something.'

'What's up, Hugh? Are you feeling all right?'

'Oh yes, I'm fine, but the boys in the room next door have been knocking on the wall and we can't get to sleep.'

'OK, Hugh, thanks for telling me – you go back to bed and I'll sort them out.'

Jack, Terry, Barney and Malcolm were in the room next door to Hugh's. I went straight in without knocking. There was an immediate explosion of movement in the semi-darkness as at least three of the boys dived into their beds and under the covers. After a brief interrogation, Barney owned up to what was happening.

'It's Clive in the room next door, Mr Seed. He's been knocking on our room and trying to get us to come to his midnight feast. I – we were just passing on the message.'

'Is he really having a midnight feast?'

'Yeh, you should see how much choccy and stuff he's got – there's a whole drawerful in there.'

'Are you exaggerating, Barney?'

'No, honest, Mr Seed – you ask Jack, he was in their room earlier and saw it, didn't you, Jack?'

'Aye, I could 'ardly believe ma eyes.'

It was at this point I remembered that I had done a very foolish thing. A week earlier, back in the classroom at Cragthwaite, someone had asked me if they were allowed to have a midnight feast. For a completely inexplicable reason I had said yes, imagining that on the last night we would perhaps let them stay up for an extra twenty minutes for an apple and some crisps. I told Jack, Barney and the others to go to sleep, and went to visit the room next door.

Here, there was not even the pretence of slumber. Clive, Wilf, George and Cameron were sitting on their beds with the light on, surrounded by a sea of sweet wrappers. They didn't say a word. I looked at Clive. Involuntarily he looked at the chest of drawers next to his bed. The bottom drawer was open. It was full of chocolate. After ordering the queasy-looking quartet to have drinks of water and brush their teeth, I decided to remove the whole drawer, heavy as it was, and take it to show Val. I switched the light off and told them I would deal with this in the morning, hoping that the warning would be sufficient incentive for sleep.

Val and I were flabbergasted at the extent of what was in Clive's drawer: there was every kind of bar, slabs of chocolate, toffees, chews, packets of gums, mints and more: it looked like half the contents of a sweet shop. Neither of us wanted to contemplate how he'd obtained it.

'Well, we've got a few extra prizes for the treasure hunt and talent show,' said Val.

I lay on my bed at 2 a.m., after the night's commotions had finally died down, and pondered how a job could be so utterly exhausting yet such fun at the same time. I was heavy-eyed but unable to sleep, the day's escapades passing through my head like a flickering cine film, with Oswalfarne's mystical sands as its backdrop. We had only been here for a day but so much had happened.

Perhaps tomorrow would be more restful? But then my drowsy mind wasn't accounting for Clive.

The morning saw us heading back across the dunes to the north shore of the island where there was a magnificent beach, to carry out some science work on habitats, and also to play rounders. The children were groggy after their lack of sleep, and most wandered along the footpaths in a quiet daze. The sight of the sea at the north shore soon revived them, however, and they carried out the planned beach and rock pool surveys enthusiastically. After a windy game of rounders, we gathered everyone together at one end of the beach for lunch. The children complained vociferously about the hotel's sandwiches, and many of these ended up with the wheeling gulls, which had moved in once more. Clive, who had been remarkably quiet, then appeared.

'I've finished ma lunch, Mr Seed. Can I go for a paddle?'

'I'm sorry, Clive,' I replied. 'You know the rules that we set at the start of the trip – no one is allowed in the sea at all. The currents are very dangerous here and the tide comes in quickly. Anyway, you'll only get yourself all wet and we've a lot more walking to do today.' He gave a quiet, 'Aww,' but turned away, perhaps recalling the night before.

Soon enough, all the children had finished lunch and were starting to explore the beach in the half hour of free time that they'd been given by Val. Charlie soon noticed that there were great piles of driftwood at this end of the shore, along with all sorts of flotsam and jetsam from passing boats, and soon most of the children were busy collecting the most interesting finds. Rose came over and asked if they could make beach sculptures out of this treasure. Val and I agreed it was an excellent idea, and I suggested that we come back later in the week when we would have more time. We were just discussing this when Mr Towler cleared his throat and pointed towards the sea. There was Clive, with bare feet and trousers rolled up, edging into the water: he just couldn't resist. Val stood up and boomed a warning. He gave a small incoming wave a desultory kick and then sheepishly went over to join the driftwood gatherers.

After a blissfully quiet ten minutes, with a jack-in-the-box sun giving respite from the briny breeze, there were whooping shouts from a group of boys to our right. Somehow, somewhere, they had found a door. Clive and Wilf were bearing it across the rocks in triumph. They dumped it in front of us, like a kill from a lion hunt.

'Look – we found a door.'

'That's very nice, boys,' said Val. 'What are you going to do with it?' There was a muddled silence; they hadn't really thought of that. We all looked at the door. It was an ordinary house door with a sturdy wooden frame, much battered and stripped of paint by the ocean. Then suddenly, Clive jumped in the air.

'Ah know! We can make a dam.'

'Yer what?' said Wilf.

'A dam, dummy – yer know, like a barrier. We can set it up in the sand and stop the sea coming up the beach – the tide's on its way in now.' A small group of children had gathered round, and I expected them to laugh at Clive's bizarre plan. Instead, there was a cheer of approval and the door was swiftly borne up by many hands and whisked down the beach towards the wet sand. Val and I looked at each other in disbelief.

'Remember, don't go in the water!' I bawled.

We had to admire the industry of Clive's little band of boys. A group of six were soon kneeling on the beach and digging with great gusto, scooping sand with their hands like a pack of dogs on holiday. Clive dug with fury, spitting out directions and demanding that a good trench be created in which to stand the door on its edge. I looked at my watch. We should have been heading back to the village now, but the sport of watching Clive 'Canute' Lambert and his gang was far too fine a diversion. Within a short time, the door was placed in the hole and some of the loose sand was packed in against the base while Wilf held it upright. Clive then ordered everyone to stand back and for Wilf to let go. The door fell over. After more manic scooping and bracing the door was finally raised, but it looked very insecure. Some of the boys began to lose interest in the project, moaning that it would never stand up to the sea, which was now rapidly approaching.

At this point Clive ran off back towards the rocks and returned holding a flat piece of driftwood. He then began using this as a spade, piling up a great mound of sand behind the door. Wilf went to look for his own wooden shovel, while the others watched the tide creep up the beach, ever closer. Clive had done an admirable job on the back of the door, and now went around to the front, piling sand up as if his life depended on it.

'Wave coming!' called Jack. Clive stood up and watched the first thin stretch of bubbly water to sail this far up the beach gently poke against the sand at the base of the door. The other boys immediately drew back, as if the water was boiling hot. Clive, however, dived back round to the front of the door and continued his shovelling.

'Wave!' called Jack once more. This time it was stronger – a swift film that climbed the outer mounds of sand, smoothing and lowering them instantly. Again, Clive watched and sprang into action upon the water's retreat. A familiar pattern now emerged: Wilf, now armed with a stubby plank, bolstered the back of the door while Clive made running repairs to the front, intermittently warned by Jack's wave watching. After three more small waves, a heavier one washed right round the sides of the door, partly filling the pit from which Wilf was digging at the back.

'Uuueergh!' he screeched. 'Me knees are wet.'

Val and I chuckled, then told the boys to come up the beach. 'You can watch how long the door lasts from up here,' said Val. The mob duly retreated, but Clive could not bring himself to abandon his project. He pleaded with arm-waving passion to stay near so that he could continue his programme of maintenance. I was surprised when Val consented to his request along with the addendum, 'But it's your own fault if you get wet.'

The whole of the class now gathered, along with the teachers, on the large rocks at the top of the beach to watch the spectacle. The waves were starting to build up a little force now, and each one washed away most of the sand from the front of the door and made inroads into the supporting piles at the rear. Clive was equal to the challenge, however. When the waves fell back down the beach he leapt into action, digging, scraping and pressing down sand with furious energy. Even when a larger wave knocked the door back a few degrees, accompanied by a cheer from the spectators, Clive wasn't dismayed: he simply scooped faster – he really seemed to believe he could beat the sea.

There then followed a quite memorable, if surreal moment. Up to this time, Clive had managed to avoid wetting his clothes, but now the door was surrounded by water all the time and he was kneeling in it while trying to bolster his faltering barrier. Each successive wave was also now giving the door a serious whack, and I sensed that Val was about to call Clive away from further calamity. Then I looked up and saw a dark line on the horizon. A bigger wave was on its way. A much bigger wave. The children saw it coming too, and started to point and shout. The wave rode in to shore, proudly, gathering height and energy, a freak offspring of a strong offshore gust perhaps, heaving and unstoppable. We were all shouting now, screaming at Clive to run up the beach. Amazingly, he took no notice, but rather dived back round to the front of the door, perhaps thinking that we were warning him of the need for additional sand.

There was nothing any of us could do. Clive had his back to the sea. He had no idea of what was approaching him at tremendous speed. We could just see his busy head bobbing above the other side of the door. There were gasps from the children.

The wave went right over him; it slammed into the door, crashing it up the beach like a piece of cardboard. Clive momentarily disappeared in a bubbling flood of foam then staggered up out of the deluge, like a human sponge. The wave surged up the beach and reached the rocks where we were sitting; everyone instinctively raised their legs and the children watched with dismay as seawater filled the shoes they had so carefully placed on the sand. Val waded out towards Clive who tottered like a gargling drunk towards us, nearly tripping over the door in which he had invested so much. His dripping arms stuck out like a scarecrow's, and Val grabbed one and hauled him on to the rocks.

Poor old Clive. He made the two-mile walk back to the hotel weighing twice as much as on the outward journey, and with no shoes, these having been washed away completely by the sea, along with his bag and lunch box. His comical straight-legged gait was made worse by the wind and the sun drying out his jeans and making them almost as stiff as his beloved door. For the remainder of the week on Oswalfarne, Clive was strangely subdued, but also commendably behaved. He cursed the wave all the way home that day, but for the rest of us, and the staff especially, it was a godsend.

Chapter Nineteen

Penny

Val Croker was a legend at Cragthwaite School. She had taught the top class for as long as anyone could remember, and she commanded total respect from colleagues, parents and children alike. I was slightly in awe of Val, from the day I started teaching: to begin with, her powers of discipline were almost paranormal – it seemed that she only had to look at a child to achieve complete obedience, whereas I and everyone else at the school had to employ a range of cunning strategies and threats. Val's physical presence certainly helped her in this respect. She was a former captain of the Yorkshire Ladies Rugby team: as broad as a door, flabless and muscled like a bear. She also possessed a voice of unlimited power, giving her long-range control of any situation when required. More than once she had made me jump when reprimanding a miscreant at the top of the playing field.

At school, Val worked the children hard, and her results were never less than astounding. She had a brain as sharp as a guillotine, and a quite phenomenal general knowledge. As I grew to know her, I soon discovered that Val also possessed a number of less apparent qualities. For one, she was far more helpful than her renowned Yorkshire bluntness suggested, although never willing to admit it. Then there was also an admirable loyalty to her class, always making sure that they didn't miss out or receive second best. For me, however, Val's greatest asset was her sense of humour, which was as dry as old toast.

Val gave her wit even more exercise than usual while we were on Oswalfarne, but as the week wore on another side of her character seemed to be stripped away by the salt winds and strange Celtic legends of this captivating island. As she relaxed with the passing days, Val became quite chatty and jovial, teasing the children and encouraging them to talk to her and tell her about their homes and interests. It was Val who insisted that we all walk back to the North Shore on Wednesday to have a go at making beach sculptures from all the driftwood and flotsam we had found there on the day of Clive's momentous wave. On the way there she questioned me about some of the children who would be moving up to her class in September.

'Who's that girl up ahead with Lucinda – is it Carol?'

'No, Carol's behind us, and she's much taller; that's Penny,' I said.

'Penny Garsdale?'

'That's right.'

'What's she like, then? I know her mum – works at the Black Swan in Ingleburn.'

'Oh, you'll get on a treat with Penny: she's a great worker and really artistic too. She's another quiet one, though, Val – she's spent every minute of this week with Lucinda so far, I notice.'

'Right, maybe I'll put her in another group for the sculptures.'

When we arrived at the North Shore, the children took great care to lay their bags and packed lunches on the big rock at the top of the beach, not least Clive, who was continuing to behave with unfamiliar sheepishness. Val then gathered the class together and put the children into six groups, telling them that they needed to work together to make a magnificent sculpture, and that they could use anything they found within sight of where we stood.

'You've got one hour, and there'll be a prize from the midnight feast box for the best one.'

There was a great cheer as she set them on their way, the children scattering swiftly across the rocks in search of the best finds. One child stayed behind; it was Penny. She looked at Val, but sidled up to me, speaking in a semi-whisper.

'Mr Seed – can't I go in Lucinda's group?'

'I'm sorry, Penny, but Miss Croker and I want to mix everyone up a bit so that you get to work with different people – if we let you change, everyone else will want to change as well, and we'll never get started.'

Val was listening. 'Go on, off you go and find some bits and pieces.'

'You'll enjoy yourself – I guarantee,' I added. She moved away, looking very doubtful.

An hour later I toured the six groups to tell them that they had just a couple of minutes to go. There was frantic activity everywhere. Barney and George were trying to drag what looked like an entire oak tree across the rocks, while Jack was making everyone in his group both deaf and irate by continuously beating an ugly rhythm on a bent oil drum with a large rock. Anita was screaming at Charlie and Isaac, who looked like they had drifted away from their group in a sulk, but elsewhere there was tremendous teamwork, and some splendidly imaginative creations now stood like vagabond sentinels on the bleak coast.

Carol's group had made an enormous seaweed dragon from a great pile of twisted wood. It was draped in greasy strands of bladderwrack and looked suitably evil. Fifty yards away, Eve was clearly in charge of a group who were busy laying out a complex pattern of stones on the sandy part of the beach. I wasn't sure what it was.

'This looks good,' I ventured. 'Is it an abstract pattern?'

Eve looked disgusted. 'Can't you tell what it is?'

I walked around it, desperately trying to make out a form. It just looked like a jumble of stones.

'Er, is it Celtic lettering?' I guessed, with a complete lack of confidence.

'It's a giant crab, Mr Seed.'

'Oh yes,' I said enthusiastically, still unable to see it.

At this point, Malcolm came running up to us to say that we hadn't seen his group's effort yet. We apologised profusely and followed him. The 'sculpture' consisted of what looked like a low seat surrounded by two flat pieces of wood and four piles of sand.

'It's an F1 car,' said Terry enthusiastically, jumping into the seat and pretending to drive. I was glad he told us. I then saw Penny standing away from the rest of the group, who were all boys, and all making screeching engine noises. She looked very miserable.

I tried to cheer Penny up on the way back to the hotel by talking about the rest of the week's activities. I also made sure she was with Lucinda.

'It's the talent show tonight, and tomorrow there's a real treat,' I said. 'It's the boat trip to the seal sanctuary on the Lonnen Isles. 'We'll see puffins and all sorts of birds too – it'll be great.'

'I love animals, but I'm just a bit worried about the boat, though,' she said. 'I get seasick really easily.'

'Oh, don't worry,' I replied. 'We won't be going if the sea's in any way rough, and the island is only a couple of miles off the shore – the boat journey is just a few minutes really.' She didn't look convinced, and Lucinda hardly helped by recounting all the times that she had been seasick in vivid detail.

The talent show was a disappointment. The diet of late nights, fresh air and long walks seemed to be taking its toll on my class, and most of them were too tired to marshal their talents into a performance. The extroverts were the exception to this rule, of course, and the evening did feature a number of curious acts from the usual suspects.

Jack told a number of rude jokes before Eve announced that she was going to juggle with knickers. She then bent double in a fit of giggling from which she was unable to recover. Wilf stood up next and waved his arms for quiet before carrying out a scandalous series of impersonations of the school staff, which went down very well with his classmates. Barney made a heroic effort to marshal a cast for a 'play', which turned out to be a re-enactment of Clive's drenching. To our relief his requests fell on deaf ears although Fergus did volunteer to be the door.

It was a considerable relief when I looked out of my bedroom window the following day and saw a great sheet of blue sky. At breakfast, despite many puffy eyes and booming yawns, there was great animation at the prospect of the boat trip to see the seals off the Lonnen Isles. After a short bus journey across the causeway and south along the coast road we arrived at Bamwick, the scruffy little fishing town that advertised 'Pleasure Cruises, Fishing Trips, Seal-Spotting Expeditions and Delicious Crab Sandwiches'. There was barely a ripple across the surface of the sea, so once the children had stepped off the bus, I headed for Penny.

'There you are. It's about as calm as it could be – not a dab of white on the water.'

'Which boat is ours?' she asked, pointing to the harbour, where several large, brightly painted fishing boats were tied up.

'I'm not sure, Penny – Miss Croker's going to check. It's bound to be one of those big blue and white ones, there are over thirty of us to fit on board.' Val soon came into view carrying a long strip of tickets.

'Right,' she called. 'Everyone follow me, we're on that small red boat over there.'

Once we were out at sea, excitement took over, even for the nervous Penny. The boat's hypnotic sway, the throb of the diesel engine and the sharp sea air were too wonderfully removed from our stuffy mobile classroom back in Cragthwaite for this moment not to be enjoyed by everyone. Within minutes, the houses of Bamwick retreated to miniatures, and the first dark rocks of the Lonnen Isles came into view. There was a sudden cry from Charlie.

'Puffin!' A fat little parcel of a bird was skimming over the waves beside the boat, its wings in a frantic buzz. Within seconds, everyone was spotting birds: puffins, guillemots, razorbills, cormorants and crowds of wheeling gulls. Each child scanned the water and approaching rocks, desperate to see the first seal. The cries were soon drowned out, however, by a shrill tannoy commentary from the boat's skipper. He named every bird on view, but his north-east accent was so thick that most of the class were utterly confused, many thinking that they were being introduced to several completely new species. Val began to laugh: the situation was obviously well familiar to her, and she stood up and gave a translation of the commentary. As we approached the first black cliffs of the islands, a huge colony of thousands of guillemots greeted us with a colossal blast of squawking. Combined with the engine noise, the tannoy announcements, Val's interpretation, and the oohs and ahs from the class, the resultant cacophony was almost unbearable. The children loved it.

A few moments later we were away from the forbidding cliffs and chugging towards a group of scattered grey rocks. Here the water swelled in dark bulges between the barnacled outcrops. We were told that monks had lived for several centuries on the minute island behind these rocks; even the tougher boys seemed impressed. The rocks then began to flatten out as we edged around the island,

and the skipper cut the engine, causing us to drift in blissful peace for a few moments. It didn't last long.

'Seal, look, a big fat one!'

'Where?'

'There on the rock.'

'Let me get me camera.'

'It's massive!'

Indeed it was – a great flabby airship of a male, lying languid with its wide spotted belly on full view. Then there were screams from a group of girls to look the other way, where four or five younger seals were bobbing in the water, their whiskered heads and beautiful eyes just a few yards away. I looked to my left and saw Penny in raptures, clicking madly with her camera and shaking Lucinda's elbow as if she were a puppet.

Half an hour later we had reached the farthest island, where a lonely lighthouse stood guard. The children were quiet again by this point, having reached their limit for taking in sights. The Geordie tannoy continued its nasal twang, but Val had wisely ceased passing on the spume of facts. The boat then veered away from the rocks and the engine pounded up to full power for the run back to shore. The children entertained themselves by dodging the squirts of spray thrown up as the hurrying boat slapped into the waves. I checked on Penny again: she gave a rosy smile as I made an enquiring thumbs-up sign.

'I told you it would be good,' I shouted over the engine's din.

Bamwick was now back in clear view, just a mile or so ahead. There was also another boat, a larger fishing vessel moving towards the shore from the north. The two craft gradually merged closer and the skipper of our boat returned a wave from the trawler. Unexpectedly, he then cut the throttle again down to a gentle pulse; the larger boat drew up nearer until it was only about thirty yards away, running alongside. Like the children, I was intrigued as to what was going on. A few unintelligible shouts were exchanged between the men, and then a most strange thing happened. A heavy figure in yellow overalls stood on the deck of the fishing boat and began to swing some dark and dangly object in his hand. He gave a heave and launched the thing across the sea towards us. For three seconds, it sailed like a globular ink blot through the air and then landed with a fearsome splat, right in the centre of the tiny deck of our boat. It was an octopus.

Several of the children screamed and all of them recoiled involuntarily with shock, as did Val and I. Only the skipper of our boat stayed cool, laughing heartily and stepping out towards the poor battered creature now lying with black tentacles splayed out like an exploded alien. He picked it up without fuss and dropped it into a bucket, which he left in the middle of the deck, before hopping back to open the throttle again. The children had been rendered speechless for a full minute while this surreal episode unfolded, but as their senses returned, a great babble of speculation rose up. Wilf edged towards the bucket and peered in, before hunching his shoulders and making a comical 'eeeeuurghh' grimace. Several others followed suit, all enacting the same ritual before Val ordered them to sit down, as the boat was now bumping along at speed again. The children stared at the bucket and asked me if the creature was dead.

'I think it must be.'

Once again, I was wrong. A thin dark tentacle poked up at the lip of the bucket and flopped two inches over the side. Several children squealed, some with delight, and some with horror. Another tentacle appeared and gripped the edge of the pail. Then, amazingly, the octopus began to heave itself up. Three more suckered arms flopped over the rim and the body appeared, a dark slippery bag about the size of a melon. Suddenly, the bucket tipped and the creature slithered out on to the deck, its tangle of limbs just a few feet from a cluster of girls who shrieked spontaneously and lifted up their legs on to the wooden bench where they were seated. Val stuck out a foot to prevent the octopus moving any closer to the girls, and the skipper swiftly reappeared, scooping it back into the bucket in one deft movement. He was obviously enjoying the entertainment, and so replaced the bucket on deck. Needless to say, the tenacious animal was not finished. Once more, it raised two tentacles and lifted itself slowly upwards. Once more, the children started to scream in mock desperation. We were now approaching the harbour and the engine was cut again. As we drifted towards the stone pier, the octopus slopped its tired body on to the deck. This time, the skipper left it there, and it began to slide about, looking for water. After a quick reverse thrust, the boat stopped and was quickly tied up. With land now within reach, some of the children plucked up the courage to have a closer look at the curious creature on the deck. One of these was Penny, who, I was delighted to note, had avoided being sick for the whole journey. She bent forward to study the strange body of the octopus. Without warning it squirted a streak of dark ink towards her. The screaming started again. I shooed them off the boat like a madman.

Back at the hotel on Oswalfarne I raced to the payphone and called Barbara. It was a relief to hear that she was still at home and feeling well, although she sounded a little drained.

'The baby's obviously keen to make an appearance soon though,' she said. 'It's wriggling around again. Anyway, I'm fine – how's it going with you?'

'I haven't got enough money to even begin to tell you what happened today,' I said. 'You can look forward to some long instalments when I get home. At least we haven't lost any kids, although it's been close.' She laughed, oblivious to the fact that I wasn't joking. 'Is my mother behaving?'

'She's on great form and has cooked every day – I'm being treated like royalty. Her lemon meringue pie is heavenly. And wait till you see the big yucca plant she's bought us.'

I just had time to say goodbye and squeak a kiss down the phone before my coins ran out.

After the evening meal we walked out to the village for the treasure hunt, which passed off quietly, most of the class having been reduced to a zombified state of exhaustion by this time. The children were all in bed earlier than we'd expected, and there were no creaking doors, giggles or even a hint of a ghost story from the bedrooms. By ten o'clock it seemed that every one of them was sound asleep. I was ready for bed too, but Val looked full of energy.

'Well, there'll be no need for us to patrol the corridors tonight, so how about a swift drink in the bar? Come on, I'm buying,' she said.

Mr Towler and I followed her downstairs to the cramped little room that served for a bar. The Guinness Val placed in front of me was delicious, but only served to make me more sleepy. Mr Towler seemed just as drowsy, and we both sat quietly as Val gave her assessment of how the trip had gone and what she'd noticed about each of the individuals in my class. I listened with fascination to her perceptive observations: she seemed to know the children almost as well as I did, and was obviously weighing each one up, ready for teaching them in September. Once again, Val had amazed me.

'Well, you two are a barrel of fun tonight,' she said, draining her glass. 'Come on then, you'd better get some sleep – we've got the long trek back tomorrow.'

After a brief morning tour of the island's gift shops where the children loaded up with tacky key rings, painted thimbles and boxes of fudge, we emptied the sand from our shoes, packed our bags and waited for the coach. The return journey to Swinnerdale passed off without incident: the children were still too tired to create even a mild fuss, and some of them even slept on the coach. The trip had been a great success, but as we pulled off the A1 and headed towards the Ingleburn Road, my thoughts turned towards school, and in particular, towards poor Martha who had missed everything. I dreaded the thought of her having to put up with endless recounts of all the fun and adventures the rest of her class had enjoyed on Oswalfarne. The girls had kindly clubbed together to buy her a sweet little pottery puffin, but it seemed scant consolation for all she had missed.

We pulled in to the school drive at three o'clock. Several parents were milling by the entrance, and without exception the children were delighted to see them again. I noticed Penny's dad give her a big hug as soon as she was off the coach, and a few people saying thanks to Val, before I wandered into the building to find Joyce. She flew out of her office and enveloped me in her arms.

'Hello! Lovely you're back. How did it go then, Andy?'

'Wonderful, thanks.'

'Well, we'll meet in the staff room after school and you can tell me all about it.'

'How's Martha?'

Joyce was clearly expecting the question.

'Come with me.'

She led me down the corridor towards Class 1. Looking through the door, I could see Emma sorting through a pile of books at the far end, but no children. She gave a little wave as we entered the classroom then put her finger to her lips before pointing to the adjoining carpeted area. Joyce and I peeped around the corner. A huddle of four- and five-year-olds were sitting with quiet attention, listening to a story. It was being read by Martha. One of the smallest boys was on her lap, and there was a book in her hand; she was only nine but she looked all the world like a teacher. The bell rang for home time and Emma stepped in to take over. Martha saw us and came bounding over, spilling out words.

'Oh Mr Seed, hello, and Mrs Berry, oh I've had a wonderful time, I've been helping the little ones all week and I've really enjoyed it, it's been fantastic. Did it go well on Oswalfarne? Is everyone back?'

I could barely speak I was smiling so hard. Joyce suggested that Martha run out to see her friends before they disappeared home, and as she went past there was a whisper in my ear.

'It was Val's idea, you know.'

Chapter Twenty

Josie

It was an incredible transformation. Five months ago, Craven Bottoms had been a sorry shell of a new home: damp, empty and crumbling; every room lined with ludicrous wallpaper and ancient, dog-eared carpets. Since then, the kitchen had been completely rebuilt, the walls had been freed from damp and we had set about redecorating the whole place despite our limited resources. I had attacked it with gusto at weekends and during the school holidays, but Barbara had worked away at the endless jobs continuously with a quiet resolve: cleaning, scraping, sanding, painting, and hanging wallpaper – right up to today when she was eight and a half months pregnant. The baby's tiny room had been finished for some weeks now, but Barbara had continued, determined to finish making the other rooms presentable. And now it was done – the whole house looked wonderful, and she had finally put away the decorating boxes. On Friday, I walked into Cragthwaite after school to buy her some flowers and a box of chocolates to celebrate.

Cragthwaite was one of the Dale's larger villages, boasting two shops and two pubs, in addition to the school. The inns were well known to me from darts matches, and were known as the Top Pub and Bottom Pub, reflecting their positions on a sloping road. The Bottom Pub was a little on the rough side and beloved of the locals. The Top Pub was much more up-market, with oak-panelled rooms that appealed to the summer visitors. In between these two old hostelries was a long curving main street with a small marketplace in the middle, complete with lumpy cobbles and an ancient market cross tucked in beside the stately church. Unusually for Swinnerdale, this road was lined with three-storey houses, giving the place the air of a small town rather than a village, and it has to be said that Cragthwaite did sometimes regard itself above its humble neighbours like Chapelgarth, Skirbridge and Shawby.

I loved the place. There were wonderful secret alleys running between the buildings, revealing silent old barns and stables at the back of many of the houses, and everything was solid and uncomplicated, hewn from the stone of the surrounding hills with pride and craft. It also possessed a narrow track, running beside a gill, which sharply climbed the hillside behind, up to the moors. The views from here were unmatched – a great sweep of interlocking valleys and flat-topped limestone crags reaching for miles to the south and west.

There was only one problem with walking through Cragthwaite village: it was full of children from the school and their parents. I couldn't help bumping into someone, and today it was Josie Birkett from my own class. She was in the general store standing with her childminder as I walked through the door.

'Hello, Mr Seed.' She whispered to the woman next to her, 'That's my teacher.'

Josie was the nearest thing in Class 3 to a model pupil: she was quiet, sensible, polite, and above all, incredibly neat. Nothing was ever out of place with Josie: her clothes and hair were always immaculate, her work was beautifully presented, with copperplate handwriting, and her books and belongings were always tidied away with complete precision. In truth, I was rather scared of Josie – I even foolishly felt myself adjusting my tie as I moved around the shop looking for some flowers. Actually, it was Josie's mother I was really scared of. She was a teacher at a large school in Hauxton, and someone who didn't suffer fools gladly. Earlier in the year, she gave me what felt like a grilling at the parents' evening, despite being pleased with Josie's work. I was delighted with everything her daughter did, but Mrs Birkett obviously believed that there was always room for improvement.

Seeing Josie there in the shop also reminded me that I still had to write her end-of-year report; in fact, it had to be done this weekend to meet Joyce's strict Monday deadline, along with three other potentially awkward ones which I had put off until last. I'd actually surprised myself by how much I'd enjoyed writing my first-ever school reports. I was determined to avoid the age-old formulas of 'could do better' and 'steady progress'. I just hoped I hadn't strayed too far in the opposite direction with some of my observations. Barney Teasdale's Design and Technology report sprung to mind, for one: '*Barney enjoys cutting up large pieces of wood into smaller pieces, and sometimes these come in handy.*'

Josie Birkett's report would be nothing like that, however: I shivered at the very thought of having to write it.

* * *

Barbara was delighted with the flowers and chocs, and relieved that I was home for the weekend. She was so huge with carrying the baby that just the effort of getting up out of a chair was a tremendous struggle. Despite being permanently exhausted, she looked wonderful, however, and her spirits were higher than ever. Like me, she was still revelling in the excitement of family expansion.

'Alec Lund popped round today,' she said, as we snuggled up on the settee with two huge mugs of tea. 'He said he's going to come and see you about cutting some edges.'

'Edges?'

'Edges.'

'That's odd – what kind of edges?'

'I don't know, I could hardly understand a word he said.' She giggled.

'He does have a bit of an accent, doesn't he?' I pictured Big Alec, the giant farmer from the top of Applesett, who I knew from the darts team: he was the archetypal village character, all right. 'Well, not to worry, we'll find out later.'

It was just before eight when the noise came. It sounded like the house had been hit by a passing cattle truck. Both of us jumped.

'That'll be Alec at the door.' It was. He declined my offer to come in, which was a great relief as he was wearing some particularly noxious overalls.

'Now then, lad.'

'Now then, Alec.'

'I'm cutting Sam Burnsall's edges tomorrow afternoon and

thought maybes you could give us an 'and, like. We all lend an 'and with Sam's garden – can't manage it 'imself with 'is arthritis.'

'Oh, right – is it the edges of his lawn you want me to do?'

'Yer what?'

'Which edges do you mean then, Alec?'

'The dirty big privet ones growin' round his garden, you daft bugger. He 'asn't got any other 'edges.'

'Right, I see, his hedges.'

'Aye, his 'edges. Two o'clock then.' He turned and strode away, visibly readjusting his assessment of just how stupid I was.

Privet hedges were not common in the Dales, but Sam Burnsall's was a beauty. It was about seven feet tall, and swept around the border of his long back garden in Applesett like a green castle wall. I stood on the path by the side of his house and looked at it, then considered the rusty pair of clipping shears in my hand. Even with two of us it would take all afternoon. My plans to make a start on writing the reports would have to be put back, for sure. These thoughts were abruptly interrupted by the growl of an engine on the road outside. It was Big Alec on his quad bike. He stopped it outside Sam's house and jumped off, before slamming a big hand against Sam's front door. I went round to meet him. He started to laugh.

'Byyy, what's that you've got there, Seedy? We'd be on t'job till Christmas if we used them.' I blushed and slid the shears behind me. 'This is the bugger we need.' He walked back to the quad bike and reached into the small trailer behind it, lifting out a brutal-looking petrol hedgecutter about four feet long.

'Now then, Alec.' Sam Burnsall had appeared at the door. He acknowledged me with a nod. 'Now then, young 'un.'

''Ave you remembered we're cutting yer 'edges, Sam?' shouted Alec.

'No, but yer can do it all t'same, lad.'

Alec reached into the trailer again and threw me a rake. 'Reet, let's get 'er sorted.' He looked at me as we walked through Sam's gate. 'Don't worry – we'll 'ave t'job done in an hour or so.'

We walked through to Sam's back garden, which was full of rusty pieces of farm machinery and stacks of logs. Alec put the hedgecutter on the lawn and fiddled with its controls with his great salami fingers.

'I'll start wi' this and you rake up the cuttings,' he said. 'There's a barra round 'ere somewhere.' With that he yanked at the pull cord a couple of times, and the hedgecutter's two-stroke whined into life, sputtering out plumes of blue smoke. Alec adjusted the choke and gave the throttle a good squeeze. The engine screamed like a Formula 1 racing car and the trimmer's great ugly teeth surged into a blur along the blade. I looked at it, thinking that goggles were needed at the very least, and gloves and probably boots and ear protectors too, but men like Alec didn't believe in such things. Sam Burnsall shuffled out of the house with a folding chair and sat down to watch. Alec swung the hedgecutter towards the hedge and, with a great arcing sweep, slashed at the privet, sending branches and leaves spewing everywhere. He stepped forward and swept the blade back down, cutting at least ten inches into the hedge with each movement. I gingerly moved forward with my rake, eager to establish a serious distance from the machine before getting stuck in.

Within five minutes, Alec had completed one side of the longest stretch of the hedge. In place of the thick ragged growth of early summer was a neat vertical wall of green; I was impressed. Alec took his finger off the throttle and I grabbed the chance to speak.

'Sam – have you got some stepladders so we can do the top?' But Sam didn't get a chance to reply: Alec was back at the other end of the hedge and had the engine screaming again. To my amazement, he was holding the giant hedgecutter above his head, with the blade piercing the crown of the hedge horizontally. Once more, he simply walked forward, this time lifting the machine with rigid arms and slicing the top off the hedge in a single cut. A green torrent of privet poured down on to him, going into his collar and piling up on his head to rather comical effect. Alec just shook it off and continued striding down the hedge, holding up the blaring machine like a strange trophy. When he reached the end, Sam had a flat-topped six-foot hedge.

To my great relief, Alec brought down the trimmer and let the motor idle quietly. But then he came over to me.

'Reet, that's 'ow t'job needs to be done. Why don't you finish other two sides 'ere and I'll come back and do the outside later – I 'ave to go and feed me lambs now.' He put the machine down on the ground and shook his head violently, flicking privet trimmings off his clothes at the same time. Then he disappeared through the gate, shouting, 'And give the blade some WD-40 after a bit!' as he went.

I looked at Sam. He smiled from his chair.

'Hope your bit'll be as proper as Alec's.'

I went over to the trimmer, which was buzzing and chugging

on the grass where it had been left. It was a monster – I realised that in Big Alec's hands it had looked just quite large, but now I understood just how industrial it was. The real shock, however, was still to come: I picked the machine up and nearly keeled over right away – it weighed about the same as two full suitcases. I could barely lift the thing off the ground, never mind reach the top of a tall hedge with it. I decided to switch off the engine, which felt like it was from a Bedford van, and practise first. The handles were hot and oily, but with a firm grip I managed to heave it up to waist level by bending my knees and employing a kind of weightlifter's jerk. I then tried manoeuvring the long blade at different angles. The strain on my wrists was immense, and I kept having to support my arms by digging my elbows into my hips.

Then it occurred to me that I was wasting time – this was obviously going to be much harder than I had envisaged so I needed to get on with it. I put the trimmer down and looked for the pull cord. I gave it a tug. It came out reluctantly halfway and nothing happened. Alec had made it look so easy. I braced my body and gave it a mighty heave. The engine gave a choky cough and went back to sleep.

''Ave you got the choke out?' said Sam from behind. Silly me: I moved the choke to the on position and tried the pull cord again. Nothing.

'Cos you shouldn't 'ave – you'll flood the engine.' I moved the choke back and gave the cord another vicious yank. It coughed twice – progress at least.

'I'll go and put the kettle on,' said Sam, rising from his chair.

'We're both going to need it.' The hedgetrimmer was really making me mad now. I called it a rude name and pulled the cord with every last sinew in my body. The engine spluttered a few times and then snarled into life. Yes! I picked it up, straining my back a little in the process and stepped towards the end hedge. I was relieved that Sam had gone – I could have a little trial run. I squeezed the throttle trigger and felt a surge of power as the great steel sword of a blade fizzed into action. This thing was lethal. I dipped it into the hedge and felt almost no resistance. Then I tried a bigger branch, about the thickness of a cocktail sausage. The blade slipped through it with ease. I cranked up the revs and went for a big vertical sweep, like I'd seen Alec doing. I could only lift the blade up to about shoulder height but I found it rather satisfying, despite the muscular strain and the shower of leaves and twigs that hit me in the face. I moved forward and swept down, careful to keep my feet well clear as the machine's great weight pulled it down savagely.

I then stepped back to survey my work and to have a rest. I'd made a large, cockeyed hole in the hedge about four feet wide. All in all it had taken me twenty minutes. Sam appeared with two mugs on a tray. I hit the throttle hard before he had a chance to comment, and went back to attacking the privet.

After half an hour, I had to stop. My arms simply refused to do any more. I was gushing with sweat, and plastered with the foliage that had stuck to it: I looked like a jungle commando with delirium. I switched the trimmer off and collapsed on to the ground, my whole body aching. I had done nearly two-thirds of the short end hedge, and hadn't touched the top at all. The hedge did at least look neater than before, if somewhat uneven. Sam kindly fetched me a glass of water and even more kindly praised my effort. Then Alec returned.

'You lazy bugger. You've only done one side – and that's not finished. And you 'aven't swept up.' He strode over to the trimmer, still muttering, and pulled the cord. It started first time. He picked it up with one hand and whipped the engine into a manic screech once more. I could hardly bear to watch. Alec raced round the remaining hedges, smoothly slicing away the greenery and handling the massive hedgecutter as if it were a cardboard model. He wasn't even sweating. In fifteen minutes the whole job was done. Shame forced me to overcome my physical suffering and rake up the cuttings into piles. Sam found his wheelbarrow and soon his garden was returned to orderliness and peace. With astonishing skill I avoided all possible eye contact with Big Alec.

I staggered across the village green and into Craven Bottoms. Barbara heard the door open.

'Andy, what's happened to you? Why were you so long?'

'I'll tell you later,' I croaked. 'I need a bath.' Thirty seconds later I called downstairs. 'Barb, can you come and turn the taps on for me, please?'

The bath was wonderfully soothing, even though the water turned green and I was unable to move my arms to reach for the soap. They had seized up altogether. I couldn't even close my fingers. Then a horrible thought crossed my mind: the reports.

I didn't even attempt to write anything that evening. It was pointless. I just wandered round the house holding out my arms like a gorilla, hoping that some life would return to them, then gave up and watched telly.

'Don't worry, they'll be fine tomorrow,' said Barbara, unable to hide her amusement at my condition. 'I can always lend you a hand.'

I woke up late on Sunday still aching. Half-conscious, I mentally retraced the explanation for the discomfort and finally got to the point where my arms didn't work. Nervously, I tested one. I felt my nose get scratched – it worked. Even though I could move both arms now, they felt curiously numb, and I could only do things slowly. I held up my right hand horizontally. It was shaking. A lot. I sat up in bed and spent ten minutes opening and closing my hands in a pathetic attempt to get them up to speed. Barbara woke up and turned towards me. She nearly fell out of bed laughing.

I had a long breakfast and another bath, but I knew I was just putting off the moment of truth. I went into the kitchen and looked at the pens next to the phone. I would have to pick one up and try to write soon – I had four reports to finish, including Josie Birkett's. By this time, Barbara had stopped sniggering, having realised that I was in a bit of a predicament.

'You can dictate them to me if you like,' she said, but we both knew that her handwriting was completely different to mine and that a fuss would be made at school.

I sat down at the dining-room table with a stack of paper to practise writing. It felt ridiculous. I picked up a pencil and felt a dull ache in my forearm. I tried my signature first. Not only was it wobbly, but for some reason it was at least seven times larger than usual. It also trailed off at an angle like it had lost interest at the end. This was bad. I wrote it again. Not much better. I tried pen. Worse. I wrote out the alphabet, and had to stop for a rest after k. I went to make a cup of tea.

After two hours, I had written a rough draft of Eve Sunter's report, but I was concentrating so hard on the handwriting that the content was drivel.

'*In English, Eve has made steady progress but a lot of the time she could do better.*'

And what was really worrying was that that sentence had taken up about a quarter of the page. With practice, I had managed to make my letters a little neater, but I just couldn't seem to make them any smaller. They were massive. It made the Reception kids' writing in Emma's class look like microfiche. And every word had a distinct wobble – it would look like I'd written the reports during the world's longest earthquake. I nearly cried. I even tried writing with my left hand.

By four o'clock in the afternoon I had written three reports in rough. They took up about twenty-five pages. But I still hadn't started Josie's. Barbara popped her head round the door and eyed the piles of scrunched-up paper on the carpet.

'Anything I can do?'

'Come and look at this, please.' I held up my latest writing. 'If you were a parent and you got this for a report, what would you think? Tell me honestly.'

'Well, I would think that . . . that the writing is big.'

'Very big?'

'Very, very big.' She couldn't hold her mock serious expression any longer and her face detonated into a seismic guffaw. Two seconds later I was laughing too. Barbara had started to snort, and that always set me off.

After ten minutes of calming down and laughing again every time one of us looked at the writing, we went into the kitchen for a cup of tea. Then something came over me.

'Right,' I said. 'I am going to finish my tea and I am going to write Josie Birkett's report. Straight into neat, with pen. I am going to tell her silly mother what a wonderful girl she is and I don't care if the writing is wobbly and big. I don't care if each letter is the size of my head. That is what I'm going to do.'

And that is just what I did.

The reports were sent out on Wednesday, along with a little slip for parents to fill in to say that they had received it. There was also room for them to comment. Val told me that very few of the parents ever made a comment. She was right – I had only one. It was from Mrs Birkett, unsurprisingly. It said,

'*Thank you for all that you have done for Josie this year. This is an excellent report and we are very proud of our daughter. We are also the owners of a typewriter should you ever have need of one.*'

I showed it to Barbara when I got home. We had another, quieter, giggle.

'I'll tell you what,' she said. 'Next year *I'll* help Sam with his edges.'

Chapter Twenty-One

George

'Can you just check again please, Andy? Just to be certain everything's there.'

Barbara was in the bath and I was in our bedroom, checking that the 'hospital bag' was ready. It was now the second week of July, and the baby was overdue.

'Right, here we go: baby clothes, nappies and creams etcetera, music tapes, Thermos flask, books, extra nighties, inflatable cushion, three pairs of socks, a note to collect ice cubes and the cassette player, and about fifty pairs of knickers. What do you need all those for?'

'Don't exaggerate, Andy, there are only ten. Olivia recommended to take plenty.'

After initially regarding the leader of our antenatal classes in Hauxton with scepticism, Barbara had been fully converted to the almost military birth planning Olivia endorsed. Most of the items in the special hospital bag were her suggestions for the big day: ice cubes to make drinking easier, the cushion to counter back pain, socks for cold feet during long labours and the cassette recorder to play gentle and soothing music to calm our baby's entry into the world. It was the fifth time I'd checked the bag that week. The item that had been running through my mind for some time was not on the list, however: the twenty-five-mile drive to the hospital in Bilthorpe. This was, we'd discovered, one of the few drawbacks of living in the Dales – full-time medical care was a long way off.

'Andy!' The call was plaintive this time. Were things starting? I rushed into the bathroom.

'Can you give me a hand? I can't get out of the bath.' Bracing myself to lift my bulbous wife out of the water, something peculiar caught my eye.

'Have you seen that?'

'What? It's not my feet is it? I bet my toenails need cutting – I haven't seen them for nine weeks.'

'No, your belly button.'

'What about it?'

'What about it? It's colossal!'

'Well, it's the baby, dear – it's pushed it outwards a bit, that's all.'

'Not a bit, Barb – it must be three inches long! Does he keep his arm in there or something?' This gave me an idea. 'Hang on – call me when you're dry.' I dashed off to look for some lipstick and eye-liner.

Ten minutes later we had a photo that has become one of our most treasured possessions. On Barbara's swollen tummy, using the eye-liner, I drew two big round eyes above her comical belly button. Below it, I then sketched an enormous grinning mouth with the lipstick. We called it 'Baby's First Smile'.

'You are a nutcase.' Barbara tutted. 'Now, how about a bit of practice with rubbing my back? It's killing me.' I went to work – this was another skill I'd learnt at the antenatal classes. I wasn't sure what I'd be like as a father, but at least I felt prepared for the birth.

At school, things were now winding down as the end of term approached and the long summer holidays installed themselves in everybody's thoughts. There were still a couple of events to prepare for – the school fair and sports day – but in the classrooms the heat slowed everyone down, especially in my stuffy mobile classroom with its windows on three sides. The only person it didn't seem to affect was George Walden.

George was one of the quietest children I have ever come across, and was undoubtedly the quietest member of Class 3. George was new to Swinnerdale and to Cragthwaite School, but had already gained popularity with his peers by early October. His dad had bought a garage in Hauxton, and drove round in a wonderful old Jaguar, much to the admiration of the other children, especially when he picked up George and his sister after school. George himself was a bright, hard-working and resourceful boy – I was delighted with the way he had settled in at the school, and was also very impressed with his work. On Monday I had given him an *'I'm a Star'* lapel badge for completing a Maths book in record time. The only thing that seemed to distract him was noise in the classroom, and there were bound to be frequent outbreaks of that with characters like Barney, Eve, Malcolm and Wilf around.

If George found the noise in the classroom difficult then dinner-times must have been a nightmare for him. Dinnertime at school was not my favourite part of the day either, particularly on a Thursday, when it was my turn at hall duty. One of the problems was the design of the school hall, which was used as the dining room: it was a large, empty, echoing box, and 100 children scraping chairs, clattering knives and forks and drumming lunch boxes created a constant background clamour which made ordinary quiet conversation impossible. In addition to this, Mrs Harker in the kitchens always seemed to be hurling large aluminium baking trays around with a tremendous rumpus of clanks and crashes. As a consequence, the children would raise their voices to talk and shout between tables to attract each other's attention. This level of noise would gradually rise as the children who were being served last would become restless and inevitably start larking.

If Val was on dinner duty then her presence alone was enough to guarantee at least a semblance of order, and the same was true to a lesser degree with Hilda and Emma. Joyce usually ate her lunch in her office while doing three or four other things. Today Val had taken her meal to the staffroom and Hilda and Emma were away on an English course, leaving me alone to face the din of dinner. Except I was not alone, because there was always another person there, and one who could hardly be ignored.

Mrs Hyde had been dinner lady at Cragthwaite Primary for a great many years. I wasn't sure of her first name and I never did possess the courage to ask, because Mrs Hyde was a dinner lady of the old school: huge, fierce, uncompromising. From twelve until one, the hall was her realm, and she patrolled it like a tyrant, striding around with hands on hips and bellowing at any child, however small, who so much as blinked. And in Mrs Hyde was another cause of the shocking level of noise in the room. Because the children were loud, Mrs Hyde shouted continuously: she shouted at them to be quiet, she shouted at them to behave and she shouted when it was time to come or to go. The children regarded her barrage of demands and instructions as just another part of the background noise, along with the plates, metal baking trays and chatter, and therefore simply ignored her, and just raised their voices further to be heard above her hollering. Mrs Hyde, in all her years, had never worked out that this was happening, and therefore lifted her booming voice further, thus continuing the rising spiral of volume.

The repetition gave me nausea:

'I – will – not – stand – for – this – noise!'

'Be – quiet – now!'

'Er – I – haven't – told – you – to – go – yet!'

'KEEP – THE – NOISE – DOWN – THIS – INSTANT!'

Mrs Hyde alarmed the infants with the threat of her vast size and output, but the juniors would have given her scant respect had it not been that she possessed one terrible power: it was she who decided the order that each table went to the serving hatch to collect their dinners. When all else failed, she wielded this weapon, and every day I heard the familiar sentence of a boy or girl being given the dreaded 'you can go last'. It was a harsh punishment too, as the dinners were only lukewarm to begin with, having been cooked in another school and brought up the dale by van.

On this particular day, the children were being extra noisy. They had probably noticed that I was the only teacher present and that the level of supervision therefore allowed rather more freedom and entertainment than usual. Mrs Hyde was also in a bad mood because in reaction to this noise she had already meted out her favourite punishment to several children, and arguments were developing all over the hall, mainly among the boys of Class 4.

'No, ah just told yer Joe, I'm fourth to last now, Kev's third to last and you're second to last.'

'Yer what! I'm fifth to last, I tell yer – Kev's fourth and you're third.'

'Rubbish!'

'ER – WHAT – IS – ALL – THAT – RACKET – ABOUT? RIGHT! PAUL – LUGG – YOU – ARE – NOW – LAST – FOR – DINNER!'

'But I'm already third last Mrs Hyde.'

'DON'T – ARGUE – YOU'RE – NOW – LAST – LAST!'

The result of all this was disastrous. The two tables of Class 4 boys involved, now resigned to even colder cabbage, gave up all pretence of good behaviour and started spinning their knives on the tabletop. I went over to try to calm them while Mrs Hyde homed in on another incident near the door.

'MALCOLM – YOU – ARE – NOT – TO – MAKE – THE – INFANTS – SWAP – THEIR – SAUSAGES – FOR – YOUR – SPROUTS – RETURN – THEM – NOW!'

'But I've eaten half of this one, Mrs Hyde.'

'I – DON'T – CARE!'

I was on my way to see if it was Malcolm from my class when I was grabbed by an infant who had just been accosted by Mrs Hyde.

'Do we 'ave to listen to her? She makes you eat the gristle.' I was trying to think of a way to defend the dinner lady's authority when something caught my eye under the next table. I looked down just in time to see half a sausage skim across the floor at a speed that suggested it hadn't been dropped. A group of Class 4 girls immediately attracted suspicion as they were all hunched forward, giggling uncontrollably. The noise level was now almost painful; I had the feeling it was all getting a little out of control.

Meanwhile Mrs Hyde had returned to the older boys.

'AND – JUST – WHO – DO – YOU – THINK – YOU – ARE?'

But worse was to come. Something flashed across my field of vision – something small and white. They had started to flick mashed potato. I wanted to scream.

At that moment a calamitous bang silenced everyone for two seconds. An unfortunate Reception boy, returning his plastic tray to the trolley, had dropped it, causing a small explosion of cutlery and gravy. The respite didn't last long – there was a huge cheer from the children, which made the poor infant burst into tears; it was either that or the sight of Mrs Hyde coming to comfort him. The noise level went up another notch; I seriously considered going to find Val, but couldn't leave Mrs Hyde alone in the room, particularly as she was now bent over, scraping up splashes of mashed potato off the floor, with the jut of her voluminous rear causing further uproar.

At this moment, just as I was looking for a large heavy object to thump on a table to urge order, the job was done for me: there came one final tumultuous reverberation: a sound to stop everyone completely in their tracks. It was a high-pitched banshee screech of ear-splitting ferocity, and it came from Mrs Hyde. Every child froze, and even the kitchen clamour ceased. We all stared at the purple-faced dinner lady who was standing up and rubbing her bottom violently.

'Someone, *someone* . . . STUCK A PIN IN ME!'

Then the hall doors crashed open and in marched Val.

'Just *who* is responsible for this frightful noise?' She scanned the whole scene with boiling eyes. There were another two seconds of blissful silence and then a child's hand went up. It was George Walden's.

'I stuck a pin in her, Miss Croker.' All 100 people in the room wanted to ask him the same question: 'Why did you do it?' But George was the first to speak.

'I don't know what came over me.' He was still holding his '*I'm a Star*' badge.

The guilty party was marched off to Joyce's office, and forced to write a grovelling letter of apology, and Val was brought into the hall to supervise the children. Dinnertimes at Cragthwaite were never as noisy again, but George Walden, the quiet boy of Class 3, was more popular than ever.

It was a relief that the afternoon didn't require too much in the way of serious teaching: there were a number of things that needed to be made for the forthcoming summer fair and by two o'clock, I was supervising a small group led by Cameron, who were trying to make a ducking stool. They were very highly motivated, as I had volunteered to be the first victim. The other children were busy working on posters, and making their own stalls. It was only moderately chaotic. By three, Cameron had finished his mechanism and wanted to test it. It consisted of a bucket on a hinged base, next to a swinging target which supported it. Two girls held it aloft and Cameron prepared to poke the target with a stick.

'Oh, Mr Seed – will you sit underneath it, please,' appealed Anita, who was working with them. I agreed, even though I'd seen them put handfuls of scrunched up paper in the bucket. I sat underneath it, praying that the falling wooden base wouldn't crack my skull. Cameron duly gave the device a prod, and there was a raucous cheer as the paper fell all over me. Then Joyce appeared in the doorway.

'Mr Seed – telephone for you. It's Barbara.'

Fortunately, there were no cows on the road and very few tractors and cars as I slalomed along the twisty lanes back to Applesett. Barbara had sounded very certain about the contractions over the phone, and Joyce had pushed me straight out of the door, insisting that she would take over my class right away. I was in a strange limbo between panic and excitement. When I arrived home, Barbara was much calmer.

'I've got the bag,' she said.

'I'd better get the bag.'

'And the ice cubes and cassette player.'

'Hang on – I'm just looking for the ice cubes.'

'Andy, we'd better go – I've got everything ready.'

'Have you seen the cassette player? I can't find it.'

The drive to Bilthorpe was peculiar. For a start, I wasn't sure whether to go really fast or really slowly. More than once I had imagined rocketing to the hospital and being stopped by the police then waving the officer away as I pointed to my wife, her head lolling and her knees wedged up against the glove compartment. The reality was very different – Barbara was certainly feeling discomfort, but she was remarkably composed. I decided to proceed slowly to Ingleburn along the narrower roads; we could speed up once we were out of Swinnerdale. I thought about the number of times that this journey had been made by the people of the dale. It took over an hour from Kettleby to the hospital. Mrs Dent at Applesett shop had told us how one young mother's baby had recently made its debut appearance in an ambulance just outside Bilthorpe.

'They nearly made it,' she said, not exactly filling us with reassurance.

'Andy . . . Andrew.'

'Oh, sorry, I was daydreaming. Are you all right?' I glanced across and watched her grimace.

'I think you'd better go faster now.' She was pressing herself against the seat and clearly uncomfortable. I put my foot down and the Alfa's raucous engine made a lot of noise without actually altering the speed of the car very much. The road was clear though still twisty and I cut the corners as much as I dared before we came up against one of the dale's less speedy obstacles, the Land Rover and livestock trailer. I glanced at the dashboard. We were doing a steady 28 mph. I edged out a little to see if there was room to overtake but the road was just too full of bends. I did notice that the driver was an ancient flat-capped farmer whose head appeared to be below the level of the steering wheel.

'Come on!' I hissed, pointlessly flashing my headlights behind the wide trailer. Barbara's face was creased in a fight against pain.

'Don't do anything silly,' she croaked.

'It'll take us two days at this rate.' I pushed the horn. Barbara jumped and screeched.

'You idiot! Don't do that – I had my eyes closed.'

'Sorry, sorry; I didn't realise it was so loud.'

Suddenly the road straightened so I veered out, pushing my right foot hard against the car's rusted chassis, silently gabbling a prayer as I did so. The Alfa reluctantly chugged past the Land Rover and I shot the driver an accusatory glance but could only see two bony hands reaching up to the wheel. A lorry lumbered into view and I swerved back across just in time, hoping that Barbara's eyes were still tight shut.

She didn't answer when, twenty minutes later, I announced with relief that we had reached the outskirts of Bilthorpe and would soon be at the hospital. All her concentration was absorbed with fighting pain. For the first time I felt fear replace the confidence that nothing could possibly go wrong.

The staff at the maternity unit were superb. Barbara was swiftly whisked into the labour ward and given checks that confirmed that her cervix was dilated by several centimetres. She was also given lots of encouragement by the wonderful midwives, along with everything else that she needed, and she was now able to talk again. After the anxiety of the journey everything once more seemed to be going to plan. All except one thing: me. I didn't know what to do with myself. I just kept getting in the way. I unpacked the hospital bag.

'Would you like some music, Barb?'

'What?'

'Would you like some music?' She shook her head – there was another contraction on its way. I kept trying to breathe for her, hoping that would help.

'Just let me know when you need an ice cube,' I said. Barbara was now off the bed and walking around.

'Rub my back, will you?' I did.

'No, not there. There.' I rubbed there.

'No! There!' I rubbed everywhere.

'Is that better?'

'Whose idea was this? Because it was a really stupid one.'

'What, the back rubbing?'

'No, having a baby!' She started groaning.

'Do you need the socks yet?' I asked.

Sarah, our midwife, came in and suggested that a little gas and air might be a good idea during the contractions. I wondered if we could both have some.

Barbara liked the gas and air, and as time went on she became remarkably attached to the dangling mask and tube that supplied it on demand. Our communication hadn't been very good before, but now it was hopeless. I could still speak, of course, but Barbara could only point with one hand. It was clear, however, that her pain was increasing greatly as the contractions became more frequent. She started pointing at the hospital bag. Was it the music? It didn't seem very appropriate at this moment. Perhaps she wanted to read one of the books? Maybe not. I held up a pair of knickers, but she shook her head and kept on jabbing. It must be the ice cubes. I unscrewed the lid of the Thermos flask and tipped it gently towards the cup. Nothing appeared – the ice cubes had welded together into a solid mass. I put the lid back on and gave it a shake. This didn't work, so I opened it again and gave it a gentle tap on the bottom. All of the ice cubes came piling out, knocking the cup on to the tiled floor and then following it. I immediately pictured a consultant obstetrician walking in and skidding on them spectacularly, so I dived on to the floor and began grabbing handfuls. Several had slipped under the bed and I had to stretch to reach them.

'Everything all right in here?' said Sarah. I banged my head getting up too quickly.

'Perhaps you'd better sit down there in the corner, Mr Seed; I think I'll stay in the room from now on.'

The plan of me staying out of the way worked for an hour or so, until the baby decided it wanted out. Then Barbara beckoned me over. The pain was intense and she wanted to hold my hand, or rather squeeze all the life out of it. I felt more helpless than ever at this point, and my only suggestion – to try Olivia's strategy of counting out loud to help with breathing – was met with a loud, 'Shut up!'

This overwrought period seemed to drag on for an eternity, and then there were lots of people coming and going out of the room and I heard the word 'forceps'. I was asked to withdraw to my chair in the corner again.

There was a huge amount of blood and another long wait, and then a slimy white baby was pulled into the world. A boy. Barbara was barely conscious.

* * *

We called him Tom. Everyone had warned us how having a child would change our lives but nothing could have prepared me for that moment of seeing my own son. The wonder of looking at his face gave me inexpressible feelings I had never known before. I sat in a kind of reverie with him on my lap, babbling a quiet nonsense of thanks and love and plans for the future. Then I looked at poor Barbara, lying shattered a few feet away. She was bruised and weak, having been cut and stitched on top of the upheaval of the birth, but her face expressed a deep pride and joy that made me well up inside. My wife was a heroine.

Chapter Twenty-Two

Heather

Barbara finally came home with Tom in the last week of term. The night before I picked them up from Bilthorpe Hospital, I scrambled round the house in a frenzy, tidying, dusting and vacuuming ready for the grand return of mother and new baby. It was so thrilling. Barbara looked like her old self again after her long confinement, although she still ached from time to time, and needed to walk round slowly.

'Andy, the house looks wonderful.' I carried Tom inside in his carrycot and laid him on the floor.

'I'll go and make a cup of tea,' I said, thinking back to what the place had looked like twenty-four hours earlier. We both sat down and stared at our little son, scarcely able to believe what had happened to us. He slept peacefully, unaware that he was home, his tiny face puckered up beneath a white hat. I wanted to hold him all the time and never put him down.

'I can't tell you how good it feels to be home with him,' said Barbara.

'It's bliss – no more dashing to that hospital . . . and seeing him here it's even better than I thought it would be.'

'I've not given a moment's thought to how you managed here on your own. How was it? Be honest.'

'Oh, not too bad. I've missed you, though.'

She looked at me and sighed.

'Andy, you look terrible. Have you seen yourself in the mirror? Do you feel all right?'

'I think I'm just tired. It *is* nearly the end of term – well, the end of the school year.' I didn't want to admit that I was thoroughly exhausted.

'I'm not surprised you look like a corpse. It's been hard work, this job, and then there's been the house and the baby. You need a rest.'

'Never mind about me; you're the one who needs looking after with everything you went through.'

'Oh, I'm not too bad, but I've never seen you so pale.' She ran her fingers through my hair.

I stifled a yawn. 'Don't worry. School breaks up in just three days, then it's weeks of summer holidays.'

'Hmmm, just as well. You make sure you take the rest of the week easy: that's an order. There's not anything more going on, is there?'

'Just the staff v kids rounders match the day after tomorrow and the leavers' assembly on the last morning.'

A trace of a frown appeared on her brow. 'You don't have to play rounders, do you?'

'Course I do.'

'Well, promise me you'll take it easy.'

I nodded, thinking that it should be me telling her to take things easy but I was half asleep.

The following day, with Joyce's blessing, I rushed back home straight after lessons finished. Joyce had insisted on giving me a loud embrace right in front of a clutch of wide-eyed parents as I left the building. I tried to imagine a grisly picture of Howard Raven doing the same thing but somehow, thankfully, the image wouldn't materialise.

There had been considerable excitement at school over the news of Tom's arrival, with Eileen and Hilda leading the charge to ask me all about the birth and how Barbara was and whether we were all sleeping, but when I returned back to Applesett I could see that the village had also woken up to the fact that mother and baby were now home. In the front room of Craven Bottoms the mantelpiece was lined with new cards and, with Tom quietly feeding, Barbara couldn't wait to tell me about her day.

'You won't believe it, Andy – we've got casseroles and cakes and enough other food to last a fortnight. Half the village has been round.' I was delighted to see her looking so chirpy. 'Mary Burton's called and says she'll do as much baking as we can eat; Mrs Dent brought a huge apple pie, Iris has given me piles of baby clothes, and even "Lady" Asquith from next door popped in to see how things were.'

She then went on to tell me that the infant teacher from Applesett Primary had even called in to say that they'd put Tom's name down on the future admissions register as they always did when a new child arrived in the village. We were chuckling about this when there was a knock at the door. I opened it to see a gaggle of bouncing girls on the doorstep all wearing the navy uniform of Ingleburn Secondary School. There were four altogether, aged from about twelve to fifteen, and I recognised them all as girls from the village.

'Hello, we've heard your baby's here,' the tallest one said before I could speak. 'Can we see him?' She peered past me.

'Er, well, er . . .'

'And can we take him out in the pram some time?' This I recognised as Rosie from The Crown. Before I could answer, the youngest girl broke in.

'We can do babysitting too – we love babies!'

I asked them to wait while I checked with Barbara. She was patting Tom over her shoulder while a milky dribble from his bottom lip stretched down her back. I invited the girls in and they nearly knocked me over rushing up the hall's slope before quietly squealing and ahhhing at how cute he was.

That evening, when Tom was tucked into his cot, we mused over our initial worries about being accepted into the community as outsiders by the long-established locals with their close-knit family ties and ancient attachment to the land. It seemed that the one person strong enough break down all of the barriers was a new-born infant.

I called Heather Thistlethwaite to come and read to me. Heather was the tallest girl in the class and had legs that seemed to go all the way up to her armpits. She was also a somewhat disorganised child, and I wasn't surprised when she told me that she had left her reading book at home.

'Well, just pick something off the shelves to read this time, Heather.'

I had been extensively warned about the Thistlethwaite family by Hilda, who had taught Heather the previous year.

'Oh, they're nice enough kids, but they're all batty. And clumsy, I'm afraid. They all have these unbelievably long legs which none of them can control properly. Poor Heather's the worst of the lot, too – she's always falling over.'

Over the year, I'd been able to see very clearly that Hilda was exactly right. Heather was well behaved in the class and worked very hard, but she did seem to spend an inordinate amount of time on the ground: she tripped and stumbled frequently, and was always bumping into things. Just the previous day she had been sitting on the carpet, listening to me read a story to the class. All of the children sat cross-legged, attentively following *Charlotte's Web*. All, that is, except Heather. Heather couldn't cross her legs. Well, she could, but it took her so long and was so painful to watch that I used to let her sit with them on one side: when she tried to sit like the others, she had to thread her gangling limbs together using her hands, like knotting thick pieces of rope, and furthermore the operation required at least a third of the carpet area. On this occasion she had her legs to one side, but decided to move them to the other side. In the process she kicked at least six children and ended up kneeing Terry in the back so hard that he went flying off the carpet and under a table.

At least standing by my desk reading, she would be out of harm's reach. I was already listening to Penny read on the other side of the desk when Heather arrived: Val had taught me the trick of listening to two children read at once, and it was actually easier than it sounded.

'Right, Heather, what book have you chosen then?'

'*The Ory Jammy Zoo*.'

'Never heard of that one – is it a foreign story?'

'No, it's about paper birds and things.'

'Oh, let's see.' She handed me a large paperback: *The Origami Zoo: Twenty Folded Paper Animals to Create.*

'Shall I read from page one?' She opened the book, which consisted of dozens of complicated diagrams. There wasn't a word in it. Eventually, after a return trip to the shelves, Heather found a collection of poems and began to read. I checked on my left to see how Penny was getting along. She was reading *The Twits* and clearly enjoying the book. I asked her what she liked about the story and who her favourite character was. Penny enthused about the comic grisliness of the battle between the gross Mr and Mrs Twit. I thanked her and sent her back to her table, then turned to see how Heather was getting on. She was gone. At first I wondered if she'd visited the toilet, but felt sure that Heather would never break the rule about asking for permission first. Perhaps she'd changed her book again? Then I saw her: she was on the floor.

Heather had bumped and stumbled and lurched and tripped over things throughout the year, but I had never seen her just go straight down in this way before. She had spontaneously fallen over. Gravity had outwitted her again, and this time while she was standing and reading a book. I asked her if she was all right, but I couldn't see a face, just miles of twisted legs, like a bowl of giant spaghetti. The funny thing was that when she did rise, she just carried on reading as if nothing had happened – the poor girl was so used to biting the dust that she couldn't taste it any more.

After lunch, there was a buzz of excitement as I told my class to line up ready to go outside on to the field for the annual staff against children rounders match. This was another tradition that, I'd been told, had taken place at Cragthwaite for years. Val was organising it, and just as I opened the classroom door she appeared.

'Mr Seed, two of my class have said they'd rather not play in the match so I wonder if a girl and boy from your class would step in. Sorry it's such short notice.'

I looked around and noticed several hands in the air; the children had obviously overheard.

'Shall I pick two then, Miss Croker?'

'Actually, if it's all right with you, the captains have already said who they'd like to have.'

'Oh, OK then.'

'It's Barney Teasdale and Heather Thistlethwaite.' Barney's name I'd expected to hear, but my eyes widened a little when I heard Heather's. Val leaned over and whispered.

'They picked her cos she's big.' I nodded sagely and checked if the two children were keen to play. They were, particularly Barney, who exploded his fist into the air and immediately bombed out of the room to get changed without being told.

Out on the playing field, the rounders posts were set out and children from all the other classes were sitting and chanting with gusto. They were shouting for Class 4, half of whom were out on the pitch practising throwing and catching. They looked ominously good. In contrast, the staff team stood by the pitch nervously laughing; a motley assemblage of cleaners, cooks, teachers and dinner ladies. We were going to get murdered.

'Are you any good at this, Val?' I said as we walked out to join them.

'I can hit the ball, don't worry.'

'Good.'

She pointed to the staff team. 'It is good, cos that lot have got the athletic ability of a meat pie.'

I looked over at my team-mates and silently concurred. Joyce had on a pair of ancient tie-up white plimsolls, but was otherwise in her ordinary clothes and was doing something surreptitious with a small mirror in front of her eyes. Hilda was wearing a tracksuit, but was doubled over coughing. Sue Bramley, the infant classroom assistant, was busy cleaning her glasses, and Mrs Harker, the cook, was clearly wishing she was elsewhere – I could see a torrent of grumbles falling from her lips, and only hoped that the children couldn't hear. Another player for the staff was Pat Rudds the cleaner. She was chuckling and swinging a bat violently in rehearsal: if she connected with the ball it would certainly travel, but at nineteen stone, I suspected that she wouldn't be too fleet of foot between the bases. Mrs Hyde was trying a few stretches and bends, but I could hear the creaks from several yards away. At least Emma looked fit, and she was obviously keen too, being the only staff player sporting shorts.

'Where's Eileen?' I enquired, noticing that our invaluable school secretary was missing.

'Oh, she has a bruised ankle and can't play,' said Joyce.

'Aye, she's not bloody daft,' muttered Mrs Harker, making sure everyone could hear.

'Right, let's get under way,' called Val suddenly. 'Children – you can bat first.' Then she turned to the staff and started making suggestions for fielding positions.

'Emma, you can catch, so first base? I'll go backstop to chuck them to you. Right . . . Hilda, will you go second please, and Mrs Hyde third – nice easy job for you there. Joyce, how about fourth post? The rest of you just spread out in the field, but Andy – I think you should go deep, being the youngest and therefore the least likely to have a coronary in front of a hundred kids.'

'Shall I bowl then?' said Sue.

'Oh, blimey – forgot we need a bowler. OK then, but don't muck about with nice polite lobs. Hurl 'em hard or we'll be chasing balls all flamin' day.'

We wandered out to our positions, and the Class 4 players, plus Barney and Heather, lined up eagerly to bat. I stood furthest away and bounced up and down a few times to warm up – I was clearly going to have to do plenty of running.

'Chil-dren! Chil-dren! Chil-dren!' chanted the rows of watchers, seated well back behind the action on the grass slope at the edge of the field. A large boy stepped into the square and raised his wooden bat. Val, standing behind him, crouched slightly and spat on her hands. Sue looked round to see if we were all ready. She drew her arm back and launched the ball towards the waiting batter. It sailed about four feet over his head.

'Oh, come on – no ball!' moaned the boy.

'You should've jumped,' said Val. 'Go on then, no ball.'

Sue's next delivery was slower but at least within reach. The big boy took a neat step back and met the ball with a mighty swipe. There was a crisp crack and the ball disappeared over Joyce like a guided missile. I gave chase but the boy had more than enough time to just saunter round the track. There was a mighty cheer from the crowd, mixed with chants of, 'Roun-der, roun-der!'

I fetched the ball from near the trees at the top of the field and threw it back. Another Class 4 boy was already waiting, tapping his bat against a palm. At least he was small.

'Go Modgie,' called one of his team-mates. Sue bowled, this time low and hard. The boy's coiled arm whipped at the ball and smashed it between first and second. It passed within two feet of Mrs Harker, who gave a yelp and jumped out of the way. I could hear Val groan, as I turned to chase it. It was a long way off, since I'd moved over to behind fourth base after the previous hit. Once more, it was an easy rounder, and the crowd roared their approval. A tall girl was next to bat. She also hit the ball crisply but into the ground, and Emma, moving swiftly, managed to stick out a foot to stop it. The girl set off, running at tremendous speed to first base. Emma flicked the ball to Sue, who noticed that the girl was still running. In turn, she threw it hurriedly to Joyce at fourth. Joyce was tying her shoelaces, blissfully unaware of the situation. The ball flew past her shoulder to screams from the staff, closely followed by the tall girl, who skipped with delight at claiming a bonus rounder.

'Come on, that's three out of three!' bellowed Val.

'Sorry . . . sorry,' mewed Joyce, holding her fingers to her mouth.

A stocky boy moved into the batting square and planted his feet well apart – at least he didn't look too mobile. Sue unleashed a real stonker of a quick ball at him and he missed it altogether. Val nearly missed it too, but managed a block with one hand before whipping an accurate throw to Emma at first post. The ball flashed past the huffing boy and was neatly caught.

'Out!' called Emma. The boy's head dropped and he wandered away from the track.

'Booooooo!' called the watching children.

The next girl up hit the ball well and made it to third base, but was wary of risking a last dash after seeing some good fielding from the staff. Val clapped her hands encouragingly.

'That's better, team. Come on.'

Barney came out next, swinging the bat round to loosen his wrists. I moved back a few paces – I'd watched Barney playing rounders many times and he was a magnificent hitter of a ball. Our bowler Sue, was now encouraged, however, and clearly had her eye in. She whistled another low hard delivery towards the Class 3 boy. Its speed clearly took him by surprise and he lashed at the ball hurriedly, making a good contact nonetheless. Over 100 pairs of eyes looked up as the ball described a magnificent high arc through the air and began a descent straight for me. I tried not to panic; normally I was a good catcher of a ball. But as it fell I was aware of a string of calls:

'Drop it!'

'Go on, Mr Seed.'

'He's gonna miss it.'

'Two hands, two hands!'

The ball lashed my palms with a sharp slap and dribbled on to the grass. I could hear Barney's glee and several other howls of delight. To make it worse he ran a rounder. The next girl forward also hit a rounder: she smartly turned her body as Sue bowled, and backhanded the ball past Joyce, who at least saw it this time. Pat Rudds was the nearest in the field, but only managed a disgruntled shuffle towards the ball, murmuring as she went, 'I'm not chasing that with my ankles.' They had now scored five.

The next batter walked into the square. It was Heather. Her team shouted encouragement; I prayed she wouldn't fall over. Sue, knowing that she wasn't as athletic as the other players, sent her a generously slow lobbed delivery. Heather punched it down into the ground with her bat and set off running, her great long legs swallowing the ground at pace. Val scuttled forward and picked up the ball, hurling it to Mrs Hyde, and screaming, 'Third!' simultaneously. It was a great throw – Heather had already passed second base and couldn't go back. Mrs Hyde caught the ball too, but then she held it up with one hand, waving it.

'What do I do with it?' she called. 'Who do I throw it to?'

Val was apoplectic. 'Stump the bl . . . the base!' But it was too late; Heather was upon her and tapped the post with her outstretched bat.

'Don't worry,' said Joyce. 'I thought you did very well.' Val had turned away for a quiet swearing session. The next two players hit rounders, and then it was the big boy's turn again. I recalled that he hit his first ball over fourth base so I moved over in that direction. He hit this one meatily over first, and jogged round the track nonchalantly for his second score. Half an hour later the school team were all out. They'd scored 23, and it was our turn to bat.

'Right,' called Val as we lined up wheezily, 'Let's at least chalk up a few rounders or I'll never hear the last of this. Who's going first?' Surprisingly, Joyce stepped up.

'Oh, I might as well get this over with – I'm going to be out anyway.'

'That's right, think positive,' added a chuckling Hilda.

Joyce stepped into the batting square and was met by an encouraging cheer from the younger children on the grass bank. She waved to them and held her bat up in front of her body.

'Are you sure about that?' It was the big boy who was bowling.

'No, but bowl anyway,' said Joyce. He did, but she set off running before the ball even left his hand. Actually, it was not running at all – more of a waddling mince. Joyce arrived breathless at first post, confident that she had made it. But the ball was already there, in the hand of a grinning Class 4 boy. He greeted her with great politeness.

'Sorry, Mrs Berry – you're out.'

'Thank goodness for that,' said the headteacher, smiling as she headed to sit down. Mrs Hyde went next, and I could see that the big boy was struggling to keep a straight face, as the mammoth dinner lady addressed the ball with outstretched bat. His face soon changed, however, as she connected with a brutal 'tonk'. The ball sailed into the deep field – surely this would be our first score. Mrs Hyde set off, travelling with surprising speed, and aided by lifting the hem of her voluminous skirt. There was just one problem – she had dropped her bat.

'Oh, go back for your bat!' called Joyce from the sidelines.

'No, just carry on!' screeched Val. Mrs Hyde was in a quandary. She had thought about stopping but couldn't – and neither could she turn at first base. She simply carried on in a straight line, like an overshooting jumbo jet on an emergency landing. It was all too much for Val, who threw her bat down in despair, but it was inordinately entertaining for the watching children, all of whom had suffered years of reprimands from the grumpy 'lunchtime supervisor', as she liked to be known. Eventually, she slowed down enough to begin to turn, oil tanker-like, and headed for the track again, but by this time the ball was winging in from the outfield and she was inevitably stumped.

Val strode out next and the big boy immediately turned round and signalled everyone to fall back, even those on the posts: memories of Miss Croker's awesome hitting power were obviously still ripe from the previous year, when these children were spectators. The big boy waved his fielders further back until half of them were next to the boundary fence.

'Oh, just get on with it,' said Val.

The big boy bowled his fastest, but this only served to make the impact harder. Val twisted her torso and hammered the ball with mesmeric ferocity. I half expected it to shatter into thousands of pieces. Instead it whistled away like a tracer bullet, straight over the fence and into the field next door. Within seconds about sixty children were piling on to the rickety wooden rails to retrieve it.

'Come back! You do not have permission to climb that fence!' called Joyce, but few could hear. The ball was soon found and the match resumed – at least we had scored a rounder. Hilda went next and she managed to deflect the ball behind and past the diving backstop. She scuttled over to first base and seemed very satisfied. It was me next. The big boy eyed me over and signalled for the field to move back. My self-assurance wilted, however, when he called them to stop.

'No, not that far – come back in a bit!' I could see Barney hopping up and down, desperate to make a catch. I was pleased with the hit, it was low but hard, and went skidding away between second and third bases. Six desperate children legged after it. Without hesitating I launched myself off towards first, determined to run a rounder. About halfway to second post, at full sprint, I came across a problem: Hilda. She was running but she didn't seem to be moving forward. I couldn't overtake her either.

'Come on Hilda, get yer skates on.'

'Look, I'm going flat out – I am sixty-three you know.' She continued to trundle. I looked up the field and saw that the ball had been picked up and was being flung back. The Class 4 players were screaming for a good throw. Hilda reached third, while I hopped and jiggled behind her – for a moment I thought she was going to stop. The ball was coming in. It was going to be touch and go. I couldn't stand it any longer so I picked Hilda up under the armpits and whooshed her, kicking and chuntering, over the line. The protests were phenomenal.

'You can't do that!'

'The teachers are cheats!'

Val silenced them. 'Listen you lot: I have the rules in my room and it does not say anywhere that you can't do that.' The mutterings and grumblings continued for some time, but the children were quickly assuaged when they got out Emma, Mrs Harker and Sue with the next three balls. Pat Rudds soon joined them, leaving just Val, Hilda and me to bat on.

Val effortlessly clubbed another rounder, then Hilda came forward. The big boy bowled but Hilda threw her bat down on the ground.

'I'm not being carted round like that again – I need a cup of tea.' She disappeared towards the school. Two of us left.

'Come on,' said Val, with a voice of steely determination. 'We've still got a chance.'

I managed to hit the next ball into the field, easily scoring a rounder. The big boy ordered two of his team to stay there. Val came forward. Another rounder. Ten minutes later we had reached sixteen and were still going, if somewhat out of breath. Sue came over with two cups of water.

'I don't like the look of the sky,' she said. Murky low clouds were rolling off the fells to the north. Inevitably, we felt drops of rain.

'Does that mean we've won?' said the big boy, hopefully.

'No it doesn't,' blasted Val. 'It's only spitting.' The game continued, and our score crept up: 17, 18, 19, 20 . . . Then disaster struck. Val was clearly tiring, and the dampening grass made running more difficult. As she stepped forward for her next hit, her front foot slipped an inch, and she clattered the ball high into the air.

'Mine!' bawled Barney. He launched forward and took an athletic low catch with one hand. The children from Class 4 poured over and slapped him on the back with jubilation. Val trudged past me, gritting her teeth and raising three fingers.

'I'm relying on you.'

I was alone.

The next ball was delivered high and fast, but I cracked it hard over fourth base where the fielders were thinnest. A tall boy went after it but misfielded. I charged home to roars from the staff. It was 23–21: we only needed two more to draw level. The rain was now more than drizzle, and Emma ordered her class back indoors, despite a crescendo of groans. The big boy was firing up his team for one last great effort.

'Come on, we can get him out. He can't afford a single mistake now.' It was true.

The next ball bowled was a no-ball, but the one after that I struck sweetly towards the fence, hoping it would bounce over into the sheep. Instead, it struck the woodwork with a decisive clonk. I would just have to run it. I had always been a good sprinter, and now determined to show what I could do. I blasted towards first base with my knees pumping, and leaned to round the post at speed. Then someone took the ground away. Or that's what it felt like. The wet turf had given all the grip it was going to give for the day, and I skidded spectacularly, landing in an outstretched sprawl, instigating a festival of laughter from Classes 2 and 3. Class 4 would have laughed but they still had to finish me off. My ribs ached as I rolled back towards first post, hoping to use it to raise myself.

As I looked up from the ground, a pair of legs appeared, long legs, then a face and two arms and a ball.

'Out,' said Heather, tapping the post with quiet triumph.

So this is what her world looks like, I thought.

* * *

When I arrived home, Barbara must have heard the car engine, because she stood at the door waiting with Tom in her arms. It was still raining. The sight of them standing there, mother and newborn son, was curiously overwhelming; I wanted to capture it somehow.

'Look, here's your daddy, Tom.' I tottered in, trying hard to disguise the fact that I could barely walk. She gave me a big hug and I kissed them both. 'Was the rounders match called off, then?'

'Yes. I mean no.'

'I hope you went easy on the poor children who were playing. Did you let them win?'

'No. I mean yes. I mean no.' I sunk into a settee, my body throbbing all over and my brain clearly receiving insufficient blood to operate.

'Well, whatever happened, the state you're in I'm sure you took it very easy.'

Chapter Twenty-Three

Nathan

The Alfasud trundled into the school car park later than usual and squeaked to a halt. It was the last day of the school year. I had told the children that they were allowed to bring games to play and that there would be no work at all, apart from helping me to tidy out the cupboards and take down the displays. Joyce greeted me as I walked through the door.

'Morning, Andy. It's just as well you're on holiday tomorrow: you look shattered.'

'I feel shattered.'

'Well, there's not too much to do today – just remember Leavers' Assembly starts at ten; oh and I need to see you about your probationary year at lunchtime in my office.' She disappeared, leaving me unexpectedly distressed. My probationary year! I'd completely forgotten about it. All new teachers had to go through probation in their first year, and their contract would only be renewed if the headteacher, governors and LEA inspectors agreed that the first year had been satisfactory. It hadn't even occurred to me that I might not have a job at Cragthwaite in September, and here I was, rolling into school late on my final day, looking like I didn't have enough energy to control my limbs, never mind a large class of excited eight- and nine-year-olds. Surely I would be safe, but as I walked through to the mobile, my mind refused to do anything but show replays of the string of educational disasters for which I had been responsible in the last three terms.

Then a worse thought struck me: the governors and local authority officers would be basing their decision principally on the headteacher's report. I felt sure that Joyce would be generous but what about Howard Raven? Had he left me a parting gift in the shape of a crushing verdict? I recalled the numerous times he'd entered my classroom, tutting and pouting, and his distaste for my approach to learning. Perhaps he had damned me with faint praise? He certainly had evidence to cite. What about the rounders post?

I headed for the classroom with a heavy heart. When I arrived there were already several children there, chattering buoyantly. Eve was among them.

'Hi Mr Seed, 'ave you seen what's on yer desk?'

There was a line of small, neatly wrapped gifts. My gloom lifted a touch.

'Ooo, how exciting.'

'Are you going to open them now then?'

'Well, I'd better hang on for a bit, Eve – I haven't called the register yet.'

More children arrived, many bringing further presents and all carrying huge boxes of games to play. By nine o'clock the desk was almost covered with little parcels, and it looked like Nathan was waiting to add to the pile.

'Mr Seed, I've got a special present for you, but I'm going to give it to you later, if that's all right.'

Nathan Coates was a slim fair-haired boy of some renown in Class 3. Unfortunately he was known by all and sundry as The Boy Who Never Finished Anything. He was not slow in the cerebral sense, but in every other way he was easily outstripped by snails, tortoises, sloths and probably dodos too. At the same time, somehow, however slow he was, he always seemed to get away with it, for Nathan was a charmer. He charmed his parents when he should have driven them demented, he charmed his friends and he had certainly charmed most of the teachers at Cragthwaite Primary since his arrival as a weeny four-year-old infant.

Emma, Hilda and Joyce all spoke of him in glowing terms and with sappy faces, despite clear proof that he had never completed a piece of work in his life. His writing never reached beyond the first paragraph, his pictures only featured headless animals, legless people and carefully titled white spaces, and in maths he was an expert at stopping at the equals sign. In the classroom, Nathan frequently left his drawer open for people to crack their shins on, he never washed his paint pallet, and at the end of school bell he always left behind piles of homework, letters to parents, and smelly items of PE kit. Val, who would undoubtedly test Nathan's charm to its limit next year, had even suggested that we replace the label on the Lost Property box with Nathan's initials.

On parents' evening, I had intended to subject Mr and Mrs Coates to a barrage of concerns about Nathan's dedication to incompleteness, but instead found myself listening to his mother describe countless delightful episodes in their son's upbringing.

'Of course, when he was five I found a letter he'd written to Father Christmas. It said "*Dear Santa, for Christmas I'd like a S*". Ahhh, isn't that sweet. We never did find out what he wanted.'

And nor did I manage to tell them my concerns, particularly about Design and Technology. This was, without doubt, Nathan's slowest subject; I recalled the 'Inventions for the Blind' project back in September when he had decided to make a white stick. For some reason, Nathan chose a large rectangular piece of wood and spent five entire lessons sanding it into a narrow round piece of wood. In the end I sent it home with him in despair.

I looked up and realised that I'd been sitting at my desk and daydreaming. At least the children were all occupied: they were playing with the games and toys that they'd brought from home. It was a fascinating scene.

The greatest concentration of noise and chaos was coming from the carpet area where Tracey, Clive, Eve and Wilf were engaged in a ferocious bout of Twister. Tracey was vociferously complaining that Clive's bottom was dangerously close to her ear, but she wasn't prepared to move herself, probably because, considering the acute contortion she had achieved, she couldn't. Next to them, and quite unruffled by the fuss, Malcolm and Terry were occupied in a tense battle of Monster Truck Top Trumps. Another quiet pairing was stationed at the adjacent table where Hugh and Anita were embroiled in a competitive bout of Mastermind. There was a little more animation around the table by the door, where a gaggle of apprentice farmers – Nathan, Cameron and Isaac – were admiring huge tractors in a glossy brochure.

The strangest sight of the morning was right in front of my desk. Fergus had just emptied a large bag of joke shop purchases on to the table and was attempting to arm himself with some of them whilst alone, in order to shock his friends. He began by contemplating a disgustingly realistic rubber turd and a whoopee cushion before trying on a horrific gorilla mask and then experimenting with a severed thumb and fake blood. I could see that it was a tough decision, and while he inwardly debated, I quickly prayed that he wouldn't turn up in assembly with plastic breasts.

Behind this scene, Carol, Sylvia and Penny were arguing over an Etch-a-Sketch, and behind them Jack and Charlie were blissfully creating Lego machine guns. I was just thinking how wonderful it was not to have a queue of needy children at my desk when Barney appeared next to me. He was holding a basketball.

'Mr Seed – before you say no – me an' George just want to do a few catches – we won't do any damage – we're really good, honest – we can move these two tables by the window . . . Awww.' He must have seen my expression.

Rose moved in as Barney went away.

'Mr Seed, you haven't opened any of your presents yet. Josie and I are desperate to see what you've got.'

'OK then, Rose. I'd better open them now.' The two girls let out a little squeal as if the gifts were all for them, and Josie stepped back to pick up a waste paper bin.

Within a few minutes I had acquired sufficient After Eights to open a sweet shop, along with a box of liqueurs, several pairs of grey socks, an interesting tie, three bottles of aftershave, a can of lager, four mugs – including a notable 'I've Been to Bridlington' piece – two pens and, care of Tracey, an enormous ashtray made from seashells. There was also a bottle of Champagne from Hugh's parents and numerous cards and thank-you letters, many of which included congratulations on the birth of baby Tom. I was overwhelmed. A knock at the door made me look up: it was a girl from Class 2.

'Mrs Berry says please can you hurry up because we're all waiting for you in the hall.'

It was ten past ten and I had completely forgotten assembly.

Leavers' Assembly was, I'd been informed, another favourite tradition of Cragthwaite Primary. It was always presented by the top juniors who were leaving the school to move on to pastures bigger at Ingleburn Secondary. Val's class was presenting a drama and, as always for such events, the hall was bulging with parents, grandparents and little brothers and sisters. I had been so busy thinking about my own class moving up to Val that I hadn't really given much consideration to the far more significant transition of the oldest pupils, away from their cosily familiar village school down the dale to what was colloquially known as 'the Big School'. For these children it was a momentous day. I mouthed a silent apology to Joyce and ushered my class into the hall, where *The New World Symphony* was nearing its end. As soon as the children were seated on the floor, Joyce moved into the centre of the room.

'Welcome parents, friends and children to our end-of-year assembly. This is a special, exciting day for twenty children in Class Four, as I'm sure you know, but it's also a sad day for us, as we have to say goodbye to them. It's their last day at this school today, but before they go, I know that they've been rehearsing really hard for a special show which they're going to present for us right now. It's called "Looking Back".' Joyce clapped her hands and stepped to the side as the audience applauded, leaving an open space with a park bench in the centre. I settled into my chair to enjoy what Val had promised would be top entertainment.

After the clapping had died down, there was a rustling among the curtains at the back of the hall and out stepped two of Val's children. Everyone immediately burst into laughter, particularly the infants, because the pair were bent double, staggering comically and dressed as an ancient couple. The girl wore a frizzy grey wig, tiny round specs and a crusty green dress. Her baggy brown tights were packed with what looked like rubber tubing to give the appearance of quite shocking varicose veins. The boy wore a crumpled trilby above a barely visible face that was thick with painted grey lines and enough facial hair to carpet a mansion. He wore a long black coat of the type heavily stocked at the Oxfam shop in Ingleburn, and giant boots. Both of them had walking sticks, although immediate hospitalisation would have been nearer the mark. It took the pair a good twenty-five seconds to shuffle across the eight yards of polished floor to the bench. Their make-up was splendid, and I shot a swift thumbs up to Val who was crouched on the front row of the audience clutching a battered script.

The mini pensioners sat down on the bench and then, after some more rustling behind the curtains, a large sandwich board sign appeared. It said: *Cragthwaite, Sixty Years in the Future.*

'By eck, Melvin!' said the girl.

'What is it, dear?'

'I've just realised summat.'

'What, like?'

'Do you know that it's sixty years t'the day since we left primary school?'

'Get away – is it really? Byyyy, them were the days tho', weren't they . . .'

'Aye, they were grand days at that little school.'

'Aye, and it was 'otter then. We had proper weather in them days, we did.'

'We did 'n'all. You could fry an egg on t'pavement in those days when I were a lass.'

'Aye, you could – and that was in winter.'

'In fact, we used to cook us Sunday casserole in the back yard; we chucked some meat and tatties in a pot, put pot outside and took dog furra walk. When we came back, it were cooked . . .'

'Aye?'

'Aye – tasted 'orrible though.'

'But it were a grand little village school, wan't it?'

'That's right. Do you recall them daft cranky things we 'ad to use in the classrooms back then?'

'Oh aye, hee-hee, real old-fashioned things they were – couldn't do anything. What did we call them?'

'Computers.'

'Aye that was it . . . We all had to use computers and calculators in them days – kids today don't know they're born.'

The audience chuckled with delight throughout the dialogue before the curtains opened up once more to produce a second pair of codgers. The boy sported impressively wide turn-ups with braces, while the girl displayed a wart that was almost as large as her nose. She also wore a frumpy brown cardigan and pulled a tartan shopping trolley. The poor boy was having terrible trouble keeping a straight face as, once more, the parents went into raptures.

'How do, Melvin, Christina,' said the girl.

'Now then, Rosalind, Adrian,' replied the bearded boy.

Space was made on the bench and all four sat down and stared forward silently. For a moment I thought they'd forgotten their lines and then, with impressive synchronisation, all four crossed their legs as one. It was beautifully done, and swiftly followed by a neat re-crossing in the other direction. The hoots of mirth from the audience grew louder as the silent routine unfolded. First they scratched their heads in unison, then uncrossed their legs, then each produced a handkerchief and blew a big raspberry before the spectacular finale where their legs were crossed, crossed the other way and then slowly crossed halfway before shooting back to their starting position. The applause was thunderous and poor Melvin had to wait some time before he could deliver his next line.

'We were just talking about primary school.'

'Oh aye. Do you remember our last teacher, Miss Croker?' said Adrian.

'Miss C? Of course I remember her. She was the best teacher I ever had,' said Rosalind.

'I'll tell you what I thought of her later . . .' said Melvin.

'But we had proper schools back then, didn't we?'

'Aye, I don't know what they're coming to today, with their laser-powered blackboards.'

'And school trips to Pluto.'

'And robot dinner ladies.'

'And alien teachers.'

'Aye well, some things haven't changed . . .'

With that all four stood up stiffly and hobbled off behind the curtains to a great ovation. A few seconds later, we weren't surprised to see two more of Val's top juniors, transformed into creaky senior citizens, making their way over to the bench. This time it was Gillian and Laurence.

'Do you remember our first school then, Gill?'

'Of course. I remember all the important things we learnt, like Mrs Percival's daily cry from the infant boys' toilet: "Why can't you aim straight!"'

'Aye. I remember when the TV exploded during *Science Challenge* . . .'

'That's right – and Mr Raven exploded when he found out.'

'And what about the time that sparrowhawk flew in through the window . . .?'

'Ooo yes – Miss Torrington wouldn't come out of the stock cupboard for hours.'

'And when Rowena Jackson put her finger in the electric pencil sharpener . . .?'

'Aye, and d'you remember when Lucas O'Leary pretended to be a baboon?'

'Of course I do – that was last week.'

'No, the thing that sticks in my mind were those sex education lessons we had with the school nurse.'

'Oh, yes, Norris got sent out for giggling . . .'

' . . . But it was Pamela I really felt sorry for.'

'What happened?'

'Well, she'd been looking forward to those lessons for months, and in the end she missed them all.'

'Oh, what was she off with, then?'

'I think it was Bruce Illingworth.'

There were screams of both laughter and embarrassment from the adults and children watching, and then two more prematurely aged performers came on to replace the risqué Gillian and Laurence. This time it was a tall girl wearing dark glasses and pushing a pram, along with another girl wearing curlers and a woolly coat. The girl with the curlers sat down first and produced a packet of sandwiches, placing them on the bench beside her. The tall girl put the brake on the pram, reached over to feel where the bench was and then promptly sat down on the sandwiches. The watching infants pointed and squealed with delight. The girl with the curlers then produced an odd-shaped box, which she put up to her face. She tapped it a few times and began to jiggle.

'House!' she called, almost leaping off the bench.

'What on earth are you doing?' said the tall girl.

'Virtual reality bingo – d'you want a go?'

'No thanks.'

'Oh, is that your grandson?'

'Granddaughter actually.'

'Ahhh – what's she called?'

'Xenon Cirrus Astro Five.'

'Aye, the old-fashioned names are still the best . . .'

'True.'

'Oh look, she's got your eyes, you know.' At this, the tall girl leaned forward, peered into the pram and said, 'Oh – so that's where they are!' She reached in and then lifted her dark glasses, comically screwing an invisible eyeball into each socket, before removing the shades and blinking expansively. There were groans mixed with giggles from the parents, while Joyce and I could barely contain ourselves. Val, meanwhile, was waving four elderly junior boys on to the stage, each donning the unmistakable garb of the ancient dales farmer: flat cap, mucky jacket tied with string, torn trousers and giant wellies. Each also bore brutal felt-tip stubble, a pipe and a crook. They took their places on the bench carefully, sitting wide-legged with both hands on their sticks. There was a long pause. The audience shuffled expectantly.

'Byyyyyyyy!' said Farmer One in a rasping boom.

'Byyyyyyyy!' echoed Two, Three and Four. There was another long pause.

'Byyyyyyyyyy!' This time from all four.

'It were 'ard at school in them days, though – '*ard*,' said One, then each contributed in turn.

'Aye, not like today.'

'I remember we 'ad to do handwriting for an hour and a half every morning.'

'That's nothing – I had to learn ma fifty-seven times table.'

'You were lucky. I were kept in after school by Miss Croker until midnight, just for burping.'

'Huh, that would have been fun to me. I 'ad to sit through one of Mrs Berry's long assemblies once – it lasted three days.'

'And what about that student from college who made us copy out the complete works of Shakespeare?'

'Aye – in Welsh . . .'

'Byyy, school were 'ard in them days.'

'We all 'ad to wear string vests in winter.'

'Aye, no other clothes – just string vests . . .'

'You were lucky: remember Sports Day?'

'Do I? We had to run a marathon, then swim the river—'

'—Lengthways.'

'Aye, lengthways, then hang glide back to school for the egg and spoon race.'

'Aye, and you were blindfolded . . .'

'Aye, and that were only the infants race . . .'

'That's right, and you tell the kids of today and they just don't believe you!'

I wiped the tears from my eyes thinking that Monty Python would have fully approved. The rest of the cast returned to gather around the bench and were given one of the longest standing ovations I had ever heard.

At five past twelve I was sitting outside Joyce's office. I could hear she was on the phone, so I waited and nervously chewed over my probationary year. It certainly hadn't been dull . . . The triumphs came to mind easily: the Christmas panto, the visit to Cameron's farm, Barney's epic football match, Charlie's Easter egg – all these had given both the children and me real pleasure and a true sense of achievement.

Then, of course, there was no shortage of tragedies either: the technology for the blind, Josie's dishevelled report, the rounders match and, the one that really hurt, Martha cruelly missing Oswalfarne. Would Joyce have detailed records of all of these? Just what had Howard Raven written?

I shivered at the thought of the inspectors at County Hall finding out that I had nearly poisoned a child with sewage, almost squashed another in a donkey wheel and helplessly witnessed a third being attacked by a Northumbrian tsunami. Perhaps these things happen to every teacher.

I stood up and listened at the door: Joyce was still on the phone. Maybe she was making a last-minute call to the Director of Education to see if he would consider an appeal? And what about my wonderful Barbara at home with little Tom? What would I tell them if I failed? The year at home and in the village had almost been as eventful as the one at school. There was the whole business of settling into the dale and adjusting to life in a remote rural area; the long struggle to find a home, and then renovating the dilapidated Craven Bottoms; settling into a tight-knit village and making friends; and, of course, having a baby.

It certainly hadn't all been a bed of roses either: we had struggled to survive financially, and we were far away from both sets of parents and most of our old friends; I had found teaching utterly exhausting and Barbara was now at home on her own with a demanding baby. How had we managed? I was considering the answer when Joyce's door opened suddenly.

'Oh, there you are, Andy – I was wondering where you'd got to. Anyway, come in.'

I slumped into another seat – it was very low but at least comfy.

Joyce was propped up on her high desk chair behind a huge pile of papers. I wanted to peek at them but they were almost above my eye level.

'Well, Andy, here we are: your probationary year just about over. How do you think it's gone?'

'Well, I have really enjoyed it, and . . .' I didn't want to say anything.

'Shall I tell you what I think?'

'Mmm.'

'Well, I've only been here since January, but when I look at those children in your class – at Jack, Carol, Tracey, Isaac and the rest – I can hardly believe it. Do you know how enthusiastic they are about learning, Andy?' Clearly not. 'They have learnt so much, and what's really important to me is that they're happy too: they love school – well, most of them. That's no mean achievement, especially for a probationer.'

'You mean I've passed?'

'Of course you've passed, you daft noodle. You didn't really think . . . Andy Seed!'

She leaned over to a bag on the floor and brought out two more presents and a card.

'There's a babygro for your gorgeous little one, and a nice bottle of wine for you and Barbara. Go home, rest as much as you can with a new baby and enjoy your holiday – you've earned it.' She stood up and gave me a characteristically vigorous hug. I nearly didn't survive it, but I was a teacher.

* * *

The afternoon passed quietly, and soon every child sat ready to go, stationed with PE bags and enormous sugar paper portfolios of finished work. I wasn't sure what to say to them. I gave each one a bar of chocolate and wished them every success in Miss Croker's class, and hoped that they would have a wonderful summer. I would miss them, not just the real characters like Eve and Barney, but all of them. The shrill bell called them away, and with high shouts and whoops they headed for the cloakrooms. Only Nathan stayed behind.

'I haven't forgotten your present, Mr Seed,' he beamed eagerly, holding his hands behind his back.

'Now, this is exciting.'

'I've finished me white stick!' He whipped out a beautiful varnished folding white stick and held it towards me; I nearly fell over.

'Nathan that's amazing . . . You finished it! But it's yours – don't you want to keep it?'

'No, I made it for you, Mr Seed.' I looked at the twinkle in his eye and wondered about his remark for a few seconds, but he dashed off, waving like the others.

It was sentimental of me, I suppose, but I went to the path at the front of the school leading up to the gate to say another last lot of goodbyes. The children of Class 3, my first ever class, weren't so encumbered by emotion: they had six weeks of freedom ahead, and I also knew that kids are fickle. Most ran past and shouted 'Bye!'; only Rose stopped and turned towards me.

'Farewell, Mr Seed.' It was reminiscent of her lyrical Irish mother.

Val popped into my room with a mug of tea and told me to come and sit in the staffroom. I managed a few minutes but I was desperate to get home to Barbara and Tom. I thanked the staff for their wonderful support in my first year, wished restful summer breaks on everyone and jumped into the baked Alfa; I had hardly noticed that a broad blue sky and glorious sunshine were overhead.

It was a late July afternoon. The sun burned the magnificent cumulus clouds into gleaming eruptions of white brilliance. A gentle breeze rolled down the hay meadows off Spout Fell and brought delicious scents in through the open window of the room where I was standing, holding my little son. Hawkbit, clover, tufted vetch, and birdsfoot trefoil painted the edges of the pasture below the hill's soaring crags. My mind was drifting, free. It was the summer holidays: six wonderful weeks to enjoy the delights of the Dales and to spend time with my wife and child. At that moment a thought crystallised in my mind.

Where would I rather be?

In the Caribbean? Too hot.

New York, Paris, Rome? I was never one for the rush and bustle, the blaring traffic and sickly air of the big cities.

No, I loved Britain, and England especially: for all its faults it was civilised and safe – a pleasant land, especially in the summer countryside.

And where in England would I rather be?

The wealthy south? Not enough hills for me.

The Lakes? A beautiful place, for sure, but its arteries are clogged with tourists for most of the year.

Cornwall, Devon? Delightful and wild in places, but they somehow didn't have the airy space of the Dales. No, in all the land, the Yorkshire Dales was the place: open, glorious, quiet, and beautiful. And where in the Dales would I rather be?

Ellerdale? Wherndale? Hubberdale?

No, Swinnerdale was the one for me: wide, wooded, rich, open, full of castles, crags and waterfalls. And where in this dale is the finest place?

Ingleburn? A town of character, but busy in the holiday season, and really it stood before the dale not in it. It was the gate, but not the meadow.

Kettleby? A splendid place, but always cold, rattled by winds even in high summer due to its lofty perch at the head of the dale. It had to be a village for me – a tight community of farms, houses and gardens. A place away from the main road and bustle. It needed a green, a pub and a shop. And preferably spectacular views of the hills and valleys all around. Throw in a magical waterfall and a tumbling beck, and this was it: Applesett, the place I lived right now. There was no finer place.

And even our home, our dowdy, lopsided old house, with its great bay window giving an unmatched panorama of the village and dale beyond, was special.

As I stood there, my baby son gurgling contentedly on my shoulder, and Barbara now holding us both and looking out through the window too, I realised that there really was nowhere I would rather be.